Arms Outstr

Volume 2 of my

By Rachel

CW01584042

ISBN 978-1 291-59377-8

Text copyright © 2015 Rachel Pallitan

No part of this publication may be reproduced, stored in a retrieval system or transmitted in any form or by any means electronic, mechanical photocopying, recording or otherwise without the written prior permission of the author.

Printed by lulu.com

Dedication

I dedicate this book to Jesus Christ who has faithfully led me through some very dark experiences and brought me out safely, though it has not felt safe, so far. He has been such a friend battling with me, standing by me, watching over me and helping me come to terms with the savage fight for my soul.

Acknowledgements

I wish to express my thanks to Samantha, my youngest sister - for being at the end of the phone during the process of writing this book. You have added the strength I have needed to persevere to the end of this vast project. Your faith in my ability to reach this goal has been of monumental importance over the years.

To my other sister, Peggy: You have unwittingly pushed me in getting a move on with this work. Your starting to write your own autobiography was the trigger I needed to get on with mine. Thank you.

Thank you Susan Hill for your help in preparing the final stages of the publication of this book and the support you have been in getting it into book form.

I thank you also my brother, Alan, for the invaluable advice you gave me for my first book, it has overflowed into this one too.

Thank you Bjarki Clausen for the cover layout, you have worked, with great patience, in getting it perfect.
www.merkiverk.net Email: bjarki@merkiverk.net

Last but not least thank you Reverend Daniel Ebbworth. You have been a great support since rendering both my books to you for your opinions.

The image on the front cover was purchased and licensed from www.123rf.com.

Contents

Prologue

My first book, *Is Anybody Out There?* is the story of my childhood to my early twenties. That book explains my distraught life without going deeper but I have discovered a complex and even sinister reason behind my tormented existence. It is an important introduction to this book.

Arms Outstretched follows on from there and speaks of what happened after I gave my life to Jesus Christ and the problems I faced. It shows how Jesus has been faithful and very close to me throughout the many ordeals. It also shows why I believe my problems did not begin when I was born but before that fateful day. Persevere through this book and you will discover a locked door just waiting for a key to be turned to set this prisoner free.

As in Is Anybody Out There? italics represent my thoughts in most cases.

Disclaimer

As in Is Anybody Out There? most names and places are fictitious while others have merely been changed to protect people's identities and for legal reasons. Anybody recognizing the true whereabouts or identity of people in this book are not permitted by the author to disclose them to any other person at risk of legal action. You are kindly requested to keep such in the confines of this book. Thank you. Year dates have been omitted for the same reason. It must be stressed that what I have experienced involved only a handful of people and not the entire church as an organization. Therefore, the church cannot be held responsible for what a minority have done. The people in question are forgiven and are not the main the reason for the writing of this book.

Foreword

I have known Rachel Pallitan since our dramatic meeting at Willow House which is recorded later in this book. Her story begins much earlier and is written in her first book *Is Anybody Out There?* Rachel has suffered much abuse, rejection and oppression by evil forces. Given the unrelenting nature of her battle, it is a miracle that she has survived to write her autobiography at all. Rachel has recorded her struggle in a skilful, detailed and, at times, humorous way. Rachel's books are a moving testimony to her courage, determination and, above all, her faith in Jesus Christ who has walked with her all the way on her long journey to wholeness. May *Arms Outstretched* open our hearts to a deeper compassion for those who have been abused and who need our patient unconditional love.

Reverend Daniel Ebbworth.

Introduction

This book is written to bring an understanding of people who have been victimized in their lives and not only for the victim but the abuser also because something has gone wrong in their lives too. We are all under an enormous battle and would rather forget that we are not alone but are surrounded by hordes of demonic spirits attempting to invade our lives. Jesus Christ came to destroy their works and bring us back to Him. He loves each and every one of us. No reader of this book is exempt from coming to the Saviour of the world.

In the Bible, John's gospel chapter 3 and verse 16 says:

'For God so loved the world that He gave His only begotten Son that whoever believes in Him shall not perish but have everlasting life.'

Chapter One

Back to Nursing

Leaving Apple Ash, that splendid halfway house set in twenty five acres of land, was not an easy thing to do, even with its bad memories. In my new home I suffered from extreme homesickness and cried for a fortnight, then prayed,

'Please, God, will you move Karen to phone me.'

As soon as I finished praying the phone rang and indeed it was Karen to ask how I was getting on. God had answered me immediately! Her call soothed the homesickness and brought a good deal of emotional relief.

Samantha and I got on well in the bedsit together. She was nursing and I cycled twelve miles to Cantrin to work at Chingles china and glass shop. While there, during my lunch breaks, I wrote my memoirs of Apple Ash. The shop was dark and creepy. Down in the stock room the white plastered walls were more like a crypt than a place to keep top of the range goods. I looked forward to getting home more than anyone can imagine but first the bicycle ride had to be faced. Bringing my bike up from the cellar at closing time was the first challenge, getting it round the corner of the pillar that held the stairs in the middle of the shop, was the second. It was plain wheeling then to the door, outside and round the corner. I mounted and peddled towards the sea. When the evenings darkened before five thirty *(closing time)* there was generally a fierce wind pressing against me. Feeling tired and unwilling to face the hassle of tackling the weather I let out an angry sigh and tried to come to terms with the evening ritual. *It has to be done, just keep calm.* Turning right, into the biting wind and pressing one foot down after the other on the pedals, I bent forward almost double to gain maximum push but speeding up was impossible. With wintry blasts in my face, and flapping hair escaping its imprisonment inside my hood, I rapidly lost patience. Dismounting and grabbing the bike I firmly parked it beside the pavement then gave the saddle a good hiding.

'You naughty bike, just stop mucking about. I want to get home.'

Sensing it got the message I kicked the pedal free from the pavement and remounted. It was just as hard then as it had been before but at least some frustration had been released and the bike had not screamed out in pain. Without further outbursts I arrived home at quarter past six and was ready for a hot meal.

After about a year working in Cantrin I was offered the much awaited transfer to Chingles, Ribford and so my trials of cycling came to an end.

I entered the smaller, neater shop to be greeted by Mr Radisan, the manager. He was a good boss and fun to work with but unfortunately, an alcoholic. Gloria, who was First Sales *(assistant manageress)* for a long time got on very well with him but I still could not speak or make friends. Gloria loved people and her bubbly confidence was what I needed to get by on.

A few months after settling in I took my guitar and played in the office whilst facing the shop floor, keeping an eye out for customers. Anyone coming in would see and hear my less than amateur playing. Somehow, I felt it was wrong but it was okay with Gloria when she was in charge and we were not busy. At times I wanted to play away and not bother about the approaching customer but Gloria reminded me,

'That's what you're here for.'

Oh, of course.

Though I was a decent type of girl I found Mr Radisan's drunken episodes quite funny. One day he got so drunk that Gloria and I walked round the streets of Ribford, after closing time, trying to sober him up. Needless to say he did not work for Chingles for much longer. A replacement manageress transferred from Chingles, Bramington. Gloria and I took some time getting used to Miss Curlingside's way of running the shop. When doing the paperwork, as there was no space in the office, Miss Curlingside spread a fresh layer of it on top of the carpet every day. No customer could find a place for his or her feet. Gloria and I began to realize that our new boss could not do her job properly and we became quite frustrated. When I unpacked our delivery and neatly put the stock away I would find it all messed up next time I looked. For many months we tried to put up with her and I wondered to myself if she would ever leave. Gloria became so fed up that in the end it was she who reluctantly left; having worked there for many years. I was promoted to First Sales in her place. Gloria kept in touch though and while Miss Curlingside was off one day I was in a real quandary as to how to sort out her mess. Things had gone from bad to worse since Gloria left as there was only myself and a part time worker left. Downstairs the stock room was like a rubbish dump with empty boxes all over the floor and I was pressed for time, having to get more important work done. I was on my own on the shop floor one day while the part timer was at lunch and needed to get the downstairs tidied and at the same time keep upstairs in good order and attend to any customers. Unexpectedly, Gloria rang in,

'How are you getting on?'

'Everything is such a mess. I'm inundated with trying to sort everything out. There are empty trays all over the place downstairs that I can't get anywhere.'

'Okay, I'll come in and help you.'

I did not know that it was wrong for Gloria to be there. I was grateful for all the help she could give. When Miss Curlingside returned from her day off she discovered Gloria had been in to help and was not happy with that at all and shouted,

'You should not have let Gloria come in to help. She is not insured to work here anymore!'

I was not happy with her manner towards me either because I had allowed what I thought was best for the shop.

'Well, don't ever do it again. I'm the manageress.'

'Yes, but the work just isn't getting done.'

'You just do what I say.'

I could not see her sense in anything and becoming more and more frustrated, walked out of the staff room where we had been talking over a coffee, took my keys out of my coat pocket, went back to her and stated,

'Well, there's your keys. I don't want your job, you can do it yourself,' then walked out of the shop.

Once home I got into my car, having recently passed my driving test, and drove to see Gloria who advised,

'Ring Head Office and tell them what you've done.'

'What! Tell them?'

'It's the best way because if Miss Curlingside tells them first you are at a disadvantage.'

I made my way to the phone box opposite her house and called. Their reply was,

'We'll suspend you for a week on full pay till we can get to the bottom of it.'

'Thank you.'

'Come up to Head Office on Thursday. Get to the station for half past one and somebody will be there to meet you.'

To travel to Kerryham would be a novelty but in those circumstances quite scary. *What will I say?*

Thursday came and when I reached the station at Kerryham it was pouring with rain. Nobody was there to meet me as promised so I phoned to let them know I had arrived. Eventually a man from Head Office showed up and, after a short drive, I was led into the presence of the Personnel Manageress. I stood in front of her with my hands behind my back and head down as though facing my father.

'You don't have to stand there like a school girl. You are not in trouble; we only want to investigate what happened.'

I told her the whole stressful story and was surprised by her reaction,

'Well, don't you do her work for her? You are doing two jobs. If she is not doing her job properly we will know.'

That sound advice relieved me of a lot of work but it seemed Miss Curlingside was not going to get found out and I was in desperate need of a holiday. A couple of months passed and Head Office invited me to join other First Sales on a course in Kerryham. Once there, my self consciousness did me no favours. I entered the hotel we were staying in to register. After registering I asked where the lift was.

'It's immediately round the corner to the left.'

I carried my case to the first door on the left and thought the door was a bit narrow for a lift but, anyhow, if she said it was a lift I was sure going to take it. I pushed the door and it doubled in the middle, *strange*. As I entered the first of three doors I thought, *we have one each.* I sent my case ahead of me into the one man lift, put it down, breathed in as I closed the door through lack of space and looked for a button to press. I had not experienced many lifts. As I could not find the button I lifted the awaiting phone receiver, thinking, *well this must be what you do.* It took me a good few seconds to work out I was in a phone box. The blood rushed ten times faster than normal to my face. The task of opening the door, which crammed me and my case into an impossible exiting position, took a horrid few minutes of awkwardness to accomplish. Watching men in business suits pass by, I, being sure they knew what I had done, was not enjoying the most glorious of experiences. But finally I extracted myself quickly and swiftly, yet clumsily, tugged my suitcase from the widest opening the door could manage. I turned right, returned to the reception desk and asked,

'Where *exactly* is the lift?'

On our way round the factory the following day we witnessed the process of making fine bone china. The tutor explained that while the clay was soft it had a chance of being thrown back if a flaw was discovered and reused. As it became harder through firing, however, it would be smashed as it could no longer be thrown back to the softer stage. At that point God showed up and said in that clear Voice in my head,

'I do that.'

Being thrown back meant there was a flaw of some kind in the clay. Once it was fired up and became harder and a flaw was detected, they, the plates or other crockery, were fit for nothing and smashed on the floor. I thought, *nice*. Despite that first episode and being forewarned by God what may well be His intentions towards me it was a very interesting and prestigious tour.

I had not seen God move powerfully much since I gave Him my life at Apple Ash and was dissatisfied with it so one Saturday I went on a trip to Southampton where a lady had come to lead a healing meeting. I needed quite a bit of that. God was supposed to do healings and I told Him so. My indignant attitude revealed a lack of trust in a miracleless world. A crowd gathered round the lady to watch the miracles as they took place. A man with a crooked back was receiving prayer. I happened to be standing beside him and close to her, watching as she touched his back and taking her time to pray. His back was being straightened so slowly that the process was almost imperceptible. By the time she finished he was standing perfectly upright.

'Wow, did you see that?' I asked, flabbergasted.

The people around me stood like zombies, not sharing my surprise. I followed the man practically out of the building to make sure I had not imagined it. For a few months previous to that encounter I had been going to the local Catholic Church but also travelled to London for Catholic Charismatic Renewal meetings. At those meetings it seemed Jesus, by His Holy Spirit, was present and the Masses came alive. At one of those meetings I heard a Voice in my head saying,

'Get to know your leaders.'

I did not understand at that point what it meant so held it lightly.

Often after Mass at my local church I became violent. As soon as I left the building I flared up in anger which was not a good sign. I did not know what to do about it but carried on going to the prayer meetings that were held at the church on Friday evenings. I also attended the annual general meeting at the church where one woman asked,

'Can anybody explain what the Charismatic Renewal is, please?'

I quickly stood to my feet,

'I'll tell you.'

The priest nodded as I glanced in his direction.

'It's when you get Jesus into your heart. The Holy Spirit comes alive in you and you speak in tongues.'

When the meeting was over the priest took me aside,

'Don't you ever say anything like that again?'

Shocked and confused I walked away, not comprehending why a priest and one that had attended Charismatic meetings, would say such a thing. He did watch horror films and called children little monsters after Mass so that might be one explanation. I became discouraged with that church after a while and God told me through the Bible, with deep conviction,

'These people honour me with their lips but their hearts are far from me.' Matthew 15:8.

If God was saying that then it must be true so I left and wandered around Ribford looking for another church. Samantha and I eventually visited the Catholic Church in the next town. Samantha played her guitar and the Masses were lively and Charismatic but we learned that the priest would shortly be leaving.

'Father Sunbry is coming to take my place,' the priest informed us.

'Father Sunbry? Is he from Yasling?' I asked happily.

Father Sunbry had come to Apple Ash sometimes to see Karen. Yasling was the next village to Haxwich on the east side and at times we had attended his church. His lively spirit made life seem worth living. At one point he was going to make a film of Apple Ash while I was there but that did not happen in the end. When he arrived Samantha and I helped him settle in and early in the mornings cooked his breakfast of bacon and eggs. He told us about the cold bedroom he had to sleep in as there was no heating,

'I wear my nightcap and I can see my breath, it's that cold.'

During his first sermon he declared,

'I'd like to put recliner seats in place of the pews in the church so people can lie back and look up at the stars.'

This might well be the church for us. Samantha taught me how to play the hymns on my guitar and I played together with her at times during the Mass, miming the chords I did not know. Our time there soon ended though. Father said we should attend a church nearer our home but we had already left that church because of what was going on. I did not return. Instead I wandered around Ribford and told God I would like to go to a Baptist church and get out of the Catholic Church altogether, not because I had ever been to a Baptist Church but I simply liked the word, 'Baptist'.

Samantha had made a friend, who, whilst on a visit one evening, told us,

'There's a meeting at Grace Church, Delton, on Friday night. Nicholas Blenson and Hank Sonnyman will be ministering in a healing meeting.'

We all went to the meeting where the church pastor, William Antine, introduced the two speakers. The church just happened to be a Baptist Free Church. The speakers' message was about the problem of rejection. I had never heard anybody speaking on that subject before and was impressed with both the meeting and the church so decided to go there from then on. Samantha stayed with the Catholic Church with her friend. The quaint church building held about four hundred people. At last I had found a place where God gave words of knowledge and where people were healed and cared for. I wanted to live for God for the rest of my life. After a few Sundays the pastor invited people to get baptized by full immersion so I prepared for my baptism which took place in October that year. I had already been baptized as a baby in the Catholic Church but the adult service would be different. It was to symbolize that I had turned away from my sins and that they had been washed away. When shopping on the Friday before the baptismal service I recognized a lady named Sheila from the church, said hello and we started to talk about my baptism,

'Can I hold your tail?' asked Sheila,

'What tail?

'Your tail, can I hold your tail?'

'I haven't got a tail.'

'When you get baptized.'

'Oh, my towel!' I re-accented but felt disappointed.

It reminded me of my first holy communion when my mother had not been there. Here was a stranger wanting to hold my towel. Samantha was not around to be asked if she would hold it so I allowed her to. Deep down I felt touched but would have preferred a member of my family to be present.

'Yes, you can, thank you.'

There were nine to be baptized on that special Sunday. The girls wore long, white robes. We had been asked to prepare a testimony on how we came to believe in Jesus Christ and in mine I addressed the congregation concerning the lack of love in my life. Being choked up I found it difficult to carry on reading my testimony. Pastor Antine came up from behind and put an arm around my waist, giving me the strength to carry on. When I finished the assistant pastor, Neil Ontiman, totally immersed me in the church's baptismal and I survived the fear of drowning. As

I stood waist high in the water Pastor Antine read a scripture especially for me,

'You will keep him in perfect peace him whose mind is stayed on Thee for he trusts in Thee, trust in the Lord.' Isaiah 26:3-4

Back at home my adventures with Him were about to begin. In the bedsit with Samantha I had lost my purse. It was five o'clock in the evening and I needed to go out before the shops closed.

'Please God, can you tell me where my purse is?'

'It's in the wardrobe,' I heard a quiet Voice answer.

The Voice was not audible but a voice in my head other than my own thoughts. I walked over to the wardrobe and felt in all my pockets but no purse could be found.

'Okay, God, it isn't there. Please can you tell me where it is?'

'It's in the wardrobe,' the Voice said again.

I shut the wardrobe door.

'No, it isn't, I've looked.'

At the same time I was pulling draws open in the chest of draws, rummaging through them and closing the ever opening wardrobe door, thinking it had a loose catch.

'Stop messing about, the shops are going to shut soon. I haven't got time to muck about.'

'It's in the wardrobe.'

I had no choice but to go through every coat pocket in there.

'Here it is!'

Pulling it out of Samantha's coat pocket I remembered wearing her coat the day before. Even though we were sisters we never usually wore each other's clothes. I spent the next few precious seconds opening the wardrobe door and closing it again, each time a little harder, and it stayed closed every time, until finally I was convinced,

'God's in here!'

With that I sped down the stairs, hair on end, and out of the front door with only minutes to spare for any shopping.

The second adventure was at bath time. A wasp, unaware of my schedule, sauntered up the window pane.

'God, please can you get that wasp to walk right out of here.'

In no time the wasp quick marched up the window pane then tackled the wooden frame till it reached the edge where the window was slightly open. It was easy going then across the flat part of the frame till it could march no more then spread its tiny wings and flew away.

Peggy eventually came to live with us. She had entered the convent to become a nun but left because of depression and came to live with Samantha and me. Samantha moved into the larger bedsit at the front of the house so Peggy and I shared the room at the back. One Sunday she accompanied me to see Gloria at her home. We told Gloria about Jesus and invited her to church but she declined so we left to catch the bus for the evening service. Once out of her gate and onto the main path we glanced behind and, seeing the bus coming, ran toward the bus stop ahead of us in slow motion. As the bus drew ever closer we seemed to be pressed upon by an invisible force and were pushing against it. The bus driver said he noticed our struggle and had made allowances for it.

My jaw had been causing me a lot of trouble around that time; pain seared from its base up to my ear. Such was the severity that I ran down the street, when out, to get away from it. During the night Peggy prayed for God to heal me but nothing happened except my heart was touched by her prayer. That week I asked Peggy to come with me to Grace Church. She said no and I was utterly mortified but she took pity on me and changed her mind.

Trusting was difficult for me. I found trust in God was one thing, trust in man quite another. The following day Peggy and I went into Ribford to shop. Whilst in a certain newsagents there was a display of those adorable Creme Eggs.

'Let's have one of these.'

Picking up two, I was just about to go to the till to pay when I stopped.

'Oh, we can't,' I whispered hastily.

'Why?'

'Look,' I nodded towards Pastor Neil Ontiman.

'Better put them back.'

My face turned scarlet with guilt but what I saw the pastor doing should have encouraged me. I put the eggs back where I got them from then watched Neil lay his goods on the counter,

'Look what he's got,' I whispered.

Peggy shot a glance his way. We stared at each other. He paid for his two Creme Eggs. I could not have hidden ours behind my back because we would have been next in line and he would have seen us put them on the counter. I did not want to be seen by him at all, let alone with the eggs. It was alright for others to have stuff but not us. I did not condemn him having what he had but felt certain death would fall on me if he saw what we had, albeit the same as him. We could have had a counseling session there and then. He could have told us to have the eggs and he might have even paid for them to make up for the times our dad did not buy us anything. He could have given us his. The shop assistants could have come over and asked if we had a problem with the eggs and we could have overcome once unburdening our souls. Nobody was aware and nobody offered a solution to the brain washing of my father. After putting them back we walked from the shop with none, deeply mortified.

'We'll get some at the shop up the road,' I promised.

A few months after my baptism, the usual feeling of helplessness and vulnerability got the better of me. By that time we had new staff at Chingles. A hairdresser who had cut my hair to within an inch of my scalp during one appointment had applied for the job *(without my knowledge)* and was successful. I was stunned. She was a lovely, loving person but even so it did not help me. My energy levels had waned to a point of near exhaustion. Often I wanted to get under the carpet and go to sleep. I cried out to God for a much needed holiday. If I could not have one a slight change might help. *A glass of wine might be nice.* So on my next shopping day, while coming back from the shops, I entered an Off-license. Walking over to the wines I decided a white one would be therapeutic. Not that I was experienced, I hardly touched wine. On special occasions at Apple Ash we drank it. I took a bottle from the shelf and paid at the counter. Once home I opened it, poured the watery stuff into a glass and swallowed a mouthful, then another and finished the full glass. After that I thought, *have another one.* Realizing what was happening I grabbed the almost full bottle, declaring,

'Oh no, you don't,' then poured the remainder down the drain.

Whenever I went to the shops for the next few weeks and walked past the Off-license door a magnetic pull tried to suck me in. *Okay, this is a temptation.* From then on I walked on the other side of the road.

Some months later Samantha found a lovely little cottage, about three miles away, to live in. Her move caused quite a bit of pain in me for I hated being separated from my family. When she moved out of the larger bedsit I moved in and Peggy stayed at the back of the house with her two rooms. Samantha continued training at Westport and travelled on her newly bought Moped motor bike. She visited us from time to time and vice versa.

The pain in my jaw did not abate and so I spoke to my doctor who referred me to the dentist who, in turn, referred me to a specialist at Westport Hospital. He told me I would need an operation to put it right. Two or three months later during an afternoon's work the phone rang and after being handed it from Miss Curlingside, a voice on the other end of the line said,

'This is Periwinkle Hospital in London. You are on the waiting list for an operation on your jaw. This type of operation is rare and so we would like you to consider having it done at this teaching hospital so that our students can learn.'

My holiday? As I had come to hate my job, I accepted,

'Yes, when can I come?'

'In two weeks time - on Wednesday.'

I would take anything to escape from the shop and Miss Curlingside. Hurriedly, I told her I had been given the appointment and that I should go as I would not be given another chance for the next two years. She gave her permission. I was elated. I would have a rest at last. When the day arrived to be admitted an older lady named Kay from our church, who had offered a lift in her car, drove me and my sisters to the hospital. They could not stay for any length of time so I said goodbye after a brief moment with them. Loneliness swept over me as they walked away. My bed was in the first bay on the right facing the doors. A nurse told me to fast from midnight. My operation would be at nine o'clock in the morning. I was to have a bone graft; bone taken from my hip and placed into the hinges of my jaw, which was out of alignment; the hinges were overriding. At eight in the morning a nurse approached me carrying a small tray.

'We have to prepare you now for the operation; just a small injection to help you feel relaxed.'

'Okay.'

The injection brought a calming feeling but I was determined not go to sleep. I would outwit them when given the anaesthetic later. An hour later, after the initial injection had taken its full effect, in walked two porters wearing white coats and rolling a trolley; the nurses had already put a white gown on me. Unlike the baptism gown it had an opening right up the back but was tied with the attached tapes. The men pulled the trolley up beside my bed,

'Hello, we've come to take you down to theatre.'

I edged onto the trolley, thinking of Samantha and Peggy. Once comfortable and with a blanket over me the porters set off. The ceiling moved like an upside down conveyer belt as I glided by. In the small anaesthetic room the anaesthetist asked about my life. It was time for the challenge of the anaesthetic. I would keep awake at all costs. I did not want to be half awake or wake up during the operation. The kind looking doctor asked,

'Can I see your arm?'

I extended my wrist.

'Ah, you have a very good vein here; this should be no problem at all. There will be a small prick.'

When that was done, he added,

'Can you count to ten for me?'

I can count to a hundred!

'One,' I said aloud, 'two, three, four, five,'

I'm still here,

'six, seven.....'

When I awoke in the recovery room I was vaguely aware something was in my mouth. It was quickly removed by a nurse then I was wheeled back to the ward. Recovering from any anaesthetic had always been an ordeal but once my stomach settled and I was more awake a nurse approached my bed, rummaged through my bedside locker and found the remainder of a bar of chocolate.

'Have you been eating this?'

Of course I had not and later faced another inquisition during the medication round where another nurse asked,

'Do you want any pain killers?'
'No, thank you.'
'Are you sure?'
'Yes,'
'Are you in any pain? Your hip should be much more painful than your jaw?'
'No, I'm not in any pain.'
She went away but every drug round was the same; different nurses offered me medication and one in particular became quite frustrated that I kept refusing. I did not suffer pain of any sort. Later, a patient who had come in for a breast reduction introduced herself to me as Felicity. We discussed what we were in hospital for and I told her I had had no pain,
'And you don't have to have any either,' I assured her.
After her operation she testified of also suffering no pain. God had removed it. However, I was not recovering in another way. Great tiredness and weakness prevailed and I was wheeled about in a wheelchair. A week later the stitches were taken out from my hip and jaw.
'I said I wanted alternate stitches taken out,' the surgeon addressed the nurse angrily.
It was to minimize scarring but what was done was done. On discharge, Kay, who had brought me, collected me, minus my sisters, from the hospital and drove me home. The first Sunday evening of my return I heard a knock at the door. On opening it, a huge bunch of flowers stared at me. I stared back in disbelief as they moved to the left to reveal an unknown woman from church.
'What are these?' I asked, to which the lady answered,
'Flowers from the church; we always give the flowers left after the service to people who are sick.'
'Oh, thank you very much.'
My spirit rose slightly. I wondered how it was possible for somebody to even think about me. As I placed the flowers in a vase all the years I had done with hardly a morsel of kindness swept through my memories.
When I recovered enough to return to church one lady asked,
'And did you have any pain?'
'No.'

She said nothing else but I fathomed she had been praying. I wondered why God did not heal my jaw before the operation but, of course, it was my holiday.

The landlady, Mrs Horrins, made milk jelly every day following my operation and brought it up to my room because the surgeon told me I must stifle yawns and not open my mouth beyond two inches. Mr and Mrs Horrins, a relatively elderly couple, were kind, unobtrusive and considerate; we certainly had no complaints about them.

In six weeks of convalescence I still had not recovered from the tiredness or weakness. After a visit to the doctor he diagnosed depression. I did not know depression could affect the body like that. It was another six months before I returned to Chingles but once there felt I no longer belonged. Unprepared to stay I applied to go back into nursing instead. At the interview I was told I would not be accepted for State Registered training because of my past problems with stress but the interviewer was going to give me a chance with State Enrolment. *Yes!* First though, I paid a visit to Cheshire to see a friend. Katrin had been a cadet nurse at St Chad's Hospital when I was there. She was married and had a beautiful two year old daughter called Penelope. But Katrin was cruel and, as I watched I could not understand nor recognize her from our teenage years. She had changed. She kept her child up till all hours of the night for her own company and during the day I watched her prod her two year old in a playful manner but with short, sharp digs. I felt the pain and wanted to rescue the child.

The following day we visited the nuns; some of them, including Sister Stephen who was in charge, had moved from St Chad's to Denwich; another private hospital the nuns owned in Cheshire. Katrin's daughter had been crying but she would not pick her up. She left her to scream, scream and scream until she was almost sick. I so wanted to pick her up myself but was not permitted. After leaving Denwich we finally arrived at Swanfold, the nurse's home back at St Chad's. Katrin went to see if there were any of the nuns we knew living there. The house had been converted into a convent. Were they sleeping in the same pastel green, partitioned rooms as we had done? It was hard to imagine. While I was waiting for Katrin to come back to the car I wondered what I could do with her daughter. Turning to look at her from the front seat I offered her a cuddle but she was not willing to come to me. I had to assure her that I would not hurt her. A blue smurf on the floor behind me caught my eye so I took the toy in my arms and cradled it, saying,

'I love smurf, I love smurf,' whilst rocking him from side to side.

The ploy worked; Penelope came and put her head on my shoulder. I gave her a much needed hug. That evening back at Katrin's house I mentioned she should not treat her daughter that way. Next morning on waking she appeared in my room,

'Rachel, I want you to leave my house?'

Is this my friend? It did not seem to bother her that I was far from home and had nowhere to stay. I phoned Sister Stephen at Denwich and explained my predicament. She invited me to spend the rest of my holiday with them in the convent part of the hospital. I certainly felt privileged as no cadet nurse had ever stayed inside the convents overnight.

On my return to Ribford I prepared to go to Westport Hospital for a fresh start at nursing. I suppose going back meant to be close to my mother who died before she qualified. I had to make it this time and time dragged until the first day at introductory school where I encountered many eighteen and nineteen year olds. *I could be a staff nurse by now if I hadn't had my breakdown.*

'How old are you?' asked Clare, one of the trainees.

I almost choked as the usual lump in my throat rose up.

'Twenty six.'

I thought I was far too old to be coming back to nursing and the thought was a burden throughout my training. My confidence was still very low and with each word a blush was right there to accompany it.

As always during training the quality of work was under examination. I did my best to make things perfect. Class times were a problem as I had to sit and face people. At break times I bought something to eat to make the time fly faster and avoid speaking to anyone. On my way back to duty from break one day I bumped into Miss Hammerkin, a nursing tutor,

'Hello,' I greeted her with embarrassment clearly showing.

'How are you? Have you done your case study?'

‘Yes, but how am I really supposed to go about it? Just to make sure I’ve done it right.’

‘Just write as though we don’t know anything. Explain every procedure in detail so that even a man in the street would understand. That way we know *you* understand.’

Returning home I reread my assignment, corrected it and handed it in the following week then waited for the results. To my sheer delight I came out top of the class with eighty percent and even got a mention for my work in class.

I lived opposite the Hospital. One morning whilst crossing the park in my uniform, a huge black dog came bounding towards me. It hit me as it passed with such force that my legs buckled causing me to go down on one knee; rather like a genuflect but I got straight back up. I thought to myself,

‘Though I fall I will rise again,’ quoting Micah 7:8 from the Bible.

In due course the time came for one of my practical examinations. I chose total patient care and dreaded it. I also chose my examiner and, as always, reacted in a negative way to being examined. Miss Cornsmith watched every detail carefully. I was fairly confident of passing but failed over one point; when changing the patient’s urine bag I threw it into the laundry skip, full. While Miss Cornsmith was talking with me afterwards I became sombre because I could have done the exam blindfolded. Lack of confidence made me vulnerable to failing, again. Even though I explained all my failings as I had done in Flenkton during my aseptic technique she still failed me. I proceeded to tell her how useless I was and pulled myself down quite a bit,

‘You sisters are excellent nurses and all your work is very good,’ she said.

So why did you fail me? Being well past encouragement I stood to leave before she added,

‘There’s something about you three.’

Ignoring her, I about turned and pulling the door hard behind me, shouted,

‘It’s Jesus!’ and marched off down the corridor.

Apart from that one mistake the exam went well but I would have to take it again and that would add another year and a half to my training and therefore, extend any qualification to become an SRN.

Even so, going to church had become such an attraction in my life that I began to feel nursing was no longer the career for me and especially as I had failed that exam. Being unsettled in my spirit I switched my attention more towards 'God' and wanted to be in church full time. Then I had a dream where I saw a finger hovering over the hospital with indicator lights on, leading me clearly to the hospital, I did not trust it. But as I still loved nursing and wanted to pass my finals I carried on, passing my drug and medication exam without a problem. Time was getting closer to my final exams and fear of success ran alongside the fear of failure. Together with lack of confidence with other members of staff and sometimes being short of staff on the ward I found I could manage better running it alone. I was still a good worker and developed methodical routines which I carried out quickly and effectively without others messing things up and taking forever to accomplish their duties. To prove I was right about that, whilst on duty during that period of rare confidence I enjoyed an intense feeling that I could run the entire hospital single handed and to compliment it had an extraordinary energy level I had never known. I sailed through every blood pressure monitoring, temperature taking, bed bathing and drug giving routine with the ease of blood rushing through unclogged arteries.

Once home, however, something else was awaiting me. I cooked beans on toast for supper and, in the midst of eating and for no reason a surge of violence vent through me and I threw, with great force, the plate and contents at the opposite wall. The following day I phoned the hospital to say I would not be coming in as I was not fit to care for anyone. That was my last day working there and the beginning of a journey through depression the likes of which I would not welcome a second time. Everything I did slowed down. Crossing the road in a hurry was impossible. Any approaching car would have to be a long distance away for me to think of starting to cross to the other side. It was not long before my face grew pale and gaunt so it was back to the doctor with me. A kind locum doctor had taken the place of my regular doctor for a while. He was interested in psychology so offered me a regular appointment after his surgery to talk. At one appointment he placed a cushion on a chair next to me and said,

'That is your mother, what would you like to say to her?'

I loved my mother but the doctor was convinced I was angry with her. I did not feel one ounce of anger towards anybody so stared at the cushion and remained dumb. He wrote me off sick for six weeks at a time. When my own doctor returned he referred me to Dr Biberson, a psychiatrist. As I entered Dr Biberson's office for the first time I noticed he stood unsteadily to his feet. After a greeting he offered me a chair to sit on. Exhausted, frightened and anxious I sat before him; totally vulnerable to his dictates. He continued to see me over the weeks and finally transferred me to a psychologist. I had got used to him and had opened up since my first interview when I had said practically nothing but progress had been made and now I was cast off to somebody else.

Dr Pannypin, the psychologist, tried to psychoanalyze me but I knew that was not what I needed. I was unable to cooperate no matter how hard I tried. As I walked along the street during one of those days a verse in the Bible popped into my mind about that kind of approach to healing,

'*Let the dead bury their dead.*' Luke 9:60.

Being a Christian meant God should be the one to heal me. I wrote Dr Pannypin off mentally and it was not long after that that he let me go. I tried to get healing through my pastor and, not succeeding, decided to call another pastor from a church down the road. He visited me and announced his verdict,

'Spiritually, you are to be envied but emotionally you are all over the place.'

I knew that was true but could not understand why. Surely if my spirit was good then everything else should be also. He left and no second appointment was made.

I began to feel unsafe in my own home; fears of the landlord, Mr Horrins, attacking me increased the feeling of insecurity; even asking him to change a light bulb was a mountainous task. I found it very difficult to be with any man on my own. It was another ten months of cruel depression before I ventured to the Job Centre. In the meantime Samantha had been to a Catholic Charismatic conference in Hampshire where she experienced a priest telling her everything about herself. I prayed for the same thing to happen to me. Afraid of what would be my next job I made an appointment with the DRO *(Disability Rehabilitation Officer)*. I did not feel ready for work but was willing to try. A kind looking, white haired, older man opened the door when I arrived at his office.

'Come in. Take a seat.'

The lump in my throat surfaced. He did not ask me any questions but proceeded to tell me everything about myself and finally said,

'You don't need work. You need the healing love of Christ.'

I was stunned, absolutely numb with shock. The man who was supposed to get me into work was telling me what I really needed. If the whole world could be like that! I asked if he was a Christian and was surprised when he answered that he was only a nominal one. I left his office and could not walk straight for the entire journey home out of sheer amazement. God had spoken through him to me just as I had asked and it was not in a church or conference.

At home my sisters and I did have some enjoyable times. When Samantha visited, she and I bought a small snooker table for my room. We had great fun on it for many hours. Watching the sport on television was the highlight of our lives. Wanting a bit of variation from church Peggy and I went to a proper snooker club one evening to play on a normal six foot table. It seemed a mile to get to the other end. Mostly men played and I feared getting bullied or made fun of but ignored the feeling as best as I could. At church the very next Sunday the pastor said,

'Some of you are getting involved in the things of the world.'

Thinking he meant us we stopped going immediately. I had also taken up classical guitar lessons. The tunes and method were easy and I wanted to stay but again something religious popped up and I felt I was obliged to join the Evangelical Explosion known as EE training. Both activities were held on the same night so naturally I chose to put God first. Not a soul was won and I did not enjoy it but thought it a penance for my sins and did not stay for long. Then one day I became physically sick, was vomiting and could not move much at all. My energy levels fell to near zero. It seemed that another episode I had experienced at Apple Ash was hitting me, though I had not vomited then. Samantha came to see me and read from the Bible, Psalm 32:4,

'My strength was sapped as in summer until I confessed my transgression to you.'

As I lay in bed I told God adamantly,

'Well, what have I done? I haven't done anything.'

The next day Peggy and I were going to a day conference in London where Selwyn Hughes, a well known conference speaker and minister who specialized in inner healing, was speaking. I was sure to find an answer so prayed,

'Lord, I need to have energy and to stop being sick for the whole day.'

So everything was fine all day. At the end I approached Selwyn for prayer but instead of praying he stalled,

'God says, "Wait."'

'For how long?'

He did not answer. The disappointment that accompanied his remark boarded the coach with me for our return home. Near the end of the journey the symptoms of the sickness came creeping back and nausea signaled it was time for a paper bag. As the coach approached the dropping off point I vomited into the bag and the speed of people getting off was greatly helped along. Not one person showed any compassion. Next morning I asked Peggy,

'Please will you phone Charles to come and pray for me?'

Charles was an elder in the church. She obliged and returned from the phone in the hall downstairs saying,

'Charles says it's an enforced fast.'

I thought as much and even felt privileged for a second. That evening in bed while listening to Joel Nederhood on Christian radio, as was my custom every night, he read from Psalm 32 as Samantha had done.

'Oh, well what have I done then?' I asked in resignation.

God's face lowered from the ceiling. I felt its dark, angry presence and cowered into the mattress,

'What about,' He paused a little, 'all those people you've wished dead?'

I thought for a while and the habit of wishing people dead flashed before my eyes.

'Oh, yeah…!' Suddenly realizing what I had indeed been guilty of, I added, 'Well, I'm sorry; I wish them all alive again then.'

I mentioned every person by name. With that, God seemed to smile and lift His angry face away. I was, by then, very weak with continued vomiting and barely able to get out of bed. I asked Peggy to phone the pastor, who came and stated, not knowing what I had prayed yet,

'You don't need to ask for them all to be made alive again. Just stop doing it.'

I recollected wishing Charles's wife, Dalia, dead after she offered some dud counsel not that long before the conviction. That very week Charles told us of a car smashing into Dalia's passenger side door. She had a cold so was not travelling at the time. That incident is probably what caused the visit from God. *I better not say anything to him about that.* God was showing me mercy as well as protecting Dalia from certain death. His mercy was on me because I said it in ignorance. I only really meant, leave me alone. That day I realized words have consequences in another person's life. I had learned a very hard lesson and vowed never to repeat it. A friend came to visit me the following day bearing a bottle of Lucozade and a box of very thin chocolates

'How did you come to buy those?' I asked.

'I was going for a walk, then went into a shop and said to the shopkeeper that I wanted something different.'

By that I knew the fast was over. The chocolates were ideal for helping my bruised stomach get used to food again. They were a special mild brand. God thought of everything. She had been totally unaware of my situation. And so I gradually recovered from an episode I would not like repeated. Charles and Dalia had actually been very good to both Peggy and me. I have still got a small doll ornament that Dalia gave me. She also gave one to Peggy. We started to attend Charles and Dalia's house group in their home. During one of those evenings a man who was deaf attended and I wanted to pray for his healing. I believed Jesus could and would heal him. However, I heard a Voice say to me,

'You want everything the easy way, don't you!'

It was not a question but a statement. *Well if God says so, I guess He's right.* I did not understand His attitude because I thought we should pray for the sick and they would recover. That night the deaf person had a picture of a rose whose petals were falling. We needed to know the interpretation of the picture and I believe God gave it to me,

'I think it's that when prayers are prayed they have to be prayed in love or they will not be heard.'

It gave me something new to ponder over.

I carried on pursuing God whenever I could and during a prayer time in my room one evening asked Him to heal my body from the top of my head to all the places that needed it, right down to my feet.

'I am going to sit here all night if I have to and wait for You to heal me.'

When He knew I was serious, as I sat for a long time fully expecting a huge miracle, He answered,

'No, I will not heal you now but I will heal you when I have made you as pure as gold then you will know I have finished.'

At church that Sunday, Neil Ontiman *(the pastor with the Creme Eggs)* who had a prophetic gift gave a word of prophecy, as though God was speaking.

'I can see everything going on in your heart. I am making you as pure as gold, my penetrating eyes can see everything. Then I will heal you.'

I approached Neil after the service. Another lady was speaking to him; telling him that the word was for her. I said,

'But that word was for me,' and explained why.

Maybe it was for both of us but I had surely been prepared for it. I continued my quest to get closer to God and kneeling by my bed another evening asked Him to speak to me.

'I am not getting into bed until You speak to me.'

I stayed on my knees listening in silence for a long time. Deciding He was not going to talk I placed my hands on the mattress to lever myself up,

'Okay, if You don't want to talk to me, fine.'

I was barely on my feet when the following scripture came to mind,

'Isaiah 54.'

I turned to the Bible and read the entire chapter but the words speaking to me were not very comforting even if they were meant to be,

Verse six described me well except I was never a wife,

'For the Lord had called you like a woman forsaken and grieved in spirit, like a youthful wife when you were refused, says your God. For a mere moment I have forsaken you, but with great mercies I will gather you, with a little wrath I hid my face from you for a moment: but with everlasting kindness I will have mercy on you, says the Lord, your Redeemer.'

What does He mean, forsaken me? Why has He forsaken me? I did not like the bit about the wife because I still had not been fed with childhood things. I had refused to grow into adulthood with all its implications. I wanted absolute innocence and a non threatening existence; just pure love and affection by parents. I could not think of seeking anything more. First things must come first. As in Flenkton during my training and Apple Ash with Karen I still searched for a mother figure. Nothing would or could break the tenacious gnawing at my forgotten soul.

Not long afterwards as I was making my way home from shopping and still sensing the angry hand of God, I was in deep thought. Why had He been so nice one minute and then my enemy the next? I felt utterly depressed about the matter so addressing Him said,

'Get out of my life. I don't want You anymore. I have never saved anyone or anything. I'm just no good. Go on, get out.'

That moment He left; I felt Him go. The air around me became empty and quiet. *Where has He gone?*

'You can come back again, if You want,' I quickly uttered.

I told Charles what I had done when I next saw him and he responded firmly,

'You should NEVER say that to God. You could get killed in an instant. He lifts all His protection away.'

That scared me and another lesson was learned. A few days later I was still searching for answers. While lying on the carpet reading chapter twenty eight of the book of Deuteronomy, about blessings for obedience and curses for disobedience, I saw the blessings did not apply to me at all but nearly, if not all the curses did apply to my life! I pressed the palms of my hands into the carpet. My eyes were transfixed in acknowledgement of the truth and the threat of separation from God's presence was like a kiss of betrayal. I prized my upper body free of the close proximity of the Bible as though it were my enemy. In a second I was on my feet and stepped backwards from the penetrating Sword of the Word of God. How had I been disobedient? I was just a human being like everybody else. I had been better than most trying to keep myself a good person and not to displease God. It was a real slap in the face from the God of love I thought I was getting to know. During that long bout of depression I read the Bible and other books about mighty acts of God in other people's lives. I had also bought Graham Kendrick worship records. His deep voice of supplication to the Lord comforted my troubled soul. While sitting, one day, in my big green armchair by the window overlooking the local park, which separated us from Ribford *(Westport)* hospital, I asked God what book of the Bible I should read. I told Him He did not understand me or care at all,

'Isaiah,' He immediately answered.

I started to read chapter one, verse five read,

'Why should you be beaten any more? Why do you persist in rebellion? Your whole head is injured, your whole heart afflicted. From the sole of your foot to the top of your head there is no soundness – only wounds and bruises and open sores, not cleansed or bandaged or soothed with oil.'

My eyes widened and gasping to catch my breath, I declared,

'You *do* understand!'

At last a word of comprehension of the pain and desolation in my life. As already stated my body too was malformed in some way from the top of my head to the sole's of my feet. Was I able to see that maybe it was a sign of how I was on the inside? I remembered the saying when He did not heal me the night I asked Him to, 'You will know when I have finished'. I understood that once He healed me on the inside He would also heal my entire body from head to toe. I longed and long for that moment. Those times of deep grief and suffering brought forth many poems; the first one was written when I was only sixteen, trying to make sense of things and get some answers to my troublesome existence. They also brought some creativity out of me. Taking a pencil and a sketch book in hand one morning I drew the following as I was given it by the Holy Spirit. The message was,

'I love you,'

I drew a willow tree.

'I laid My life down for you,'

I drew a heart with a crown of thorns around the centre and drops of blood falling from it.

'Can you love me that way too?'

I drew a cross on a hill.

'Take My strength.'

I drew a cobbled, uphill road knowing the way would be hard. Was I literally going to die for Him? I put the picture aside.

I sat contemplating my behaviour of violence because not a day went by without it. I noticed also the pattern of my outbursts, being unable to help the surge that erupted from within me at communion. I so often wanted to hurl the communion things across the church *(though I never did).* During worship I changed all the words around and, rather than worshipping, I sang according to my experiences and observations. Unexpected hurling of newspapers or magazines across the road that I bought after church would startle me and anyone with me. Yet in my eyes I had done nothing wrong. I only saw why I behaved that way. It was a natural progression from my past and because I was seeking love and healing. One time at church when I was not worshipping at all, somebody read the scripture verse for all to hear,

'If you do not worship me even the stones will cry out.' Luke 19:40.

Well if a stone can do it I'll do it as a stone then. A few days later I was sitting on the side of my bed and suddenly sat bolt upright, as though hit by an invisible fist.

'Have I got demons?' I asked myself.

Convinced now that this was my problem; my search for an answer began. What could I say to people? It would indeed explain my out of control behaviour after Mass. These things were out of keeping with who I really was on the inside. I did not equate the violence with who I really was. We Pallitans were decent, church going Catholics who dutifully attended Mass every week. We children especially were like broken down ships on a violent sea. Debris scattered across our hearts. When my heart tried to function it spluttered all kinds of pus from wounds inflicted by a mightier hand. It lay practically lifeless in a body trying to carry its dead weight, struggling to live from one day to the next. The demons of hatred had landed on the vacant ground left by my dead mother and uncaring, violent father. Something or someone needed to be tending to this wandering, aimless soul, but what and who could it be? What had I done to deserve such a warped personality and putrid character? Why did my mother die? Why the confusion of mind? Why the rejection? Why hated by my own father? Why was I born and when would I die?

Chapter Two

First Trip Abroad and Aftermath

Besides trying to cope with my troubles I wanted to make everything please God in my life. I had never been abroad and thought a change would do me some good. One thing was sure to please Him.

'I would like to go to Israel before I go anywhere else,' I told Him.

It was a kind of 'first fruits' travel offering. This would make all my future journeys holy and sanctified. First fruits offerings were normally meant for the harvest of crops but I wanted to include my travels as well, besides, I had no crops to offer. Peggy and I discovered a trip with a Christian group for that May. It would be my first time on an airplane. *I think I might be healed in Israel.* Everybody in the Bible was healed in Israel so why not me? So off we went. On arrival at Heathrow airport we spotted a lady from our church at a distance but she was not coming to Israel with us. Her white hair and blue gabardine made her easy to recognize. She was fast advancing towards some glass doors with her arms stretched out in front of her and had no idea she was being watched by anyone she knew. To her complete surprise the doors opened automatically and she was unable to slow down. It was the funniest thing and started our journey on a good footing.

Once through the airport system and outside we crossed the tarmac, boarded the plane and settled down for the flight. Five hours later, after a non eventful but enjoyable flight, we landed in Ben Gurion airport. I felt like I had come home. A feeling, I believe, sent from Heaven. Most people felt the same. We travelled in the dark by coach to the King David hotel in Jerusalem where Peggy and I shared a beautiful twin room. The four star hotel, in my eyes, was magnificent. After unpacking we experienced our first meal of the tour. A whole fish lay on our plates. Head, fins and tail were all included. I sat like a statue, staring and trying to work out how I was going to eat all that until our tour leader realized I was stuck with knowing how to proceed. He informed me it was a St Peter's fish from the Sea of Galilee and offered to separate the meat from everything else. I turned away until he finished. It was hard to swallow the added vegetables together with the fish due to the lump in my throat but I somehow managed to finish the meal, after which, a welcome meeting was held for the group in a room upstairs before we went to bed.

At five in the morning we woke to unfamiliar sounds coming from outside, a little way away. The wailing of human voices through sirens permeated the skies from tall minarets. It was not a disturbing, grating sound but quite attractive. Not a morning passed without that human dawn chorus. Such was the dedication of the Muslims to prayer. I had not heard any Jewish shofar blasts or Christian worship of any kind. We did not mind it. It was all such a novelty and we were, after all, little children being carouselled through our trip of a lifetime.

Jesus says in Mathew Chapter six of the New Testament: *'But you, when you pray, go into your room, and when you have shut your door, pray to your Father who is in the secret place; and your Father who sees in secret will reward you openly',* and so maybe that was why neither Jew nor Christian prayed out in the open.

We made our way down to the dining room a few hours later and discovered there was no cereal for breakfast. We had to help ourselves to a buffet. That proved a great challenge to me. In my timidity I found it hard to choose what to have so copied others and nervously helped myself. After sitting down at a table and grace was said by our leader I picked up the huge orange. My thumb nail went through the peel with unexpected ease and pulled it away with little effort. It was fresh from the tree and much larger than the ones at home. It seemed to me that in transit to our country the peel shrinks to about an eighth its size and all moisture evaporates, making the use of a knife or extra sharp finger and thumb nails imperative. The exquisite taste and what seemed non acidic juice was sweetness itself; non acidic because it did not 'bite' on the way down. The best part of breakfast though were baps completely covered with masses of sesame seeds and the taste was nothing that I can describe except I was sure God would allow such things into Heaven; both baps and oranges. In fact everything in Israel should be in Heaven. In England baps had between ten to twelve sesame seeds at the most on top. There was a problem to taste even one unless you bit into the tiny thing if you could find it in your mouth; much better to taste many and not have to work so hard.

The following evening a meeting was held in one of the rooms in the hotel. There, our leader spoke about the suffering of the Jews in the holocaust and various other persecutions. I wondered if the reason for all my suffering was so that I could understand and help them. Suddenly, a revelation popped into my mind, *they need healing!* I probably thought that because *I* needed healing. The emptiness and pain I felt even at that moment did not help gird myself into action so I tucked the revelation away together with the 'get to know your leaders' one I had back in England a few years before.

As we took days out touring the land where Jesus walked I marveled at the feeling of belonging, the beautiful scenery and the Bible coming alive.

'Wow, this is gorgeous,' I said aloud.

I gave my whole heart to adoring the land and knew God would be pleased. The next thing I heard in my head though was,

'Don't worship My land, worship Me.'

He had a point!

Next morning our destiny was Mount Tabor and a real challenge to our nerves. An Israeli tour driver climbed up the narrow hairpin bends at a daring speed.

'We might meet a taxi coming down in the other direction,' I said, as if he would not have known.

He reassured us that he was the best driver for the eventuality. The mountain road was hardly wide enough for a donkey let alone one car. Once at the top we gazed down hundreds of feet to the patchwork valley of Jezreel. Suddenly, at three o'clock in the afternoon the voice of God was heard in an awesome thunderclap. There was no lightning or rain and we knew God had acknowledged our hunger to have Him along with us and experience His majesty. The following day we visited Masada, ascending the high battlement via cable car. It was there that in AD70 the Jews committed suicide against the attack of the Romans. The height of the fortress made me turn pale. A single, waist high rope was all that prevented us from falling to the depths of the Roman camps far below. Even holding onto the rope for security was enough to send anybody's head spinning round. The high waterfall of En Gedi, on our return from Masada, sprung from rocks down to the crystal clear pebbly pool at other tourists' feet. Bathers refreshed themselves under the mighty spray, I did not. Opposite, goats stood regally in the crevices of rocks at En Gedi. I wondered how they managed to get up or down as the rocks were almost vertical.

We went on other tours including Mount Hermon where I had the great opportunity of holding a soldier's rifle. The weight almost had me on my knees. After our short visit there it was on to the Dead Sea, in which I nearly drowned. It is the saltiest of seas and keeps everything and everyone afloat that enters it but not me! Peggy floated well but I could not get the gist of lying back and trusting it to hold me up. It was funny that I should feel so threatened in a sea that, to my knowledge, had never had one record of a drowning in its life, or rather – death. Speaking of death, I felt suicidal on the trip as the depression had not lifted just because I went abroad. I did expect to be healed but it did not happen.

When the tour was over and we were almost home, I gazed out of the plane window at the scenery of England. I could not believe how cramped the land was. London seemed to be struggling for breath as its buildings jostled, trying to find their space. In only ten days of being away the difference had an incredible impact on me. To see police in blue shirts and Bobbies' black helmets felt stranger than strange. We had got used to soldiers with guns and rifles all over the place in Israel. The fruit stores in Israel were packed with so much produce, filling the streets with vibrant colours and smells. In England the stores are sparse and lifeless in comparison.

Once home it was back to business dealing with my health. Peggy came into my room one afternoon and said she had met a man named Roy Herpson and that he could deliver people from demons. Immediately, a voice within me retaliated,

'I don't need him.'

Then my church suggested I should spend some time at a home of healing in Devon at their expense so I gratefully accepted. Purple Heathers was set in a lush area where pine trees lined the streets. It was an immaculate place of utmost beauty. The large, white house stood elegantly at the end of a short driveway but everything frightened me. I was shown to my room on the first floor; a small one at the end of the corridor with a sink at the far end. The wooden box fixed above the headboard was a tannoy which the following morning came on at ten to eight with music. The resident warden gave out a thought for the day which was most welcome and so often it spoke directly into the condition of my circumstances. Purple Heathers was indeed a safe place.

Leslie Ridgehurst *(the warden),* a Methodist minister, wore a long blue cassock. He walked slowly through the house. His gentle but deep voice made me feel secure, such as I would expect from a father. A bell rang at dinner time. Residents formed a neat queue outside the dining room, which daunted me. So many people! Again the lump in my throat surfaced. Fear and anxiety shook me still. Allowing everybody to walk past I stood frozen to the spot. Leslie beckoned me but I could not advance. He stood beside me and asked,

'Are you alright?'

'I can't go in.'

Discerning the fear he invited me to sit at his table. The round table was set with knives, forks and the usual things including water jugs and glasses. White starched table cloths hung neatly to chair seat level. I had taken my napkin from the cupboard on the way in. Each person was assigned a napkin ring with their room number inscribed on it. I sat in silence for the entire meal. Every person an ogre surrounded the table. I dared not look at any of them. Even moving away from the table after lunch when Leslie said the grace was a terrifying event. *Where do I go now?* Of course I had to move but when I did it was very slowly and each step taken as though walking on water. *Am I doing the right thing?* And so I carried on fumbling my way through the day. In the evening after a chapel service the caretaker led me to the altar and while we both knelt, he wept. His compassion spoke of a possible rescuing answer from God and I was deeply touched by the man's love and care. He was a caretaker in every sense of the word.

The following morning during an appointment with Leslie in his office I mentioned my grandfather, Thomas Plowder, to him,

'Do you know if anybody knew him?'

'Ah, yes, I knew Tom Plowder.'

He called him Tom. All at once Leslie became my grandfather; the one that was never there for any of us. Leslie was not aware of his transformation but I am sure he respected me more for being a Methodist Minister's granddaughter. Because I was poor, on benefits and my stay paid for by my church we talked about improvements. One of them was the question of riches. Leslie announced confidently,

'In fact, you are going to be *very* rich.'

Those words took anchor in my barren heart and the hope of them coming true remained with me more than anything else he said. I mentioned to him about the episodes of paralysis and 'effort syndrome' that I experienced at Apple Ash and he, in turn, told me about a story of a girl he knew who had come to him once,

'She had had her hand amputated because it was paralyzed and as her finger nails grew they embedded into her clenched fist and could not be cut. They were damaging her hand. Now the reason for her hand being cramped like that was not because of a physical illness but because of hysteria.'

My heart went out to the girl who had to live without that hand for life. How it could have been avoided if only her dilemma had been diagnosed correctly. It was hysteria *(not to be confused with hysterical)* that caused the 'effort syndrome' at Apple Ash as Sandra, a resident there, had shown me in her nurse's dictionary.

That sunny afternoon I ventured outside *(my energy gone completely)* to find a vacant area of grass. I rounded the corner of the chapel and noticed an older couple sitting there but before I could turn back a face looked up at me from a deckchair.

'Hello, I'm Ruby and this is Archie, my husband.' I smiled and, being polite, lay on an area of grass not too close to them. 'Where are you from?' asked Ruby.

I sensed she would not harm me so told her.
'Where are you from?' I returned.
'Mackton.'
Mackton? That's where Roy Herpson lives.
'Oh, do you know Roy Herpson? My sister told me a bit about him.'
'Yes, I'm his sister.'
I nearly swallowed myself whole with shock. *God must be showing me I do need him after all.* I unloaded my problems onto Ruby whose response was,
'You can come and stay with me for a while if you like and we can minister to you.'
'Do you deliver people from demons?'
'Yes, Roy can come over to our house and pray with you.'
'Okay, thank you very much.'
I returned to the same spot the following day. Archie and Ruby were not there then. I lay down exhausted and while I relaxed, God spoke,
'I will take you far and wide.'
I could not see that happening in my condition and wondered when it would ever be.

As soon as I returned home I prepared for a visit to Mackton. At first, I only went for an evening. Victor Entwist, one of the elders from my church, drove me to Ruby and Archie's bungalow. The deliverance ministry impressed me as Ruby used accurate words of knowledge for my condition,
'I will make you a pure virgin bride,' Victor prophesied, as though God was speaking.
I felt embarrassed but knew God would take away the shame of my father's sexual abuse. Confident in this and, feeling no threat from Ruby, I accepted a further invitation to stay for a week with her and Archie. After becoming more familiar with them my behaviour deteriorated as my need became more apparent. During my stay I became frustrated because of a communication problem. I could not adequately express myself. My real need was just to be loved and understood. Having been told by others that I would never get the love of parents I was not prepared to express it to Ruby, at least for a while. I shouted at her at times

and could not listen to her many misunderstandings. At other times I was so frustrated when she said things that did not apply to me that I took my glasses off and threw them across the room. If people argued with me or offered something other than what was along my own understanding I felt I could not make any progress. I could not understand what they were saying to me. They wanted me to act normally but I could not, even though I wanted to.

At times I helped Ruby with her gardening and housework and that part of me, as usual, was fine. Being very troubled and praying to God about myself I needed an answer. One day while in the bathroom I read from a scripture calendar Ruby had put on the wall,

'Do not be afraid, I know that you seek Jesus.' Matthew 28:5.

It stood out more than any other verse. I felt comforted that God was going to do a major work of healing in my life and that I would find Jesus. At the same time I wondered why He was telling me I had not yet found Him even though He was with me.

Ruby had already spoken to Roy and told me of his plan,

'Roy and Brenda said you can live with them for a while.'

'When we were praying the other day I had the word anorexia,' I informed her.

'No, you are not anorexic so that can't have been right,' Ruby insisted.

I did not know Roy and Brenda and was upset that Ruby could not continue to have me. I became unsure about living with them because it meant leaving Ribford so I arranged an appointment with the Disability Rehabilitation Officer to see if I could cope with some work. If not successful I would go and live with the Herpsons

'You can go to a rehabilitation unit in Surrey. You can live there for six weeks and see what kind of training would best suit you,' said the DRO manager during my interview.

That appealed to me so I left his office feeling it was an opportunity to pursue. Walking along the high street on the way home I passed St Paul's church and decided to go in. The door was unlocked. I walked down the centre aisle and slid into a pew half way down the church. There, I sat and stared at a huge cross at the front. After a few minutes I came out, went home, phoned Ruby and told her I had been at the church. She asked,

'Did God say anything to you?'

'No.'

But almost immediately, out of the blue, the memory of what He had said came flooding back. How can something that you did not even know happened come flooding back? But it did.

'Oh, yes, He did. He said, "People - will not be patient with you but I will be patient with you. People - have not suffered as you have but I have suffered and I will be patient with you. I can do in a few days what it would take humans a lifetime to do."'

Pondering that memory I knew I was not in for a happy time where people were concerned but I also knew that He was with me and for me. He understood what I would go through until He decided to act whenever those few days would come. A couple of weeks later I was off to Surrey for the training. I was unsure how to find the place and coming off the train with my suitcase, ventured onto a huge field. Glancing over to my right I noticed an airplane was taking off. *Oh my goodness, I'm walking on a runway.* The plane was not that close as it was not exactly the runway but still the field did belong to the airport. *I better get off it quick.*

The rehabilitation centre consisted mostly of single story accommodation buildings. I was shown to my room where a dark haired girl sitting on one of the beds greeted me. We exchanged an introduction. The whitewashed walls and spartan furniture; only a bed, bedside locker and a wardrobe at the end furthest from the door, spoke of a temporary stay. A big, chunky radiator stood in front of the window opposite my bed. Huge concrete slabs stared from beneath the whitewashed walls. No wallpaper or anything fancy there. Settling in was a problem due to my lack of confidence and the feeling of not deserving anything. Uncertainty about my future and the fact that this was a rehabilitation unit undermined my hopes and did nothing for my dignity. At meal times I found I could not eat more than a couple of mouthfuls of food before feeling sick. When nobody was watching I threw the remainder away into the bins provided and disappeared to my room.

During the first class, next morning, I started making a plastic letter opener,

'You can choose the colours you like. Choose your pieces of plastic and return to your workbench, I'll come round to help you all in turn,' said our tutor.

I chose a white blade and would create a black handle with a red strip running diagonally through it, front and back. The red strip was the most important as it signified the blood of Jesus breaking darkness and demonic forces. The white blade sandwiched inside the handle would emerge as a cutting edge, signifying light and the sharpness of the Word of God. It would ensure victory and take full control of the job it was made for. First, we drew the shapes onto thin slabs of plastic then cut them with a small saw. After that we sanded them down and then glued the red and black handle parts onto the blade. Finally, we polished the entire knife to give it a good shine. One of the boys made a harness for his but I did not know how to make one so did without. It took two weeks to make the knife.

Meanwhile I was losing weight because of the new eating problem. I met a Christian lad who invited me to a prayer meeting held at a pastor's house. There I renounced all the works and associations with the Devil and after prayer did not feel much better so went back to the centre disappointed.

After the spell of time in the 'plastic' factory I was due to do some typing training. However, I could do no more than put my head on my arms. My energy was diminished yet again but it was no usual tiredness. I phoned Ruby and told her about the events unfolding before me and that I could not sit up during class.

'Roy will be on a course up in that area; in Napsome, actually, next week. I will have a word with him. He may be able to pick you up.'

That was all too much of a coincidence but because of my health I accepted the proposal to go and live with the Herpsons.

Chapter Three

Desperation

I left Surrey before my six weeks was up. Roy picked me up and drove me the long way to his bungalow. After staying there for a week I went back to Ribford to pack some things in a case. On my return to Mackton by bus I felt uneasy about the decision I had made. Was it right?

'Put your cases down,' I heard that Voice say in my head.

Oh, I'm going to be happy here then? I crossed the road and ventured towards the small bungalow in Norcombe Lane. On arrival Roy carried my case up a narrow, metal ladder to the loft and put it on the floor next to my bed,

'Now you can unpack and come down when you are ready.'

A few days into my stay I walked into the lounge to a sight that stopped me short. Roy was over the other side of the room with his arm around his much shorter wife and both were staring at me with a mocking expression. They were posing just for me. It seemed like an accusation; testing to see my reaction but they would never see it as I tucked it well away from them. Up in the attic bedroom that night I found my tablets and took the lot. Again I was admitted to hospital for the usual stomach washout. Roy, who was also a pastor, came to the hospital and stood at my left hand side. I lay on the trolley and as he leaned over to ask why I had taken the tablets I grabbed his hand, merely because it was the only one available. I squeezed it like I was drowning in a sea of desperation,

'Help me, please, please help me.'

A psychiatrist arrived and admitted me to the local psychiatric hospital in Easingborough where I stayed for three weeks. My days were spent watching television with my legs swinging over an arm of a chair. No visitors attended me, not even the Herpsons. The place was a far cry from Fareacre and All Saints Hospital in Rombourne *(see book one)*; a dilapidated complex and not at all conducive to a patient's wellbeing. It was not the place for me. When discharged three weeks later Roy came to collect me and I tried to settle with him and Brenda. A few days into my stay one of the ladies in the fellowship came round to see them and to meet me. While we were all gathered in the kitchen she told Roy and Brenda,

'I had a picture while I was praying, of Rachel. There was a funnel and God was saying that continuous love needs to be poured into the funnel.'

Her message encouraged me so much. I really would get what I needed because God had shown them.

Brenda was nine years older than Roy. A quiet, non intrusive woman and, I thought, without character. She worked in the house making sure the meals were cooked and housework done. I kept my room tidy and helped in the house at times.

Roy and Ruby prayed for me on occasions and I still helped sort out Ruby's garden. It was not long before Peggy came to live with Ruby. We did not see too much of each other though. I had left most of my belongings with Peggy at Ribford but as she was in the process of moving I had to bring my things over as well. Ruby had said I could store some of it in her loft and after taking the last of it up there I closed the hatch. Peggy stood in the lounge doorway watching. Suddenly, she pushed me with such force that I lost balance.

'What did you do that for?' I shouted.

The loft door powerfully swung loose and blood gushed from one of my fingers as it swept past.

'You could have been killed. I saw the door coming open.'

It was not the only time she stepped in to save my life. Her compassionate heart blessed me even though I could not appreciate it fully because of my impacted pain, broken heart and terror filled life. Nevertheless, any act of kindness towards me never went unheeded. I loved my sister. Ruby turned the cold tap on in the kitchen, ran my finger under it to help stop the bleeding and put a dressing on.

My behaviour had not improved since arriving at the Herpsons. If I could not sleep at night I crept down the ladder, whose noisy creaks could not be avoided, to the toilet. Roy, whose bedroom was downstairs and almost opposite, came out and waited in the kitchen. He made a drink and we chatted for a while. The scenario became a regular routine.

On Sunday mornings church meetings were held in the village hall. Roy packed the acetates and sound equipment into his car. He also took us on Thursdays to Cantrin Community Centre where Ryan Hovling, a renowned leader from Bramington, held meetings once a week. The meetings did not offer much help but I looked forward to them because it meant travelling a few miles in Roy's car but I was always in the back seat; a sure reminder that that's where I belonged; at the back of everything. I was fed up with being a runt so, back in Mackton, took off for a walk towards the seafront, not the part I usually went to but as I walked I pondered my life situation and thought I heard God say,

'Humble yourself in the sight of the Lord and I will lift you up.'

It was not an encouraging word at that moment but good enough to keep me going for a bit.

On Wednesday evenings prayer meetings, which I found boring, were held in other people's homes. I expected Jesus to be present but He was not. Mostly, people chatted away for hours before any prayers were said. I became frustrated because I needed to be getting better. Healing and deliverance did not seem to be a priority on their agenda. The chatting went on and on and on and one time I sat fuming away on the inside. When the fuming reached a peek I stood up with a jolt declaring with a mighty hint to the others,

'Well, I'm going to get my knitting.'

Off I went home, brought it back and knitted to my heart's content. Nobody heard my cry. There was no prayer that night and I began to feel trapped in Mackton. We had to travel seven miles from Mackton just to start any journey. I had a life to live. I did not want to stay there for the rest of it.

'You will find your husband here in Mackton,' said Roy.

I was not even looking for a husband. I still needed parents. The little girl inside of me needed to be loved and cherished without any overtones of uncleanness in any way. Roy was affectionate on occasions but Brenda was not.

One night as I tried to sleep in my attic room I had a vision of my mother. Her long flowing hair was not the truth. She did not have long hair. But there she was by the sea with beautiful locks hanging over her shoulders. *I must go to my mum.* For a while I lay there scanning my entire life. Anger rose to a crescendo and I was going to get the Devil for what he had done to me and my family. Deciding not to go out entirely in my night clothes I quickly descended the ladder and hurried past Roy and Brenda's room, took my coat from the hook and very quietly opened the front door. Once clear of the bungalow I turned left and made my way to the top of the lane. Once there I looked behind me at the many detached bungalows on the opposite side of the road. It was like a Flintstones movie when all was still and quiet, until I shouted with all my might in the most defiant rage,

'Say-t-a-r-n!!'

There would be a fight between him and me and I would win. I imagined all the lights down the lane coming on but not one sign of life appeared. Thank God. *They haven't heard me.* I hurled my voice into the air a second time,

'Say-t-a-r-n!!' and waited.

I was a sure match for him. No devil could defy me now as I braced myself in the pitch black. In deadly silence I waited for his arrival but as I stood motionless my adrenalin decreased so much that in the calmness I imagined the arrival of my foe. *What have I done?* Remembering he had no good in him whatsoever and would probably come with the hoards of hell like locusts to devour me, I was filled with horror. *I have to get back quick.* Relinquishing all bravery I walked as quickly as I could to reach the caravan that stood outside the Herpson's bungalow and sat on the steps. I called on God to save me from the inevitable visit from His, and my, opponent. Hoping for His answer I gazed into the sky and imagined drinking the blood of Jesus down in gulps. Had God visited me in the Devils place? Was the blood the antidote to a night of sheer desperation? I do not know but that night was real, the fear was real, the spiritual tangibility was real. I cannot remember the front door opening to me but I knew, for sure, I was in big trouble with the Herpsons. Roy must have come out but the moment of re-entry to the bungalow is one blur of a memory. What had I done to deserve such an existence?

Ruby often took me for walks along the seafront. There was an uncanny pull on my mind and body to walk into the sea and drown. Ruby, noticing what was happening, grabbed my arm and pulled me from even going one step out of line.

'This happens to quite a few people who come to Mackton,' she explained. 'There's witches who live in Tangletown, the next village. I think they have something to do with it.'

What have I got myself into? How do I get out of this place? Things were not going as I had expected when I arrived at Mackton and one afternoon Roy and Brenda decided they wanted a break and told me quite plainly,

'We are going to see Jungle Book.'

'Can I come?' even though I would be disturbed during the film.

'No.'

'Why not, why can't I come?'

Roy smiled mockingly so I hit his chest as hard as I could. I wanted to enjoy things just like anybody else. They got into the car without me. *It's me who should be going to see Jungle Book not two middle aged people.* Roy reversed the car into the road, ignoring my pleas. Slowly they turned and drove away. In my long blue and white dress I ran down the middle of the road after them. Wild rejection filled the atmosphere. They picked up speed and disappeared. I returned to the bungalow and dialed 999.

'Emergency services, what do you want; fire, ambulance or police?'

'Police, please.'

After a pause a policeman picked up the phone.

'I want to hand myself in for assault and battery.'

'Okay, I'll get somebody down to see you shortly.'

When the policeman arrived I told him my story and he said,

'Well, I'm not going to arrest you. You have not done any damage and he has not pressed charges. You just settle down and things will be okay.'

Fine.

As well as being a pastor Roy was an artist. He painted landscape pictures in oil. In his office he painted one for me of a fishing scene and I was staggered by such a gift. It was not a picture for a female, I thought, even though I had longed to go fishing with a dad many times but, nevertheless, it was the 'thought that counted'. I puzzled why he gave it to me. I would love to be able to paint like that.

The bungalow was not a comfortable place and needed a lot of improvements. Roy set to redecorating it and taught me how to paint walls and doors. He was trained by McAlpines. I enjoyed learning the new trade. Again my expertise in being able to turn things to gold at a touch came to the fore. If only inside I was gold. Once the redecorating was finished an evening prayer meeting was held at the bungalow, at which, I still longed for Jesus. While we were praying I had a picture of His face over England. It covered the entire island. There was one thing wrong with it though. He was unrecognizable; so marred were His features. It certainly explained why I was experiencing the cold, callousness of the 'caring' church. Yes, my behaviour was all topsy turvy but there were good reasons for it. Instead of receiving the love God told them to give I was dished out an unwillingness to heal and deliver me. If only I could have been myself, who I really was deep inside and not this awful tormented whip of a thing. God had told me to get to know my leaders years before and I was certainly getting to know this one. He was not all bad and his congregation loved him but I wanted more. The only reason I was in Mackton was to get set free but I found myself in a frightful situation.

As in fairy tales Prince Charming, I mean, Prince Charles, arrived on the scene in a dream one night. I arrived in my air force blue coat, long brown woolly scarf, equally woolly knitted hat and matching gloves at our village hall. Music emanated from the entrance so I ventured to open the door slightly. A most glorious sight caused me to open it wider. I stood watching as the hall was full of ladies dressed in the most wonderful dance costumes. I had never been to a ball and silently carried on watching the professional looking feet whirl about the floor. Prince Charles chaperoned their movements as they weaved gracefully, grasping and letting go of his hands as they glided past. Then something caught his eye; me, standing in the doorway! He left the ladies to dance among themselves and strode towards me. I waited. He extended a hand and offered so unexpectedly,

'Can I teach you the steps?'

Despite my not having the correct apparel to dance with a Prince I took his offer and away we went. Sadly, I woke up but the message was clear. Jesus, the Prince of Peace would teach me how to live one step at a time, not bothering what my outward state was. He has to start somewhere with every one of us. I hid the message in my heart as it was highly unlikely ever to happen, in my view anyway.

During that first summer the entire fellowship attended a Bible Week where everyone camped in a field and meetings were held in a huge marquee. I had never heard of such things. I slept in an awning attached to the Herpson's caravan.

The following year at the Bible Week Roy arranged for me to sleep in a tent of my own. One night about midnight I woke suddenly. My eyes just popped open to a great awareness of evil. I had never screamed before in my life and lay frozen to the spot. It was not a windy night but my tent flaps hit the sides of the tent. I swallowed. *What is that?* Holding my breath I listened some more. The flaps made another dull thudding sound against the upper portion of my tent. *If that happens one more time I'm going to scream.* The flap raised and lowered itself rapidly. Fear of screaming was more intense than fear of the noise. Then with an increased intensity of the evil presence a scream rammed loudly out of my throat and into the eerie atmosphere. Almost instantly Evelyn, from the fellowship, was at my bedside.

'It's okay,' she said, 'we know. I watched the tents all being flapped like that; one by one, not all at once. But then it seemed to rest at your tent. When it found yours it left everybody else's alone.'

Why, why would it come to me? Despite feeling awkward when people helped me I allowed Evelyn to stay until I had been to the toilet and returned. She prayed with me and then left. At least, I believed, they knew how much I was targeted and that my condition was serious. I was not play acting or looking for attention but had a real, deep need to get set free from all the torment. That morning when the fellowship was awake and dressed for the day Evelyn was telling Roy and Brenda,

'I came out of my tent to see what was going on. All the tents were flapping one by one but when it got to Rachel's it stopped and kept on flapping hers. The Devil was coming towards me and

I was about to run but God said to me very firmly, "Stand and face your enemy."'

Thankfully, she obeyed and I was rescued. It goes to say that a person has to witness and be involved in a situation to really be of help to another person. I wonder if the outcome would have been the same, when *I* told them in the morning about the visitation, if I had not screamed and the others had been sleeping throughout my ordeal. Would they have believed me? I may not have been there to tell the tale at all. What would the Devil have done with me? Better not to ask or even try to imagine.

Later, at one of the daytime meetings in the main marquee, I was standing and feeling vulnerable. My eyes were closed and all was very dark. I saw a picture of God's shirted back. I grabbed the white material and while holding it tight, heard Him say,

'You stay *that* close to Me.'

I held on as He led me slowly through the darkness. There was no light anywhere except for His shirt.

At that Bible week God moved in my life in a way that was not common. I felt His powerful touch. He had heard my cries and come down to help. During one of the meetings somebody prayed for me and I fell to the floor where I rested for a while under the power of the Holy Spirit. Nobody else experienced the phenomenon. I overheard somebody ask,

'Is she dead?'

I had visions of being taken out of the marquee and put in a mortuary and panicked but thankfully nothing like that happened and I got up later.

Just before leaving the Bible week Roy and Brenda went for a walk and said I could go along with them but they walked on ahead. As usual I walked behind in rejection and became more and more morose. They had not turned to me once to see where I was. Eventually, when I reached them, I asked,

'Why did you just walk off and not wait for me?'

Roy mocked my behaviour so I kicked him in the shin. That hurt him and I was glad. They were putting me through agony. I decided not to go home with them but instead to walk back! Leaving them, I wandered off alone. Two hours later while walking towards Mackton I was thinking they must have gone and even be home. *I don't care.* I did not know where I was and naturally came to the point of telephoning them for help. Neither of them was amused by my absence. Roy came and picked me up. They became even colder towards me. Because they were refusing to deliver me my behaviour worsened. They were so deaf to my cries for love. One day when returning from a church meeting at another congregant's home a member of the congregation who was walking along with us told me,

'Mothers can become jealous of their daughters.'

I had been trying to be a daughter to them and pondered what she had said,

'Why?'

Such tension arose. I wanted pure, innocent love and to be free to express and receive it without any form of misunderstanding or filth. Other people's thoughts were being forced into mine and I could not stand it. It was not long before I became exhausted and slept for hours into the day. Unable to move, again the Apple Ash syndrome hit me. For three weeks I lay unable to recover. It was only when Brenda said she had had enough that I was made to get up and do something about the exhaustion. Gentle movements at first rehabilitated me but I did not agree with her getting me up and about so soon. The grief of not finding Jesus had taken its toll. A few days later another prayer meeting was under way at the bungalow. The usual first hour or so of talking bored me to tears. Why could they not sense the desperation and anguish? *I know what I'll do,*

'Excuse me.'

I left the room. Once into the hall I reached for my coat, turned the door knob quietly and stepped outside. Pulling the door softly and knowing they would not miss me with all the chatting, I turned right and kept walking until I reached the Off-license. After entering and scanning the bottles I asked,

'What is your cheapest wine?'

I took the delicious sounding apricot wine home with me, silently opened the door and sneaked into Roy's office. Great! I opened the bottle and drank the contents without stopping, no matter the unexpected disgusting taste. While watching the level of wine getting lower in the bottle I was pleased that it was not affecting me. I was in big trouble if it was. Not long afterwards though it dragged me downwards and made me very sleepy. *Oh, this is nice.* Another mouthful had to be the last. My body could not cope with any more. I had drunk three quarters of the bottle; a disappointment to myself as I wanted to finish it entirely. Finally, Roy made his way out of the lounge in search of my whereabouts. Seeing his office light on he stepped inside,

'Where have you been? What are you doing?'

My heavy head had fallen onto his desk, still attached to my shoulders I must add. My left arm hung lifeless from its socket as I sat in his chair.

'Are you drunk?'

'No, I'm not drunk. I know exactly what I'm doing and saying.'

'What's all this about?'

'Where is Jesus? He isn't in the prayer meeting.'

'We are going to pray soon. Come in when you are ready.'

'I won't be long,' I answered, quite coherently.

Roy left and I took no time in getting to my feet. *I must get in there with Jesus.* Taking my first step I slowly walked towards the office door. Thankfully, it was ajar so that was no obstacle. My body by then felt like it was swimming in syrup. As I neared the lounge door I took a deep breath. *I am fine.* My hand reached towards the door handle and grasped it for steadiness. I pushed the door and walked in. Knowing that nobody would notice I stood in the room and glanced around at the people. The room was full and Peggy sat next to my empty chair in the corner. A well of compassion rose in my heart towards her. Aiming my gaze towards my chair I was determined to walk in a straight line and not to veer left or right, even by a quarter of an inch.

'And I love Peggy,' I stated as I passed.

I made it to my chair without incident and felt a surge of victory. The prayer meeting got under way and I thought I would get some deliverance or healing but no, I was ignored. After everybody left Brenda made me a cup of extra strong coffee; so black it would pale even the colour black to white then held my head, after dragging me to kneel by the toilet, blocked my nose and forced me to drink it until I was sick. Next morning Roy and Brenda suggested I get a job but in my condition I would never have done so as I had not had my deliverance and healing. I knew work would take me along a path unsuitable. However, I had no choice being under their roof. Within a week, after travelling the seven miles by bus to get there, I was in Easingborough job centre. Perusing the cards on display boards I noticed an advertisement for a shop assistant at the Lamton Rooms in the Rich and Richer stores. The Lamton Rooms were equivalent to Chingles shops. *Well, at least that is familiar to me.* I applied for it and was offered the job on the grounds I had already worked for Lamton china and glass in Chingles of Rockminster, Cantrin and Ribford. On my first morning Roy accompanied me all the way to the store because I would not go on my own. He even came up to the door of the back entrance because of my fear.

As I had been taking prescription drugs for depression and not slept for ten nights trying to get off them I was not in a fit state for anything. In what little amount of bravery I had I walked through the store alone until reaching the Lamton Rooms on the ground floor. It did not take me too long to get acquainted due to the familiarity of the job. The manageress was a lovely younger lady and easy to get on with. That was a change for the better in comparison to other management I had experienced so I stayed and even succeeded in remaining off the drugs.

After that first day of getting a lift I caught the bus to and from work where I met a girl called Bessie. She also worked at Rich and Richer in another department. We started travelling home together in the evenings. One of those evenings she made me an offer that changed my life for the better.

'My cat has just had kittens. Would you like one?'

I was delighted. As soon as I saw Roy and Brenda I asked if I could have it,

'No, definitely not,' said Brenda.

Okay. However, on my return from work a couple of evenings later Roy was standing at the bus stop with his compassionate look. Almost crying, it seemed, he said,

'You can have the kitten.'

So I prayed to God,

'Please may I have one that does not get on your lap, putting hairs all over you and one that does not meow?'

The following day after work I went to Bessie's house to choose him.

'You can't have that grey and gingery one. I'm keeping that one and somebody else wants the black one.'

That left two ginger tabbies. One was lying on its own in a basket with its back to us, just like me; the runt of the litter!

'I'll have that one.'

'You can't have him until he is six weeks old.'

So after six weeks I bought a mesh cat carrier and proudly took my new kitten home to Roy and Brenda's. He was mine. I was so chuffed but I knew Brenda did not want him. She had made a sacrifice. Starting with the letter A I went through the alphabet to choose a name for him, Andy, Bandy, Candy, Dandy, Fandy and on up to when I reached Sandy. That's it, Sandy. He was the perfect colour for such a name too. I remembered a time when Brenda showed a bit of compassion. I was picking raspberries at a local farm and all day a little sparrow hopped about at the foot of the canes, keeping me company. I dared not get too close in case it flew away but gave it freedom to get as close as it wanted. On returning home after the day's work Brenda asked if I had had a good day so I told her about my little visitor. She explained that she had prayed to God asking if He would send me a squirrel or something to cheer me up. How thoughtful. If only it could have been like that every day but what of my future? On one of my days off whilst riding on the top deck of a bus one empty day, I begged God,

'Take this hope away!'

I could see no future. A constant dead end reaching into infinity kept giving way to a tormenting perseverance only God could have provided. The treadmill of despair led to many moans and groans until one day God said,

'I know what I am making,' or words to that effect.

During that summer friends of Roy and Brenda, a married couple, came to visit. The lady had all her sewing equipment out on the floor in the lounge. I sat in the green armchair near the fireplace watching my kitten playing with her pin cushion. He gracefully and gently pulled out a pin with his tiny mouth then caringly placed it on the floor. He extracted about twenty more pins one at a time from the foam they were sitting in, in exactly the same way. If only I had had a movie camera on hand. I almost cried as I witnessed my kitten prophecy for the Lord. God spoke to me when all the pins were removed,

‘That is what I am going to do with you, remove every pin that has been stuck into you. Every wound that has caused you so much pain will be removed.’

I understood God’s heart for me that day. God can speak in many ways and one way is through dreams. One night I dreamt I was driving a plane, sitting in the cockpit steering the huge aircraft through the streets and stopping at red traffic lights. I wondered how I would miss the houses and buildings because of the gigantic wings. When I woke I wondered what the dream meant until God shouted,

‘You’re not on the runway!’

The meaning, I presumed, was that I was not yet ready to live the way He wanted me to.

Another dream was that I was pushing a little girl in a pushchair. I walked in front of her to give her something to eat but looking at her face I saw how impossible it was to feed her with anything. She did not have a face; just a blank piece of skin covered the entire head up to the hood. I wondered what the dream meant until God said,

‘You don’t know where your mouth is!’

I wanted to get fixed up and during my desperation something came through the post. I had not sent for it but on the cover it read,

‘God is not in a hurry.’

‘No,’ I said, ‘but I am.’

I did not have any friends in Mackton except for dark, curly haired Queenie; a humble woman who lived round the corner from us. She was part of the dance group. I was invited to a ‘Worship in Dance’ teaching weekend by Lottie, head of the group in our fellowship, even though I could not dance. Four of us arrived in Nobovan, Dorset, on the Friday night by car. The following morning, our first session, was to draw a picture of what we thought our ministry was. I sat on the floor with a blank sheet of paper in front of me. My pencil rested on the floor. Ten minutes later while the other girls were drawing away I sat with my companion the lump in my throat. Inside my skull not a thought entered my brain, ideas were dead and buried as to what I should draw. Linda, the Worship in Dance leader at Nobovan said for the benefit of any who could not even start,

'Just start to draw, anything, it will come.'

Sure, knowing it never would. However, I slowly reached towards the pencil and picked it up. With my left hand I placed the point on the paper and started to draw a tulip. It lay prostrate on the ground. I then drew a house with a wide, jagged crack down the middle. Lastly, I drew a broken heart with drops of blood falling to the ground. Above them I put in a thunder storm. All these were on the left hand side of the page. Next was a mountain in the middle of the page with a person kneeling on top, their hands raised towards Heaven. On the right hand side all the broken images were drawn with nothing wrong with them. The heart was healed, the flower upright and the house no longer disjointed. The person at the top was an intercessor and prophetic Christian who loved Jesus and who brought hope to all afflicted by misadventure and hopelessness; quite an impressive drawing from nothing.

That night trying to sleep together with ten other females was a great trial. My problem with sleeping had not yet been overcome. I could not work out how other people could get to sleep within two minutes of their heads touching the pillow. A lady started to snore. *Oh great, I'm not even nearly asleep yet. Could she not have waited for three hours?* Keeping my thoughts to myself I waited for her to stop but she continued unaware of the torture her sweet sleep was causing somebody else. I became more agitated and angry with her as the night crept on because we were in for a busy day in the morning. Eventually, I could not contain my emotions any longer,

'Oh why can't she just shut up!' I blurted out loudly in an attempt to cure the situation.

Lottie sat bolt upright, swung her heavy legs out of bed, passed other sleeping ladies and dragged herself over to me. She moulded two tiny balls out of the white cotton wool in her hands and demanded,

'Don't you *ever* let me hear you say *anything* like that ever again. Here, put these in your ears.'

Fear ripped through my bones but her actions were taken to a place in my heart that desperately needed the mother's touch.

Strangely comforted I lay back and relaxed when all of a sudden my eyes seemed to turn over; as though looking out of the back of my head. I stared and stared in forced concentration. At first I saw absolutely nothing but then, as my eyes focused, I made out a very faint line of light, then another and another in various parts. When they were all visible I looked a bit harder and recognized a dimly drawn face. *That's Jesus!* Shocked, I wondered why I saw the image,

'That!' said a Voice, 'is how much light you see in Me.'

God was not too happy with me again. He turned my eyes back over and I immediately fell asleep. After breakfast next morning while we were in the hall Linda read from the Bible,

'God is light and in Him there is no darkness at all.' 1 John 1:5.

I was stunned but sat until I had an opportunity to tell her what happened. At least I knew then that the supernatural event really occurred. We did learn some dancing but as my confidence was too low I could not grasp much of it. Any movement made me feel like a humpback whale; my slim body grew to an enormous monster that filled the room. On the last night Linda asked to have an appointment with us. It would make us late home but that was alright with all concerned. As we sat in her presence a few problems came to the surface and after some encouragement and prayer from Linda, Queenie was first to speak,

'I had a picture of an apple that looks perfect on the outside but on the inside it is bad right through.'

Philomena had something else to say,

'I saw we were in a river but were wading upstream. The tide was against us and then I watched it freeze over. I know why it's like that.'

'Why?' asked Linda,

'It's because we don't want Rachel.'

Her words struck my soul with the thrust of a cruel sword. I already knew I was not wanted but, if so, why did they bring me to the dance workshop? My hopes of improving came to a sudden halt. Tears in my soul made by unseen claws confronted my orphaned state once again. Not wanted, always not wanted. But God had spoken and He had frozen their walk with Him because they refused to love me as they had been shown when I first arrived at the fellowship. My sister also needed their love but we were left stranded like battered ships on a deserted island. That night I left their company in my heart, that is, except for Queenie. She did not have any nastiness in her and remained my friend. I explained one evening whilst visiting her in her home,

'You know, in a prayer meeting Jesus should be there. People are always talking. We never get to pray and let Him in. I wish I could have Him here all the time not just at a Bible week or some special meeting.'

'Yes,' agreed Queenie.

Well, how do I get out of here?

Not so far from Mackton, in the village of Reppington, lived Roy's aunt who notified him that a friend of theirs died and I went along with them to the funeral at a church in Tangletown. Roy let me drive part of the way. I parked in the car park and out we got to go into the church. After the service and wake Roy's aunt and her friend went to sit in the car. Roy followed quite a little while later and went on ahead with a friend of his. I trudged along after them on the gravel while looking straight ahead towards the car. *What are they doing? What's the car doing like that?* There, lying back in the upturned car were Roy's eighty year old aunt and her eighty two year old friend. As they had eased into the car and rested against the back seat it rolled backwards until it came to a sudden dip at the edge of the tarmac. The back had found a platform on which to rest; the front wheels proudly raised in the air and the car, perpendicular. They looked safe enough to me. At least they had not disappeared down a steep cliff. I laughed as I watched two elderly ladies trusting the car to hold them in the reclining position. Totally vulnerable and at ease were they but Roy and the men who helped him lift the car were angry.

'You should have put the handbrake on. They could have been killed,' Roy snapped.

'But I did, I always do.'

Who does he think I am not to do such a thing? Roy's aunt and her friend found it highly amusing and a change to their boring lives. They welcomed the adventure with the simplicity of children. Once the car was upright Roy took the wheel. The aunts and I talked about the once on a lifetime experience until we could talk of it no more.

As the frustration at the bungalow grew to boiling point during another confrontation, I picked up their phone, smashed it against its holding, breaking it and then went into the lounge, took off my shoe and hit my right wrist as hard as I could with it over and over again. Roy walked in to see what I was doing and encouraging me, said,

'Go on, keep on doing it, keep on bashing it.'

So I did with even more energy till I could bash no more and, as I continued, a deluge of unexpected cold water was thrown over me by his unsympathetic wife. She had filled the largest pan she could find. *What kind of love is that?* Not many days from then, as I hated the deformity of my right hand, I stood in the kitchen greatly tempted to cut it off. I don't think I hated it that much because I overcame the impulse but only by a hair's breadth.

Months later Samantha drove down to see me for a week in Sunshine, her small yellow Fiat. She told me she was going to attend a Catholic Charismatic Conference. I was keen to go as well, glad to get away and hopefully for good. Whilst there she met her future husband, Dean. As for me, I continued to seek God for an answer to all my suffering. On the third day of the conference I became heavy and sad. My mood changed to one of deeper depression and fear. At first I could not explain why so went and sat in the chapel to pray. I asked God,

'Why am I feeling this way?'

My thoughts became focused on the fellowship in Mackton. God answered,

'There is coming a time when I will speak to My people about their love. Their love is like gravity, it holds you down, it does not set you free.'

Then I understood why I had become unsettled; I was going back there to face yet more of the same hostility. During one of the Masses I received ministry from one of the priests; Father Bothwell. He was the same priest who told Samantha all about herself two years before. I waited for him to speak and when he did it was what I already knew but could not describe about myself,

'You don't live, you exist.'

The usual rising of the lump in my throat was all I could respond with and as we walked up the aisle towards the back of the church, he added,

'You want to cry, don't you.'

The love at the conference was almost tangible and I felt safe. The end had to come though and a few weeks later, on my birthday, Samantha became engaged to Dean, though not as a present to me, of course. It just happened that way. They set their wedding for the following year. Peggy, myself and two other girls were to be their bridesmaids. Samantha wanted to buy her wedding dress and the bridesmaids' dresses in Bramington so we all had a day out. The first ankle length bridesmaid dresses on show were bright peach, laced with small white daisies and transparent laced shoulders and sleeves. Samantha approved of them and chose her white dress for its similarity to ours. It had a short train and simple shoulder length veil.

Before the wedding, Peggy and I stayed at Samantha's new house. All three of us dreaded the arrival of our father. We counted the minutes and started guessing what time his car might arrive. The terrified trio or at least duo *(Peggy and I)* did not know where to hide. My insides swam in a pool of panic.

'When we see his car shall we dive under the table?' I anxiously asked.

But we had to bravely face him and show no fear. Out of scrambled thoughts and flaring emotions we did manage, on his arrival, to conceal our true feelings. I was shaking. There was no escape, no running away this time. The busyness of the wedding was an ideal getaway from too much interaction with him and especially as it was the first time I had seen him since reporting him to the police thirteen years before.

A few months later Samantha invited me to attend a Catholic church in Yorkshire where an amazing anointed priest ministered healing. I gladly accepted and we went along on a coach. During communion the queue was so long that I anticipated the healing line would take much longer as the priest needed to pray for each individual. At communion you just take the host and after saying, 'amen', you go back to your place. Surely the queue for prayer would go on until the next day. When we joined the healing line, however, I was staggered at the speed the priest prayed. Nobody told him what they needed. He simply laid a hand on them and they left just as at communion. *Okay.* At my turn, though, he stopped and took his time in silence. Not knowing what was going on, I waited. After a few minutes of him laying hands on me I left but his stopping did not really surprise me at all. The silence was what surprised me and that he had asked no questions. He simply knew my case was different. The following day I was fit for nothing and for three days lay completely exhausted on Samantha's sofa, wondering what on earth God had done to me but I did know that it was good.

A year after Samantha's wedding she offered to sell me her car so I was free to give up the bus rides into work and back. It would get me to work quicker and I would not have to walk from the station. I would also be able to go for outings and escape from time to time. On the first day of driving to work I watched carefully the driver behind me. *If that car stops behind me I will know that I am not invisible.* The driver did stop and so that is how I found out that I really did exist. A confirmation of that fact came whilst driving back to Roy and Brenda's from work one twilight evening *(the time most dangerous for drivers).* I was heading towards Norcombe Lane and noticed a grey car parked on the left. Heading in my direction was a white van. I judged its distance and made ready to overtake the car. As I pulled out the car, with no indication, moved slowly away from the curb.

'What is he doing?' I asked myself aloud.

As he edged me into the middle of the road I was in for a head on crash with the white van. My body went limp and I was ready to die but a few seconds later I found myself parked at the side of the road. The driver of the van stopped. Before I knew much about anything a heavy thudding hammered the roof as he banged with his fist, shouting,

'What were you doing overtaking a moving car? We could have been killed.'

I explained what happened.

'No, he didn't.'

I knew what I had seen, being right behind the car. Suffering from shock I managed to drive the rest of the way home. Later on, Emma, a member of the fellowship, told us it was her father driving the car, he had admitted everything. The van driver was not there to hear it or to apologize for what he had done to my roof.

New Home

The following spring Roy and Brenda informed me quite out of the blue,

'There's a chiropodist called Iris who has a two bedroom flat in the village. She is offering a room for you. We have arranged that you move in with her.'

I had already told Roy I believed God wanted me to move back to Ribford. My idea was that he would help me move. I was not strong enough nor did I have the resources to do it myself, emotionally or otherwise, but he was unwilling to let me go. At that point I felt like I was in exile and wondered how I would ever get out of Mackton. I had no choice but to move in with Iris. *Why has God exiled me?* I remembered how Israel was put into exile by God as stated in the Old Testament. *Maybe He wants me to identify with them?* I tucked the thought away for the time being. The fellowship I trusted to give me life was bringing a slow death instead.

Having to do my own shopping and cooking after so long was a new experience and somewhat daunting. On my first shopping trip I bought far too much for my needs and wasted quite a bit of food. On my second trip I stopped at the fruit and vegetable stall just inside the doors of the store. *I think I'll have a salad.* After placing lettuce in the basket I thought, *I need half a cucumber.* My eyes scanned the provisions but no half cucumbers were available so I prayed silently, *Lord, I only need a half a cucumber because if I buy a whole one it will get wasted.* I thought about the whole thing of salad, *maybe I'll have baked beans instead if I can't find half a cucumber. No, I'll have a salad.* Looking back at the stock I reached for some tomatoes, put them in a brown paper bag and then into my shopping basket. At the same time I looked into the basket hanging over my arm. In the corner behind my elbow was half a cucumber! *What! How did that get there?* I would have been very angry, having no tolerance at being touched, if I had felt it. A walking volcano ought not to be tampered with. So there was that half a cucumber. I checked the stock in front of me; there were definitely no half cucumbers. My head swiveled to search up the aisle, nobody was nearby who could have put it in. For ten minutes, it seemed, I pondered the situation. Having done all, I looked towards the entrance; it was the only place left and there, in the doorway, stood a huge man dressed in a long, dark brown gabardine and hat. His head was just touching the top of the door and he was staring at me with a straight, serious look on his face. Not a word was spoken. He looked out of place and certainly was not shopping. I looked back at the stock then back in his direction but he was gone; vanished in the twinkling of an eye. *That was an angel! Why couldn't Jesus have come and done it Himself?* The cucumber was wrapped in cellophane and had a small speck of red fluff on the end. I thought of the blood that Jesus lost on the cross for us all. The event stunned me for the rest of my shopping. I spoke to nobody about it but when I neared the cashier, thought, *what will she say*? *'We don't have any of those, how did you get one?' Do I have to pay for this?* I watched intently as she drew it out of the basket. She charged me as if nothing was amiss and I had not found the courage to mention it.

Despite that miracle I was unhappy in my new home so after a few days looked for somewhere else to live. A lady from round the corner advertised in a shop window for someone to live in one of her rooms. I applied for it and within a week moved in. Her large, detached house was set a little bit off the road. As I lay in bed one night I heard strong screams coming from the pit of my stomach but they never reached my mouth. The new phenomenon never ceased. So far, my suffering emotions had found no proper outlet but this was coming to an end and beyond my control. During a visit to Queenie we talked about how Jesus ministers to people. Later that night before going to sleep I asked Him,

'Can You minister to people during the night?'

That very night He answered in a dream. I was walking through a forest with a woman who was linking my arm. She did not speak but simply accompanied me. Thunder sounded in the distance. We were walking straight towards a storm. As we approached a clearing I feared being struck by lightning but, encouraged by my companion, I kept walking. Suddenly, a bolt of lightning hit me. I dropped to the ground. The 'friend' lay beside me. I woke up still clinging to her arm with my right arm pressing hard against my waist. Electricity pinned me to the bed. I could not move for some time. When recovered slightly I moved my head to the right expecting to see my friend but there was nobody and so I was convinced, Jesus could minister in the night! While lying in bed another night I heard what sounded like a hurricane outside. As the wind howled I lay frozen with fear. There was something different about that wind. It did not seem to be blowing anything about. I only heard the viciousness of its roar then suddenly realized, *It's the Devil trying to frighten me.* The fear left and the wind stopped immediately. On yet another night in the same house God gave me a dream in which I was walking towards huge golden domes. One after the other stood ahead of me in the distance, each one surrounded by darkness. Was I about to start on a more prosperous journey? Were good times ahead at last? I turned, again with somebody linking my arm. A huge void of darkness stretched to infinity. I would not, at any cost, return there. Once I encountered a few of the golden domes they too would be behind me and I would have a few bright and good memories to look back on but as for now there were none.

After six months I had enough of living there. Peggy became concerned about what was going on and she too was looking for accommodation, together with Olive *(a couple's adopted daughter in our fellowship who had little to do with me)*. I, in despair, was settling to remain in this unhappy, less than desirable house when Peggy came running in to see me,

'Rachel, I've got a house. We can share it and rent it for a year. It's a three bedroom house just over the road. Olive will be sharing too. Come over and see it.'

Happy to be invited we toured the house and moved in the following week. Peggy chose her bedroom at the back of the house so I took the front bedroom and Olive had the attic. It even had a drive and garage for my car. Roy and Brenda still had Sandy but I had a home of my own now so took him back to live with us. Walking up the drive to the front door on the first night I noticed the roses in the garden were infested with black fly so prayed,

'Lord, I cannot afford to buy spray for those flies so please can you get rid of them. I command all you flies to get off the roses now, in Jesus Name.'

Next morning not a single fly was left on the bush. *How did He do that?*

The massive garden at the back contained five eating and two cooking apple trees. There was a patch for vegetable growing just outside the kitchen in which I sowed a variety of seeds.

We had not long settled into our various routines when, whilst driving to work one morning, I had just cornered a bend. A scene set before me required immediate spiritual intervention. On my left a motorcyclist lay face down on the grass verge. A person standing by the body stared into space. Opposite her a van with a smashed windscreen had been vacated and somebody stood nearby on the grass verge. It was not a good thing to stop. I stood up, keeping my right foot lightly on the accelerator so as not to lose control of my speed, and prayed earnestly,

'God look what's happened here. Why did You make that happen? If that body is dead, put that soul back in there right now,' I visualized the soul coming back across the fields and entering the corpse, 'and please make sure it is the right soul coming back.'

I sensed my prayer had been answered as there was movement in the atmosphere. However, as I continued driving, an ambulance, which was still quite a few miles from the accident, dawdled along. *Well, it must be dead if the ambulance is going that slow.* My spirit sank. That evening, when relaxing at home in the lounge with Peggy, I told her what happened.

'Well, she came back from the dead twice then. Dr Matthews from the other fellowship was in the ambulance and when they picked up the body it was just about alive but died in front of him. He prayed to get the girl back to life and she came back. She lost some fingers and broke some bones as well.'

So even in the midst of despair God can answer the prayer of faith offered on behalf of another.

My searching for answers continued and I went to various meetings when aware of them. One I went to at Ribford Assembly Hall had a delayed effect. Somebody had laughed during the meeting. Not because a comedian had acted up but because God had touched them deeply on the inside. I had a secret longing to be that person but mildly scoffed instead. I half believed it was God. Tuesday was our delivery day at work and I was in for a surprise. A few customers were browsing around the store. We had moved the office desk sideways to make room for sales goods. The manageress went for lunch and I was left to unpack the delivery trays. A customer bought some mugs and she would call back later to collect them. I wrapped one mug carefully and put it on top of the desk where it promptly dropped down the back onto the floor and there was no way of retrieving it. My normal reaction was intense frustration but instead I said,

'It's got to be funny.'

Then the laughter came, showing the gap in my front teeth. No way was it welcome and in any case I was not allowed to laugh. There was no control over me being stone drunk in the Holy Spirit but I did manage to get on with the unpacking. Leaving the mug where it was I approached one of the trays and reached in for another mug to check it for soundness. As I grasped its opening I wondered why it had not got a base. Comprehending a mug with two openings, one at the top and one the other end, was rather difficult but I had only put my hand in the top, not in the base of it. I roared with laughter wondering how I had come to such a conclusion. Next I drew out a plate for display and absentmindedly put a wall hanger on the back of it then put it on a display stand. At first it looked good but after unpacking other things I took another glance towards the plate, at which my laughter filled the room. *What are you doing with a hanger on your back but resting on a plate stand?* A customer came along next needing help. I was just about to offer it but burst out laughing instead,

'Excuse me,' I managed, 'but I've got to go into the stock room and laugh.'

I left her standing alone facing the closed door. I laughed it out then somewhat composed myself. That lady was one happy customer. I continued to laugh even when mounting the stairs to the third floor to get a break and go to the ladies. Perhaps I should not have gone, as there were more people to encounter. I grinned and tried to hide the gush of merriment as I emerged from the ladies and made my way back to the second floor. The stairs were wide and so there was not much to hold onto to steady myself. A woman in front of me tripped and I started to laugh all over again,

'God,' I said, 'this isn't funny anymore. I shouldn't be laughing when people fall on the stairs. It could have been serious.'

The three hour long laughter finally stopped. At long last I was human again. God had taught me not to mock things I did not understand but He also gave me what I secretly longed for.

The next step in my search for Him was attending Nicholas Barwin's healing conferences. He was a man of great Christian standing and brought a wave of new miracles, a brand new method in dealing with people and administering the power of God. From the USA he came to Bramington Town Hall one time. I stood like a stone statue watching a spastic man with white hair and wondered if God could heal him. His arms flopped about uncontrollably. As I watched he stopped shaking and became normal then danced with all his might. God was helping me to get to know Him better. My brain knew He could do miracles but my heart wondered if He ever would. Because of that miracle my longing for a few myself, reignited. After all I had plenty of opportunity for God to straighten out my own body.

At Nicholas's invitation I and some other people went up onto the stage. After he prayed I fell to the floor and began to choke as though a noose was around my neck. My face turned scarlet as the veins in my neck bulged. Eventually, members of the team lifted me to my feet and later, whilst back in the main auditorium, I was again lying on the floor and screaming. I had not screamed all my life *(except the Bible Week experience)* but now it was all coming loose. The trapped emotion and pain erupted. I continued to scream and writhe in agony on the floor. A while later a lady from Nicholas's team came over. By then most people had gone home. I was almost alone in that vast auditorium. The lady crouched beside me and spoke above my screams,

'Clear all the blood away, Jesus. Clear all the blood away. Stop the bleeding.'

The screaming eventually stopped. It had to as the auditorium was about to close. Somebody drove me home in their car and another person drove my car back to Mackton. One man from the Mackton fellowship, who was also at the meeting, asked indignantly when I next saw him,

'Why do you want to make such a fool of yourself?'

I thought it better to be a fool than carry crippling pain around all my life and there was plenty more where that came from.

Back at home Peggy wanted Olive more than she wanted me. She wanted to play tennis with her. I had invited Peggy to play the game many times, even when we were living in Ribford but was refused. Because she never came I never played. The rejection only caused my behaviour to decline some more. *Nobody wants me to be happy.* I discouraged Peggy from playing with Olive, thinking God would not be pleased with her and that she would eventually go astray and backslide. So there we sat, Peggy wrapped in her blanket day in and day out. I occupied myself with knitting. Months passed then speaking to Peggy one evening I said,

'Peggy, I can see you as an old woman sitting there without doing anything with your life.'

I think she took it to heart but we were both far from happy in our big house even though the home had so much potential for a happy life.

Peggy had become accustomed to rejecting me. One day she said no when my request was quite normal. I could not understand the rejection. It caused great bewilderment and frustration in my spirit and produced more aggression towards her. Without the love I needed I snapped and went for her with all the strength I could muster. All I needed was for her to return some of the love I had towards her. I went, with pent up rage, to strangle her but her strength far outweighed mine. She fought me off yelling,

'What are you doing?'

'You shouldn't keep on rejecting me,' I shouted back.

Next thing my neck seized up, as though an angel had got hold of me by one of the muscles and squeezed it so hard that I could not move with the pain. Immediately, compassion rose up in

Peggy and she helped and nursed me. I did not deserve it after such an attack on her. She called the doctor and I lay on the couch until he came and tried to sort me out. How sad for the love we had for each other to be thwarted by abuse and neglect in our earlier, most tender, vulnerable years. How tragic that we could not enjoy one another; play tennis, snooker, go swimming, walking or simply chat till daylight without all the host of hell at work against us. But one day I thought an angel played with us. While messing about I kicked my right slipper off into the air. Peggy stood facing me by the lounge door. We waited for it to come down but when it did not we only stared at each other in puzzlement. *Where is it?* Neither of us could speak nor could we look around the lounge while waiting for it to reappear. What seemed like a minute of staring at each other, it popped out from nowhere and dropped onto Peggy's head. She was highly annoyed but I found it hilariously funny. I tried to stop the laughter because of her annoyance but it was impossible; an eternal mystery.

Even though I had moved out of Roy and Brenda's house the problems continued between them and me. William Antine, my ex pastor from Ribford, was called to help sort the problems out. They discussed me in my absence and the outcome was that I was no longer allowed in any of the fellowship meetings. Roy became ill and suffered a nervous breakdown. Then I remembered a word God had given to me when I first came, about what would happen to him, though I had long since dismissed it,

'Beware, the Lord is about to take firm hold of you and hurl you away, O you mighty man. He will roll you up tightly like a ball and throw you into a large country. There you will die and there your splendid chariots will remain--you disgrace to your master's house!' Isaiah 22:17-18.

Does it not feel like you are being rolled up during a breakdown? So that seemed to fit but as yet he had not been thrown into a large country. Roy told the others in the fellowship not to talk to me and so my life became a living hell, filled with terror, as if it was not already. I returned to my old church in Ribford, driving over to their services every Sunday. I also started to see Pastor Laurence Perkston for counseling. He had joined the church while I was living with Roy and Brenda and was an assistant pastor. He and a woman talked with me together and told me I should take antidepressants which I loathed to do. I did get some from the doctor, however, but refused to take them.

Peggy and I both sought Jesus for peace and healing often. It was a huge battle to get to Him sometimes. We decided something more needed to be done so Peggy suggested we embark on an Esther fast.

'What's an Esther fast?' I asked her.

'You do without food and water for three days.'

The first day we both managed well but on the second day I could no longer do without water. Peggy went the three days without both. When we told my counselors at Ribford they only mocked and asked,

'Did anything happen?'

'No.'

How were we, or they, to know God had not noted our fast and written it in His book to answer later on? I did not understand the spirit world very well. All I knew was life was hell for us and especially for me with my behaviour problems. During one of the evening services I sat wondering how to kill myself. Once I reached home I would take a knife and cut myself into tiny cubes. As I was contemplating it a man approached the lectern and read from the Bible,

'For God so loved the world that He gave His only begotten Son that whoever believes in Him will not perish but have eternal life.' John 3:16.

I knew the verse well. Pastor William Antine was about to leave the fellowship to pastor another church. After the service I asked to see our new pastor, Horace Hatherwell. When he arrived at my pew I told him what I was planning,

'Just repent.'

He said a quick prayer but I felt dissatisfied and went to my car. Peggy was not with me. Once in the car I slumped onto the steering wheel and sobbed, unable to stop. Strength seeped from my body and I was quite frightened. I opened the door of the car and walked round to William's house where he asked,

'Who prayed for you?'

'Horace.'

'Well, go back to Horace.'
I reluctantly returned to the church but Horace had left so I walked round to his house, knocked on the front door and waited. When he opened it his other hand held a plate of food and he asked what I wanted. My face was still red and wet.
'I can't stop crying; please can I come in till I calm down.'
'No,' he said firmly, 'we're having our tea.'
'I can't drive home like this. I'm always doing it.'
'Well go and do it again,' he ordered and closed the door.
I turned, unable to believe what he, a Christian minister, had commanded me to do. The only support I had left was the wire fence opposite his door. I clung to it for a while and then walked back towards William's house. Rather than go back to him I phoned Peggy from the corner phone box,
'Will you phone Laurence for me?' then explained why.
I felt Laurence had a softer heart and cared for people. After phoning him she phoned back and told me what he had said,
'She's going through an emotional response to a spiritual experience.'
That was it! At least he had taken the trouble to explain and on that tiny morsel I drove home.

Later on in the week Esther Rantzen was doing a programme on television about child abuse and how people could apply for criminal compensation damages. Immediately, I wrote my whole story out to her and that, unlike the people in her programme, I never had a mother to go to or anybody for that matter. In due time, I was sent a form from her department to fill in and was confident that I was highly eligible for compensation but when I received the reply it was far from encouraging. It explained that because I had been living with my father at the time of the abuse I was not eligible for the compensation. At only eleven years old how could I decide where to live and how could I know that I would be abused in such a way? I loved my family, even if my dad had abused me in the past. I always lived in hope that he would change. I felt badly let down and as a result my struggle went on. Because of the stress I had to leave work again.
While driving to Ribford with Peggy the following Sunday morning for the service and passing through a small village on

the way, I felt the car pulling to the right of its own accord. Thinking it was a problem with the steering wheel I carried on driving.

'We'll make it,' I assured Peggy.

But just as we reached Ribford, on a hill, I pulled over to the side.

'I think the car tyre is flapping onto the road.'

We got out to investigate. The tyre was shredded; part of the chrome rim had penetrated it.

'I think I better keep going till we get nearer the church. Please God help us to make it.'

Stripped of a motorist's dignity I slowly drove the extra few minutes to church.

'Will you ask Horace if one of the men can change the wheel? I asked Peggy.'

'No, you do it.'

'No, I'm scared.'

'Well, I am too.'

'Let's both go together then.'

After talking to Horace he relayed our message during the notices,

'Two ladies have asked if any gentlemen can help them change a wheel on their car. Can you two stand up please?'

The mocking tone infuriated me. I stood in a silent but defiant mood. *I'll do it myself.* Immediately I left the church, leaving Peggy inside. On reaching the car I opened the boot, grasped the spare wheel and jack and jacked up the car. Using the special spanner I tried to undo the nuts but they would not budge. I called to a man passing by on the other side of the road for help. In no time the new wheel was in place and, thanking him for his trouble. Job done I proudly rubbed my hands together and was free to go back to church. After the service a man from the congregation approached us,

'Did you want somebody to help you change the wheel?'

'No, thank you,' I smiled, 'I've done it.'

We made our journey home without further problems.

God can speak anywhere and at any time but I was not expecting Him to speak the day I went alone to the beach. It was a warm and sunny day when I gathered my beach mat and walked towards the sea. I had the beach to myself and settled to read a book. As I read quietly, without a soul nearby, a smell of cigarette smoke disturbed the peace. I looked up and around but, seeing nobody, continued to read. A few moments later the smell returned. I again looked up. The only people in view were tiny dots a long way away. It could not be them as the wind would not have been able to blow smoke from that distance to right under my nose, besides it was not windy. I turned back to read. A third time the smoky smell assaulted me and I thought it must be God trying to say something, I waited.

'Smoke - is a stench in My nostrils,' He said.

Olive, she smokes. I prayed for Olive to stop smoking but no sooner had I prayed for her and went back to my book than the smell returned again. *Well, what now? Did I ever smoke? I've never smoked... Oh yes, I did.* During the time of deep desperation at Roy and Brenda's I bought a packet of cigarettes. After smoking about six I reminded myself I was a child of God and because of that I ought not to be doing it. Then there was the first time I ever put a cigarette to my lips at fourteen years of age. William, my brother, had offered me a puff of one he had got hold of from somewhere. Taking it off him I blew with all my might but could not get the end to glow fire red. I gave up so perhaps that memory did not count.

'Okay, it was me. I did smoke. Well, I'm sorry I smoked God. I'll never do it again.'

The moment I confessed to what I felt was a trivial thing I started to shake uncontrollably as God cleansed my body. I had barely smoked twenty in my whole life. Why was God so fussed about so few?

About a week later while feeling tormented and suicidal *(still working out my salvation)* I drove to Ribford and knocked on Pastor Laurence's door. His wife answered,

'Hello, is Laurence in?' I asked politely,

'Laurence is having his tea but will be out at about quarter past seven to go to a meeting.'

'Thank you.'

After she closed the door I walked back down the path and stood behind the pillar at the end of his front garden. It was taller than me and hid me quite well. I waited until the door opened then popped out in front of him when I was sure the door was shut and started to tell him about my problems. He was having none of it and I was again left stranded with the terror. A vision of my mother's legs hanging in the sky invaded my mind and I wanted to grab them,

'I want my mum.'

'Oh, so that's a new thing now, is it?'

Needing her was the crux of my problem. If she had not died I would not be going through such hell. I reached up to grab her, in my imagination, but it was no use. Laurence threatened to call an ambulance which only served to panic me. I was trying to come to terms with my existence, not to cause trouble and would not leave. He walked back into the house and a little later Horace arrived. He frogmarched me by the arm to the car park threatening to call the police if I did not leave the premises.

'I'll have you arrested for trespassing on church property.'

He threw me into the car, slammed the door hard and walked away. I was left to drive home in a pitiful state. *Why can't anybody love me?*

Weeks later, I was watching a programme called Police Psychologist at home. The episode was about a man who wanted revenge on people who hurt him and it caught my attention. The man wanted to blow his guilty ones sky high. *Is this what I am? Am I a psychopath?* Every thought the man had and the secret plans in his heart were hidden away in mine. I got on my knees and prayed,

'Oh, Lord, please forgive me. I am a terrorist in the making. Help me.'

When finished, I started to shake uncontrollably.

'Peggy!'

She came downstairs to see what I wanted,

'What?'

'I know what's wrong with me now? I'm a psychopath. Now I know what is wrong I can ask Laurence to pray for me and I'll be okay.'

Getting excited I asked her to ring the church office, thinking they would not speak to me.

'See if Laurence is at home, just ask if he's in but don't say why.'

'Laurence is at the church office,' Peggy said, after putting the phone down.

'Alright, please will you come with me and then I'll be okay.'

We got our coats on and left for Ribford. I drove in the sunshine through the country lanes. The roads were clear but my car inexplicably lost its grip. The car floated across the lane on a bend towards the right. There was nothing wrong with my car. It was the Devil trying to stop me going. I took a risk and continued with no further problems except when a car waited to come out of a side road just before Dunham. Eagerly I drove on without a care in the world. As I approached the side road the car pulled out rapidly across my path. *What is she thinking of?* I watched as she sailed by oblivious to my presence. It did not affect the hope that flooded my soul. I drove without further ado to the church car park hoping Laurence would still be there. We had not warned him of our arrival in case he did not want to know. Peggy and I approached the black side door of the church and knocked. Laurence opened it,

'Laurence, please can you pray for me,' I asked after he showed us to his office.

We remained standing.

'I know what's wrong with me now.'

'How do you know?'

I repeated my experience of the programme. In no time I would be walking out a new woman. However, I misinterpreted the look on his face. He took a deep breath and shaking his head said slowly, in broken tones,

'I wipe - my hands - off your case,' he wiped his dry hands together, 'God does not speak to people through television programmes,' was his firm reply.

My blood plummeted at his unbelief.

'Well, He did to me?' I said, absolutely stunned.

He had made up his mind and I would remain the same and there was no way out, again. *What am I going to do now?* Taking hold of my Bible by one corner I lifted it high above his waste paper basket and dropped it in.

'Well, that's it then.'

So much for doing my part in getting well. I walked from his office in despair. Poor Peggy would not get the relief she desperately needed either of a tormented sister. I would not be able to love her the way she needed me to. I hated myself furiously as we walked across the hall and back towards the door we had entered. Laurence opened it and in my perplexed, hopeless state I walked out onto the concrete. Peggy, following behind, stood on the step. I turned, looked at Laurence in the doorway, angrily hurled my bag and car keys at him, ran across to the car park and sat in a heap against the wall. My thoughts were for Peggy but what was I to do? I could not do two things at once and my hopes of being free were the most important thing to me and to be able to get on better with my sister. Pain filled every fibre of my being. Peggy followed me into the car park. After she handed me my property we got into the car and sat together utterly astounded at the lack of the tiniest bit of help or concern. I was deeply grateful to Peggy for accompanying me. *If only I could do something about all this. I know what I'll do.* Thoughts roared through my mind like cars on a racing circuit. Getting out of the car and, leaving Peggy, I ran over to the phone box and dialed Roy and Brenda's number. Roy answered. I shouted at him for failing me while living with them and for what had happened as a consequence. I continued,

'And you can come to my funeral and if you don't, I'll go myself!'

Slamming the phone down I realized what I had just said. At least I was able to give a little chuckle. I drove home unable to calm down. It could have been so different. I kept silent about my plan. Once in the kitchen I picked up Sandy's feeding bowl. He meandered round the kitchen, ignorant of the problems surrounding him. I scooped his dinner from the tin into his bowl. Peggy had gone upstairs.

'Here you are Sandy; this is your last supper from me.'

I lay the bowl down again gently. Unafraid of what I was about to do, my thoughts shot to and fro. I knew why Laurence had insisted on the tablets. God had known I would reach this point. He was in control of it all. I walked upstairs, grabbed my bottle of Miansarin tablets and returned to the kitchen. The cap came away easily as I twisted it. Filling a glass with water and glancing at

Sandy eating without a care in the world, I thought, *how can I tell him anything?* How could I explain to the cat that from now on his life would change and I would not be there anymore? I took the tablets one by one. Remembering the time I took them in Rombourne *(see book one)* I made sure to drink water with each one. Soon I would be out of this world. After swallowing twenty or so with the added bulk of water my stomach was filled and I could take no more then waited fifteen minutes for something to happen. *Why isn't anything happening? Why aren't I scared? Why so calm?* The Devil wanted me dead and removed all fear to make things easy. I forced my mind to take over from the missing emotions. Needing help I made my way to the lounge which became a waiting room to die. Getting increasingly edgy I wandered out of there to the bottom of the stairs and shouted,

'Peggy, will you phone the doctor?'

'No.'

'Please, I've just taken an overdose.'

'Well, why don't you get a knife and do the job properly,' she shouted.

'Nothing is happening. Something must be happening but I can't feel it so I could die really suddenly. Please phone the doctor. If I do I'll just get told off.'

She came downstairs and reluctantly phoned. The doctor asked her what tablets I had taken. After she hung up, she said,

'The doctor has phoned for an ambulance.'

'Will you come? I don't know what's going to happen to me.'

Again, reluctantly she decided to come and went upstairs to collect some things of mine for the hospital. After twenty minutes or so the ambulance arrived. I still felt alright. The ambulance men were good, not abusive. We left the house. In the ambulance Peggy and I sat side by side. An ambulance man sat and observed how I was doing while the other one drove. My eyes grew heavy and started to close.

'No, try to keep your eyes open,' the ambulance man ordered.

Every now and then he repeated himself. Peggy sat in silence. *If only Laurence had listened to me. Neither of us would be going through this now.* We arrived at the casualty department where I was ushered into a cubicle. There I waited until a doctor arrived. Lying down, wondering where Peggy was, I listened for approaching footsteps. A nurse wheeled a machine in on a trolley and put it beside the bed, to my left.

'What's that for?' I asked.

'It's an electrocardiogram, used to assess heart damage.'

A numb wave pulsed through me. *What have I done?* The doctor arrived in his white coat.

'Hello.'

After the kind greeting he asked why I had taken the overdose. I glanced at his name badge which read, Dr Burden *(his real name). I can't believe it! I can't even get away from my problems in hospital.* I chuckled despite everything. He put electrodes on my chest and took a reading. I watched the needle making patterns on a long strip of paper, rather like a shop's till roll. After seeing the results the doctor recommended I be admitted onto a ward. Once there, the two legs at the bottom of my bed were placed, by a nurse, on bed blocks.

'What is that for?'

'Your blood pressure is low.'

As it was Friday I had to stay on the ward until Monday when a psychiatrist would see me. If I were to be released from hospital I would be in no fit state to cope or behave in an acceptable way. My pastor had distressed me greatly and life was not worth living anymore. As I lay in bed prayer was not far from my lips.

'Anyway,' I said to God, 'it doesn't say anything about suicide in the Bible.'

To which God immediately responded by giving me a picture in my mind; lots of sand as in a desert and two slabs of concrete rose from that arid ground. On the slabs were written,

'Thou shalt not kill.' (Exodus 20:13)

I only thought that meant not to kill others and that it did not include oneself. The Devil had blinded me to seeing the truth. When well enough to get up and about, though I did not think so, I went off to the bathroom for a wash. The mirror fixed to the wall above the sink reflected my unrecognizable face. It looked like it had been moulded in white plastic. My eyes were as black as ebony. Death looked imminent. *Can't they see what I look like?* I said nothing and dreaded the psychiatrist's visit. What would he do with me or tell me to do? Would he put me back in the local psychiatric hospital? Tuesday came and I sat before him in a side room in my dressing gown and slippers.

'Do you want to go to Peacock House?' he asked. 'It's a place where you are treated roughly by confrontation with other patients. Not an easy place to be and you have to be tough with each other.'

Up to then I did not know much about choices, having always been a victim of circumstance. Where people said I should be, I went. Blown around with the inevitable times I was dished out; a weak wreckage I lumbered along. Without parents to guide me caused a great feeling of vulnerability and aimlessness. My abusive and neglectful father had brought so much misery to my life which was one tragic merry-go-round. The psychiatrist and I spoke at length and most of the time he stared out of the window, appearing not to be listening to anything I said but in a world of his own.

'You don't have to go there,' he suddenly announced. 'You can choose.'

Was I letting him down if I said no? I usually did things to please others. If this was his job I was rejecting his kindness in offering me the place. He had given me permission to turn his recommendation down.

'No, I don't think I'm strong enough to have all that happen to me.'

'I'm going to discharge you today. You can go home.'

I thought of all the physical pain in my body. My back, chest and head wracked with it.

'But what can I do about all this pain?'

No sooner had I asked the question the pain suddenly stopped. Not knowing what to do, I stared at him in total silence; afraid to tell him. A minute later, tears fell and I sobbed uncontrollably. He left the room as I wept and sent a nurse in to sit with me. I cried for over twenty minutes. God had touched me deeply. When I arrived home I experienced great freedom in my body, bending every way I could imagine in total flexibility unlike before the overdose even. Peggy saw the change but her pain was still with her. She had spent the first night of my stay in hospital wandering around the grounds. It had been too late for any transport home. I was not pleased with the hospital for not looking after her. Laurence was to blame for all this. Peggy and I went to church the following Sunday. When we arrived home after the evening service I placed my Bible open on the kitchen worktop. Later, I wandered over to pick it up but, instead of picking it up, peered down to the page it had opened at and read,

'Do not say, "I'll pay you back for this wrong. It is mine to repay, says the Lord, wait for the Lord and He will deliver you.' Proverbs 20:22.

I was satisfied with that.

Peggy and I continued to live out the year of rental contract on the house, towards the end of which, Peggy found somewhere to live in a shared house in Easingborough. I found nowhere and could not function even to look for a place. Time was running out and I felt massively lost. No direction at all. Having lost the Herpsons and the fellowship through their disobedience I had only One Person to trust – Jesus. As the house was only partly furnished when we arrived we had to sell the comfortable three piece suite we had bought, one that had served us well. I prepared to put an advertisement in the newspaper but on reaching the printer's shop found that the printer had broken down.

'Sorry, we can't get it done in time for you,' they said.

I then asked a counselor at church to put up a notice regarding the suite instead. The phone rang shortly afterwards. Peggy answered,

'It's for you; it's about the three piece suite.'

I took the phone.

'Hello.'

'Hello, this is Mrs Enrithson. I am Mrs Enrithson's sister from your church. My daughter is interested in buying your suite. When can we come and see it?'

'When can you come?'

'Next Wednesday. I'll come with my husband.'

'Okay, that's fine. Bye'

I went to tell Peggy,

'Someone's coming to see it next Wednesday?'

'At least we've got somebody to buy it,' Peggy said.

'Yes, let's hope they do.'

As promised Mr and Mrs Enrithson came round to see the suite,

'When do you have to be out?' asked Mrs Enrithson.

'On Saturday,' we both said together and laughed.

'Where are you going to live next?' Mr Enrithson asked.

'I'm going to live in Easingborough,' explained Peggy.

The usual lump rose like a knife in my throat. I swallowed, trying to dislodge it as I stared at Mr and Mrs Enrithson.

'Rachel hasn't found anywhere yet,' said Peggy.

I felt like ten orphans rolled into one, completely devastated at my predicament. What has happened to all the promises of God? Peggy did not want to live with me. She had had enough of my outbursts of anger and frustration and I was very much misunderstood by her.

'You can come and live with us,' said Mrs Enrithson, kindly.

'Oh, thank you.'

I sighed in relief. Next day Mrs Enrithson rang to say,

'My daughter would like to buy the suite but you can't come to live with us. I hadn't asked my husband first. He doesn't want anybody to live with us.'

My stomach overturned. Just when I thought I was blessed the blow came out of the blue. Meanwhile, a notice had been put up at church about my need for accommodation. A lady contacted them to say I could work for her by being a resident carer. Peggy came with me to see the lady. We knocked on her door and waited. A while went by. The door eventually opened but nobody was there, until we looked down. On the floor sat a woman who asked us in. I was staggered by what I may have to face. We followed as she slid along the floor unable to use her legs. I did not feel up to that at all.

'I have a cat and lots of things,' I informed her, trying to put her off.

The room she offered was tiny. My cat could not have been swung by half a tail in that space. Not that I would try. We left the premises.

'You are not going there,' Peggy said bluntly.

'Well, where can I go? I have to go there, God is punishing me. I have to accept His punishment. He never stops punishing me.'

'He's not punishing you,' she tried to counsel me.

'Yes, He is, I have to go.'

Greatly discouraged with my impending future I sank to deeper depths than previously. If I did not take up the offer I would end up on Waterferry Green sitting on a bench with all my things around me. We told Mrs Enrithson about the lady.

'Well, only if the lady doesn't have you, you can come here. It is a last resort in case you have nowhere to go.'

I prayed like never before. I would have nightmares and all kinds of emotional problems living with that lady. *Should I really be praying to a God who is punishing me?* On Saturday Peggy was packing her things confident in her new home in Easingborough but I had been told by the lady to ring her that morning. Unfortunately, we had had our phone cut off so I trudged next door to ask if I could use theirs. *Please say no.*

'Yes, of course you can, come in.'

Aaarrrggghhhh! I hid my feelings of horror.

The number I dialed rang and rang. *Yeah, please don't answer it.* The longer the phone rang the better I felt. At last I knew she was not going to answer so phoned Mrs Enrithson and explained the situation.

'Well, you will have to come to us then. We'll come and get you when you are ready, and you can have your cat.'

All of a sudden I was the happiest person in the universe. Wiping the sweat from my brow I allowed what joy I could experience flood my soul. *God isn't punishing me.*

Chapter Four

Life in an adult care home

Even though I was allowed to live with Mr and Mrs Enrithson I felt a burden to them. Mrs Enrithson was a motherly woman and baked delicious chocolate brownies and Sunday dinners but I ate my meals in my room away from them because that is what her husband wanted. The day after I arrived, being Sunday, they both went to church. I stayed behind. On their return Mrs Enrithson informed me,

'I prayed to God about your being here. I was not at all sure and my husband was not sure, as I said. This morning, however, God spoke to me at church, "Don't be afraid to entertain strangers, because you may be entertaining angels unawares," so now I am quite happy to have you,' she smiled.

I had been promoted by God Himself! To be likened to an angel lifted my spirit. God rarely spoke up for me like that but as soon as Monday came Mr Enrithson wanted me to seek another place to live. Both he and Mrs Enrithson went out flat hunting. I left the house later and met them on their way back,

'We can't find anywhere.'

Being pleased about that I thought maybe they would have me more permanently but Mr Enrithson pressurized me to keep looking. I could not look after myself in a flat so bought a newspaper and while they were out that evening spread it out on the floor and searched through it thoroughly. An advertisement by the Rape Crisis Centre caught my eye. *Well, I haven't been raped but I have been abused.* I felt it was the only way for me to go. The lump in my throat rose up again. *I'll have to ring them, no other choice.* People say you have choices in life. That was not a choice but a forced necessity. I had no real guidance on the matter and certainly no support. Even so, Mr and Mrs Enrithson left glowing reports with the pastor at my church and said I had been a pleasure to them and certainly no trouble. My pastors only knew me when in church. Roy and Brenda Herpson had deliberately disobeyed God as to what to do with me so consequently there was a lot of friction in the house. They had tried to fit me with a remedy that was not of God and I could not wear it. It grieved not only my spirit but also the Spirit of God. I called the Rape Crisis Centre giving them a summary of my life and present circumstances.

'Can you come in for an appointment and a chat some time?'

'Yes, when can I come? I have to tell this couple I'm doing something to get a place.'

'Tomorrow afternoon, about three o'clock.'

When I arrived at the centre a middle aged woman greeted me. Her round face wore a sympathetic smile. During our discussion she offered,

'I can phone somebody. There are places where people live in order to try to get their lives sorted out. Do you agree that I ask them?'

'It's a matter of having to really. Yes, please do that.'

I left her, feeling like Peter in the Bible who came to Jesus walking on the water. Total instability but total trust in what she may be offering. She called the following day to say there was a vacancy at 21 Spearmint Street, Ribford and would I like to go with her to an interview with the house warden.

'Yes, but I'm really scared.'

'You don't have to go. You do have a choice.'

I don't have a choice. She picked me up at half past three. I had not lived the other side of Ribford before. I did not know there was another side and felt out of my territory as the car slowed down but reasonably safe with her half hiding me. We stopped opposite the big white house with the black door. A woman came straight out while we sat there. I watched as my carer got out of the car and approached her. They chatted for a while. My lady returned and looked through the car window.

'Do you want to come and look around?'

No.

'Yes, okay.'

The lump in my throat came along with me. It always told me I was disadvantaged. I wondered again what I had done to deserve such hopelessness. As I left the safety of the car I looked behind to make sure it was still there. The lady at the front door looked like a witch in her long, black dress and short, ruffled, white hair. With that conviction I had to show some bravery.

'Hello, I'm Janice,' said the unexpected sweet voice.

She smiled warmly. *Perhaps not a witch?*

'Would you like to take a look around with me?'

Together with the lady who brought me we walked first to the lounge. Chunky inviting armchairs sat majestically just beyond the door. Looking round behind the door there was a settee to match. A television and video player stood in the corner and a coffee table in the middle of the floor. *I suppose it isn't too bad.* We left the room, turned and Janice opened the door opposite.

'This is the games room.'

A pool table stood in the centre. It was a far cry from Apple Ash with a proper snooker table *(though not quite full size)* and huge rooms. I noticed, through the window, how small the front garden was in comparison to Apple Ash's twenty five acres. *Not sure.* Next was the small dining room just beyond the lounge. A table with ten chairs around it stood in the centre. A white hatch at the far left hand side with its doors open gave me a view of the kitchen sinks. We left the dining room and walked along the hall to the kitchen. There was a good deal of space in there. The red floor reminded me of Lincrest, the children's home in Campton Range.

'The residents take turns preparing meals. You cook for nine people.'

Nine! What if I can't do it? I swallowed hard.

'You soon get used to it and the staff will help you at first.'

'How long do we stay here?' I asked; eager to leave already.

'Trencham, the people who own us, say you can only stay for two years,' Janice explained.

Opposite the kitchen was the office where Janice, her sister-in-law Sabina and other members of staff stayed during the day. A different member of staff slept in the bedroom attached to the office every night.

'There's no point going upstairs but you can if you like.'

I wanted to see but all we saw up there were the bathrooms and they were fine. I could see the house needed cleaning though.

'I've got a cat. Can I have him with me?'

'Of course you can.'

With that we left and, once outside, it felt good to be in the fresh air. A taste of freedom and at least I was able to leave.

'What do you think? Will you come here?' asked the lady who brought me.

'No, let's go. I don't really like it.'

'Okay then, I'll go back and tell Janice.'

I waited in the car. On her return she said,

'Janice said you can come if you change your mind.'

'Well, I'd better change it now then because I haven't got anywhere else to go and I have to leave the house where I'm staying.'

Depression covered my dejected shoulders. I pressed my temples to stop the pain.

'You sure?'

'Yep, got no choice.'

'I'll go back and tell her then.'

'Okay, I can have Sandy at least.'

So that was it. The next stage in my travels through life had arrived. Would I ever have a normal life? Sorry to be leaving a proper home of relative security I moved into 21 Spearmint Street. Perhaps I should have had faith that God would speak to Mr Enrithson and he would change his mind but he was adamant. Janice took me straight to my bedroom in the attic and left me there; I placed my case on the floor and stared at the unmade bed. The room had not been prepared at all. Gravel topped the bare, grey mattress. Feeling frightened and insecure I froze to the spot for a while. *Should I go and ask for the hoover?* That would let them know I was not satisfied with the bed; even so, I had to be brave and ask. *Apple Ash was clean.* I did not understand them. *Now I am stuck here for two years.*

After the first week of being allowed to get used to my new surroundings I was put onto the rota for chores. Once I started those they soon took notice of the superior cleaning abilities I had. Even though I was terrified of everything and everyone the quality of my work never deteriorated. I was a perfectionist.

The following week a famous Christian speaker came to a church just around the corner from the home. I attended eagerly, hoping to escape the home and sat in the second from back row on the right. I glanced behind for a second and to my sheer astonishment people from Mackton Fellowship were sitting on the back row, right behind me. I froze with fear. *What if God wants me to go forward, I won't be allowed. They will try to stop me and say awful things about me.* One of the leaders prophesied from the front,

'Don't be afraid of those who are behind you. You come to Me.'

Wow, but the fear remained. I tried to be strong and respond to what God had said. The rest of the meeting went alright and I left unscathed.

I had never learned that people should trust someone before laying their lives out before them. Institutions are open to all and sundry. Privacy was hardly an issue as I was continually looking for help and so divulging my every need. One day I handed Janice the memoirs of Apple Ash that I had written at Chingles, Cantrin; hoping they would be able to understand and sympathize with me a little better. A few days later I asked for them back but she did not return them. I could not understand why, neither did I know anything about rights so they were lost. I often wonder what happened to them.

I continued to go to Grace Church on Sundays where, at the first meeting, a lady prophesied by the Holy Spirit,

'I can see all that is going on in your heart. Tears are rolling down My face for you. I can see those who have failed you and I am watching them. Come into the future with Me.'

I had only half listened and was staring into space when my head jerked as somebody slapped me hard across the side of it. I looked around, people were standing nonplussed. Nobody looked guilty to me so I was convinced God had walloped me. *How can He do that?* After the service I found the person who had given the word. I knew her. She had taken me into her home for six weeks after my breakdown that ended my nursing career.

'That word was for me,' I told her.

'No, it wasn't.'

I learnt then that the person who gives the word is not God. God only used her as a spokesperson so that I could hear what He was telling me. She was unfruitful in her understanding because she had not lived my life. God, however, was with me all the time and was the One True Witness. I left feeling more vulnerable than ever.

As I was no longer earning a wage I had very little money and my car had to be sold. In its place I bought a brand new, pale blue bicycle. Every Sunday morning I cycled to church even though some mornings I did not want to bother. My legs always took the initiative of getting out of bed, not my upper body. Once they had swiveled and my feet touched the rough carpet the rest of me had no choice but to follow. Meanwhile, Laurence and my counselors remained the same. The odd thing was the counselors did not seem to want to hear the cry of my heart. They only seemed to want to tell me what to do.

'I need parents,' I told them.

'Let Jesus be your mother and father.'

'How do I do that?'

When watching small children with their parents in church services my heart cried. A few years earlier Pastor Antine had given a word of knowledge,

'… you know I took them away and they are with Me.'

God was talking about my mother. I had hung my head and cried. The tears flowed and flowed, my shoulders shook with the strength of them. Minutes went by as the grief poured out. Two women took me into another room. No one was given to me in my mother's place; just a few words then I was left just as alone afterwards as I had been before. Minutes turned into hours. The crying had left me with a bright red face and neck. I did not recover that evening. It was a hunger nobody understood. Frustrated with the constant misunderstandings in the counseling room I often took off my glasses and hurled them across the room; just like I had done at Ruby's in Mackton. My words could not have been any simpler. Why could they not grasp what I was saying? I was happy to have Laurence as a counselor. He was a father figure and we had made up since my overdose episode. What I could not give my father I gave to Laurence, including writing him a note one day. Amongst other words, I wrote,

'… I love you….'

I saw nothing wrong with that. After all he had spent much time counseling me but the next meeting was far from good.

'There are undertones in your note, Rachel,' he accused.

I was shocked to the core.

'From now on you will be seeing Marianne with Olive.'

What crime had I committed that was so bad for Laurence to reject me? I used to write Mother Stephen notes and one or two other people who crossed my path in the hopes of fishing out a parent or two. In addition I had also knitted Laurence a soldier doll. Laurence was colour blind and saw the pink face and hands as white. He had appreciated that. I knitted a lot of dolls from Jean Greenhowe's book; scarecrows, clowns etc. Now my childlike trust was shattered. The Bible said God would give us mothers and fathers and not leave us as orphans in distress. I was not a child orphan but nevertheless an orphan and had felt bereft all my life. The pain was ever with me. If I was his daughter would he treat me that way? When she told him she loved him would he throw her away to strangers? If she lived where I lived would he want to rescue her? My note, which was meant to bring some kind of permission to be accepted and loved back, turned out to be a trap into a new world of intense opposition from then on. Self defense did not save me. My black hole sucked me in deeper and deeper. There was no hope of ever being understood. Yet my problem was so simple. Had they not heard the glowing report from Mrs Enrithson? Was I just an inconvenience? Was I supposed to be born at all? Questions about my existence were forever at the surface of my mind.

'It's like a bottomless pit!' exclaimed Marianne, angrily.

Is that my fault? I stood in total shock at her words. Not only her words but the look on her face as she turned her curly head to sneer at my misfortune. *If they understand so well about my bottomless pit, why can't they help me?* Like others, I gave prophecies in the meetings, feeling responsible to be open to God if He wanted to say something; wanting to serve Him with all my heart. When they could not change my behaviour Marianne eventually ordered

'Sit at the back of the church and do not move or speak for three months.'

I had to obey; such was the strength of their impenetrable authority. I continued praying and crying out to God. During those three months there was a guest speaker who announced that somebody was there suffering from rejection. I, having been told practically not to exist, was not about to answer so sat motionless. However, I watched as a lady responded by coming out of her place and walking to the front of the church but the speaker said there was somebody else and all of a sudden the wind of the Holy Spirit blew in from behind me and rested on my hands. I asked if the person sitting next to me could feel it but he said no. *Well, I better go then.* In spite of the fear I walked to the front. The speaker prayed for me and, as I was overpowered by God's presence, I lay on the floor and got stuck to it. The leaders of the church became impatient as I was there for a long time. Eventually, Olive commanded me to get up but I could not. She yanked me off the floor in a rough manner causing me to become very afraid then threw me into the pew and commanded me to sit there. I glanced around and, seeing Michael, whose house I had been visiting from time to time, begged,

'Michael, save me.'

He did not stand up for me so that was the end of what should have been a healing and loving time.

As I continued counseling sessions with Marianne I expressed a desire to be visited in the hostel where I lived. She did come one day and what she gave of herself fed an enormous need. We played on a small game computer I owned. I knew she was not enjoying it by the look on her face and the lack of patience but better than nothing. *If she does this every week I might get well.* She never repeated her visit.

Michael and Kate were a pleasant couple who cared for disadvantaged people. I had been attending their house group. How I wished I had a home like theirs! They were sitting one evening with about six other people watching one of Theobald Petland's videos. Theobald is a great teacher of the Bible. After the video they invited me to some powerful Christian meetings in Bramington where Matthew Minnerton ministered every Tuesday. Before that, however, Michael told me that I could get healed at home on my own but God had said through Theobald Petland's teaching that I would have died if I was made to do that *(he was speaking generally but it answered Michael's statement regarding me that very evening).* Matthew was filled with the Holy Spirit and gave accurate words of knowledge which helped people respond to God and go forward for prayer. I was hoping for a miracle and God did start to minister to me through him but not as powerful as I would have liked. Every week I attended the meetings. During one of those evenings, he said,

‘I can see somebody covered in blood. I’ve never had this kind of picture before. You are covered from the top of your head right down your body in blood. There is not one space left without it. Come forward and I will pray for you.’

His words hit me with lightning force. Nobody moved but I waited to see if anybody would respond. God had not meant somebody had been in an accident; the blood Matthew was describing was internal. I stood amidst a hall full of people and, knowing their thoughts against me, I could not respond and waited to see if he would ask again. My hope was that he would single me out to help me own up but he did not.

‘Is there anybody this applies to?’ persisted Matthew.

I lurched forward as if pushed by an invisible hand but fear of persecution from the crowd held me back. I could not possibly face the onslaught of verbal conflict afterwards. Surely everybody knew it was me anyway or they knew I would say it was. *If only somebody would take me to him.* But it had become too late so after the meeting I approached him,

‘You know that picture you had of the blood?’ I said sheepishly. ‘Well, that was me but I was too scared to come.’

He sympathized but the opportunity for prayer had passed. I had ‘blown it’. Dread and disappointment took its place. As Michael and Kate drove me back to the hostel I did not speak and had to carry that awful feeling of missing a great opportunity for a very long time. They also took me to see a couple called Elsie and Jacob who lived a few miles away and did not go to our church. I sat in their lounge feeling vulnerable yet hopeful that my disturbed behaviour would be rectified. Yes, he indeed understood but after two sessions they saw me no more thinking that once prayed for, that was that.

Other meetings were held in Bramington where anointed visiting speakers were invited to preach and minister. One of them told me, when praying for me,

‘Your prison is so small you bang your head on it every time you move.’

That is exactly how it felt. Just prior to his meeting I had gone to the ladies toilet and when washing my hands the glass light shade came loose and missed crashing on my head by an inch. God was surely watching over me that night.

In despair at the home I took some of the expensive china and crystal pieces I had bought while working for Chingles at Easingborough and Ribford and threw them into the dustbin. It was a Sunday morning and as I reached the hostel after church on my bike I stopped just opposite the gate. I could see the bins and watched a member of staff removing my treasure from them! Sabina was taking my small china teapot and other things for herself. What timing! I witnessed the callous way I was really being cared for.

'Why are you taking my stuff out of the bin?' I demanded as I approached.

'You threw them away, so anybody can take them.'

I had not thrown them away because I did not want them. I hurled them in anger because I felt so hopeless about my life and suffered a great deal of unending inner and bodily pain. *That should not be happening where people understand your problems,* I screamed to myself.

During the week I attended the Beech Day Centre at Westport Hospital where I tried a different approach to try to fix my problematic behaviour. The best experience was when eight staff and patients clasped and interlocked hands; four on each side facing each other. The person who was learning to trust stood on a table and jumped into the matted hands. At my turn I stood for a long time debating whether to jump,

'Come on, you can do it,' encouraged Victoria, who was in charge.

'Okay, I'm coming.'

After five minutes of standing still and taking countless deep breaths I let myself fall into the surprisingly firm mattress. The subsequent feeling of security was indescribable; nothing at all to worry about.

'Can we do this every day?'

'No.'

'Why not?'

Nobody answered.

In another session we play acted one another and watched ourselves on video. Seeing myself was far from enthralling. My clumsy body and sinking soul showed more than any clothes I wore. *I'm not watching that again.* Next thing, Victoria brought in a stress measuring gadget; a small oblong machine. The measurement was accomplished by holding it in the palm of your hand. When it was handed to me I sat down not knowing what to expect. Victoria left the room as part of the test and I was unprepared for her return. I held the machine being unaware that she was already approaching from the corridor, as she had closed the door behind her. The needle rose to an alarmingly high read. I did not feel the slightest bit of tension but there was the proof that people scared me at quite a disturbing, unconscious level. No wonder I had trouble with people sitting beside me.

Places like that made allowances for people to behave 'badly'. They understood the deep pain of emotions and how it affects some of us. They did not, however, understand me. I could not let go of needing parents. It was all I needed. Neither could I comprehend that there were so many parents out there who could give me a year of their lives but never offered. I could recover from my forlorn and empty way of living, get an education and be encouraged in a safe home, even at my age. But there I was trying to cooperate with the only establishment that was available, except that of the church.

Determination ruled, so off to the library I went to research the occult, the root of what was most likely to be the cause of all the trouble. Upstairs on the reference shelves I found a set of old encyclopaedias. Their size and weight staggered me. Was it just plain grief that affected my behaviour or was something more sinister the key to my becoming well? I took out a volume and opened its pages to everything I could find on the subject. Discovering a whole lot of symptoms associated with it in one of the entries I wrote them down but lost them during one of my many moves. I do remember part of one entry: 'To the extent a person has been associated with the occult they will be affected by being loveless, lifeless, barren, hopeless.' There were more than those and I saw all of them in me. Just like when I had seen the curses in the Bible I could not understand why I was sentenced to such an awful existence. Somewhere in my life there must have been some terrible things carried out in the occult realm that I certainly was not aware of. All I knew was how much I felt the impact of the darkness of hell all the wretched days of my life. What could be done about it? I told no one what I found. The spiritual side of life is not one that is considered most of the time but there, in the books, was an explanation of all the years of fruitlessness even though I had worked so hard. I served everybody to the best of my ability and reaped nothing but pain and heartache. Satisfied that I had found a hidden gem of knowledge I walked back to the hostel.

I spoke to some of the people in the hostel about Jesus but it was hard going. I even mentioned Him to Janice. I could never tell what was going on in her heart. Her chain smoking was a veneer of protection; apart from that both she and Sabina took great care of themselves. Janice wore lovely clothes and I envied her not having to live my life. My only escape was to cry out to God for blessings. The longing to be treated like an ordinary person increased. Week after week the Gospel was preached at church. Jesus was my Saviour but He was not saving me and I knew my pastors would never come to visit the hostel. I hated institutions. I make no apology for repeating myself because that is what always went on for me. Institutions were a dumping ground where people are forgotten; a place where nobody ever has to think about them. I constantly longed for my mother and my family. I had lived in institutions most of my life and longed to put them far behind me.

As time went by Janice wanted me to do a word processing course. It sounded like something quite out of this world. I was terrified that people would see my deformed hands and so said a firm no to the suggestion. Anything to do with my hands had to be in total privacy where nobody could see them. I was lacking encouragement from somebody close to me. Strangers encouraging me seemed wrong. There was no bonding or love and I thought they only said good things to get rid of me. As I chewed over the pastors' unwillingness to have anything to do with me I suddenly had an idea and later mentioned it to Janice,

'I know what will get the pastors to come here. They won't touch us with a bargepole but I know they will come if I cook them a meal.'

Janice agreed that I invite them. The following Sunday I held out my bait.

'Laurence, would you and your wife like to come to the hostel for a meal next Wednesday? I'm going to invite Horace and his wife too and I'm going to cook it myself.'

I never saw such a quick smile in all my life.

'Yes, I'm sure we'd all love to come.'

Secretly nodding to myself I faked a smile in return. *Yes, I thought so.* Trencham Housing paid for the food but I chose the recipes. I would feed them till they wanted no more and show them the real Rachel if they only gave me a chance of a normal life. I would give them the best I could offer. For starters I prepared a fruit salad. The main course was something Peggy *(who was also invited)* called ratatouille, though I'd never heard of it. Dessert was a delicious apricot meringue with apricot sauce. I bought fresh apricots and made the meringue from scratch. Everything was hand prepared by me with no help from anyone. As if that was not enough I bought lots of different cheeses and savoury biscuits to go with coffee at the end of the meal. Four courses had to be enough to impress them. Their facial expressions gave them away, they were happy to be in my presence, or rather, the food's presence. I even gave them leftovers to take home. But that was the end of it? Nothing ever came of their admiration. What more could I do? Okay, it was a test I wanted to prove to myself. They will only ever come to anybody if they are going to gain something good out of it. They were not prepared to suffer. Yet they were all too willing to give me a hard time for my pain.

When alone in my room I prayed often. My faith was relatively new and I discovered the power of God working on many occasions. One sunny day I was sitting slightly to the right of the open window in a chair, reading my Bible, when I heard what sounded like a distant lawn mower. The humming noise grew louder and louder until, as though being drawn by a magnet, I rose to look out of the window. There was nothing at first but suddenly a huge bee appeared and upon seeing me it hovered in mid flight. Unprepared for such a meeting we stared at each other until I commanded with teeth clenched and without moving my lips,

'In the Name of Jesus turn right around and fly right out of here.'

It hovered for a while as I repeated the command then suddenly turned and fled.

Not long after that, lying in bed one night, I became aware of a presence in the room. It came over and lay face down on the length of my entire body; head to head, arm to arm, leg to leg, foot to foot,

'We are one,' it said and entered uninvited with the ease of air, three times.

I lay motionless and compliant not understanding and later wondered if it was all in my imagination. As I sat in prayer the following day God gave me a reading from the Bible; Revelation chapter one,

'Do not be afraid, I have the keys of death and hell.'

Then He commanded,

'Do not make a pact with them.'

Whatever was happening was totally outside of my control but well within my senses. I had not invited the 'guest', it just helped itself; whatever it was. Next morning at church the experience was verified. God always spoke to me at church when I asked Him to. Sometimes I did not even have to ask, just lifted my spirit to Him and He was right there. One of the pastors read from Revelation chapter one, the exact chapter and verses that I had read! It was confirmation that what happened was a true experience. The battle was unceasing. Week in, week out I went to church changing the words to suit my mood and all kinds of things were going on in my heart. I was not really at peace with God but was walking with Him, and He with me through all of the nasty experiences.

Homes, always in homes: children's homes, adult care homes, hospitals and so on. I could not even imagine a better life, ever, but one night during the hopelessness I had a dream. I was standing outside the side gate of the hostel when the sound of a plane in distress came from overhead. I looked up. A one pilot plane was hurtling my way. As it spiraled to earth I heard the pilot quoting a famous verse from the Bible,

'God so loved the world that He gave His only begotten Son that whoever believes in Him shall not perish but have everlasting life.' John 3:16.

As the last word was uttered the plane crashed into the house next door. Convinced the pilot had no chance of survival I ran inside to tell Janice but no sooner had I entered the hallway than the pilot, a little blackened around the face, marched in very much alive. Totally untouched by the effects of the crash he made friends with me, sat down, took a pack of cards out of His pocket and played a game. On waking I meditated on that scripture. Yes, I understood the parable of the dream but what was so striking was that the pilot, who I understood to represent Jesus Christ, did not go on to tell me to work. He was lifting a vast amount of childhood pressure from my shoulders and saying, in effect,

'It's okay for us to play together.'

'God,' I said, while walking to church one day. 'I'm fighting with You but I want You to win.'

'It is as much a command for you who find it hard to believe as it is for those who find it easy,' He replied.

I was certainly stunned by that remark. God could not change His word but at least I understood that it was nigh impossible for me to believe. *I must believe God for who He is, not for who I think He is.* Church, as far as I was concerned, was who portrayed Jesus to me. God worked through them and it was their job to allow Him to do whatever He wanted in my life. Many times I asked for a miracle but one day a lady who sat in front of me recited a part of the Bible where Jesus had asked God the Father to take away the cup of suffering that He was about to drink, adding,

'Nevertheless, not my will but Yours be done.'

As with everything, I felt that word was for me because I was always sensitively listening for His voice. God was not about to take the cup of suffering away. *Why does He want me to be like this?* I lived one horrible day at a time. What power did I have to change my life? Life did get too much for me as a Christian. I was not actually living the Christian life but working out my salvation with Jesus, trying to shake off the kingdom of darkness that clung to me and that brought me and others a lot of sorrow and misery. I attended all the meetings I could and still not a lot was happening as far as I was concerned. Worst of all nobody understood what I was trying to do. They seemed satisfied with a Sunday service that gave words of prophecy and knowledge and nothing more. I wanted and needed much more. God had to penetrate my life and set me free. I did not want to be a false Christian but a true light. I wanted to be like Kathryn Kuhlman when I lived with my sisters; at least, that is what I told God. Peggy and I read many books about the miracles of God in those days. She brought one after the other for me to read. All we wanted was to live for Him. But it was as if He did not want us to live for Him in the same pure, innocent faith. Feeling discouraged one afternoon because I did not feel I was improving, I said to God,

'I might as well go into sin. I haven't done anything wrong. I've never deliberately sinned or anything and yet look at my life. Nobody wants me. Everyone's horrible to me and You aren't doing much Yourself to heal me. I might as well go and be a prostitute or a thief or something; go on drugs, become an alcoholic. At least then You will be able to save me properly.'

If I did that I would have to renounce Him and all He stood for but no sooner had I said that than God answered,

'You shall not put the Lord your God to the test.'

'I just can't win with You, can I?'

There was no turning back. I had to keep going. If I did not I would not be fit for the Kingdom of God, *'No man, having put his hand to the plough, and looking back, is fit for the kingdom of God,'* Luke 9:62. Many times my physical strength was sapped and I had difficulty climbing the stairs. Nobody witnessed how I bent forward just to put one foot on to the next step and the exhaustion that followed. It was difficult to keep seeking the truth.

Meanwhile, Samantha had given birth to her first daughter and I went to visit them. One morning she came downstairs and sat at the table where I was having breakfast. Her face, with gentle eyes, made its way closer to me. She placed her hands on top of each other. I watched and waited for what she was about to say,

'I had a dream last night. In it I was experiencing a lot of terror and could not get rid of it. The terror was as if it was me through the whole dream and even as I woke up I was saying to myself, I am Rachel, I am Rachel.'

I stared at her in amazement. God had given her a revelation of what it was like to be her older sister.

'Samantha, I am like that all the time. My whole life is one of terror. It never goes.'

I wondered if our relationship from then on would be one of more understanding and returned to the hostel feeling closer to her even though we lived miles apart.

At one point I dared to venture from the hostel to try an evening creative writing course and discovered I was a good writer. Once there I wrote a fictional story based on my early teens at home but instead of the cruelty I used drugs as a reason the police raided our home. Writers encourage a person to show what they know and I was sure the tutor thought I was a drug addict. She told me how good my piece of work was and that I could enter it for a women's magazine. I did not take her advice. If any editor was to discover who I was underneath it all and where I had come from they would surely discard it. In a way I wrote the story as a plea for help. *Perhaps she will rescue me from the hostel?* Then one evening, as I stood in the games room looking out of the window and feeling angry, she passed by but refrained from knocking on the door. What was she afraid of? None of us were that bad. The residents were not the kind of people many folks made them out to be. They simply could not cope with their lives for one reason or another and had entered those places because of it. If she had knocked on the door and asked for me I would have run and invited her in with a big smile. All anybody really wants in life is to be accepted. Perhaps I should never have written about drugs when I was not qualified to do so? She did not know me and was not bothered to be of any help. I watched her turn the corner and waited to see if she would turn back but I had a long wait.

A year later Janice left the hostel to run a similar home down the road and so a new warden, Colin, took her place. He was a red head like me and young. Peggy and I met quite a bit and decided to go to a camping Bible Week. Colin drove us there with our tents and equipment. I had made cheese scones, rice salad and other nice things for the week's food supply. After the tents were erected with the help of a mallet and other people *(we had never put one up before)* we rested.

In my troubled state and yet listening to God I had an experience that may or may not ever come true. It happened at our meal in the evening of the second or third day. Peggy and I were sitting outside and I had not quite finished eating. I tore off a tiny bit of a cheese scone which was still fresh, even at two days old, and absentmindedly threw it onto the grass. I repeated the performance and had no idea Peggy was watching but not too long into the ritual she asked,

'What are you doing?'

'Oh, I'm feeding the five thousand,' I answered, equally absentmindedly.

At that I burst out laughing and could not stop, even though it was offending Peggy. It upset her that much that she stood up almost indignant and marched into the tent. When she reemerged later I asked,

'Where've you been?'

'To look in the mirror to see what you were laughing at.'

I was not laughing at her. God had spoken. I hardly ever laughed; my life was much too serious and painful to embark on laughter. Was He talking about what I would do for Him in the future? Perhaps I would feed five thousand of His 'sheep' with only a tiny bit of spiritual food. If it was a revelation from Him it certainly has not yet come true. So many people had told me,

'God is really going to use you.'

They seemed to think I could go ahead and be used by God without as much as a morsel of help while I was so desperately in need myself. I could not give what I had not received. Left totally alone, accused and even spiritually abused, was I supposed to somehow prepare myself for ministry?

While we were packing up to leave, Peggy and I volunteered to help pack the main marquee away. As we helped my temper got the better of me and I heard one of the pastors bellow in front of many people something about anger not being right. I felt humiliated and utterly vulnerable. There was no understanding or protection, just preaching the cold hard word. I felt its icy blast against my soul and shivered. Why could he not have come and talked gently like a parent or caring pastor? What was he afraid of? I would have responded well but he never gave me a chance. The only reason a person gets obnoxious or bad tempered is usually because they are treated like an outsider or pushed away. Perhaps they have been so used to it all their lives so that any form of acceptance is an invader and, though it is good, is a very hard thing to get used to. I needed time to adjust to a normal life but nobody was giving me a normal life. They thrust me into care and threw away the key. They wanted me to change with a word of rebuke. I had no foundation for it, no stability and no assurance that I was accepted. Their rebuke only made me feel condemned and more rejected than ever.

I encountered some bizarre behaviour in myself that year at the Bible Week. God had come closer to me; at least, I thought it was Him. Some people prayed for me and said I needed deliverance. While they were praying I had pictures in my mind of people dressed in black gowns with pointed hoods and I doubled up in agony on the floor. Growling and screaming I clung to the leg of a chair for safety; my knuckles white. Were these black entities the key? It was my first deliverance encounter and barely enough.

During that period in my life I did not want anybody around me. But I did want them around me at the same time. Deep in my heart, a massive cry was reaching out to those in ministry. I wanted them to be able to read my heart without me having to tell them. I wanted them to take the lead and tell me I needed prayer instead of asking me if I wanted it. I was totally incapable of coming for it at times. I felt it was wrong of them. If I could not receive the help all the church were doing by keeping silent was showing me they could not care less that I was perishing. It was not their fault but the way they had been trained to behave. I did not want to be left alone. They were judging me wrongly. I said one thing with my mouth and behaviour but quite another deep in my heart. If they sat down and talked with me they would have found a very cooperative person. If they could not discern my problem then they could not help me. Colin came to collect us and we returned to Ribford rather dejected.

The following year I returned to the Bible Week alone, put up my one man tent and spent the first night awake. An uneasy feeling that my tent was being lifted supernaturally from the ground with me inside and moving to another part of the field, kept me alert and frightened. The terrible head on battle for my soul was under way. Either that or I had moved into a deceived Christianity where demons picked on ignorant leaders. Had I come to a place where Jesus was preached but not allowed to work in the power He intended? Were demons doing that in His stead, trying to mimic Him like a wolf in sheep's clothing and so bring about a false Christianity and devour the true faith? Even though that awful stuff was happening I could not escape the fact that the sun shone brightly within the camp but not in the surrounding area. It spoke of an open heaven and God's favour.

Once back at Ribford I continued attending my church. Even though there was no progress I sensed God wanted me there but one day I heard a certain Theobald Petland Ministries would be leading a conference in Bramington. I had never been to a conference like it before but sensed I should go. I arrived, via a lift in somebody's car, on their second night. Not long after entering the hall during worship I heard Theobald say,

'Let's laugh at the Devil.'

'Don't you laugh at me,' replied an indignant voice in my head.

I stood with a scrunched face and shoulders, defiantly opposing Theobald. Deep down though I knew I had come to the right place but that was it for the night and rest of the conference for me. I could not attend any more as I had no way of getting there. So life went on and one day Colin asked the residents if they would like to do a course at the adult education centre. He gave us a local newspaper to see what was on offer. I had given up on life so did not choose. Later, as the deadline came around for bookings I tried to dredge up a little bit of hope. *Perhaps I can do one?*

'Colin, I'm sorry but can I do a painting course?'

'Well, you should have let me know before now. I'm not sure Trencham will let you.'

He tried to get me some allowance and succeeded. I applied for a beginner's watercolour course which would be held in the hall at the corner of the road. I was petrified. I did not need any materials for the first lesson, except myself. Again, just like at school I felt like a huge monster entering the class which was mainly full of older people. *Maybe I've done the wrong thing*. I sat with my elbows on the table, hands dangling in front of me just below the edge. I wanted to walk out and leave the whole thing. Just at that moment a cool breeze swept across the palms of my hands. God was there and saying it was okay. The tutor arranged teasels in a vase before placing them on our table. I had always wondered what those were. I sat a little straighter, took a pencil and started to draw. One line after another, without a mistake, I sketched a perfectly formed teasel. *I can draw!* Encouraged with that I carried on and completed the course.

In time a psychiatric nurse called Beatrice came to work at the hostel, much to my delight. She was one of the staff from Beech Day Centre and believed the best in people, loving everyone. She tried to help me but I did not have the love for myself to be *able* to improve. I could not fathom what she was saying when complimenting me. She also used pendulums, a little thing on a chain to foretell the future and I, having been taught that using those things was wrong for a Christian to dabble with, did not feel confident about it. One day I asked if she would visit Apple Ash with me and so she took a day off and drove me over to Haxwich. We had a good day exploring once again the huge gardens, house and fields. Everything was as it was when I left eight years before.

'I think you should live in a village,' said Karen.

As I heard that whilst sitting in the lounge, which was mostly out of bounds to residents, I wondered if she wanted me to return to Apple Ash but thought, *no*. She had become a born again Christian by then and told me about the day I had my experience with Jesus *(see book one)* that it filled the whole house. She also revealed,

'When you were trying to cut your meat that day on the patio, I sat thinking, if she is putting that on then leave her to it but if she is genuine then God help her.'

My mind went blank. Emptiness and the vastness of it threw itself down to taunt me. How could she possibly have thought I had put on an act when before her very eyes I had been unable to walk, had considerable loss of energy, was absolutely exhausted and the physical sight of my muscles wasted to nothing? It seemed that any opportunity for people to help me was swiped away by what they thought about me. Yet they knew my problems and what I needed because I told them and were they not in all my medical records? *Would they treat their children like that? Who am I? I'm made of flesh and blood too, aren't I? I have bones, nerves and feelings just like them. I don't treat them this way.* The questions about my existence were always before me. I remembered the words of Father Bothwell at the Charismatic conference with Samantha, when I lived in Mackton,

'You don't live, you exist.'

When we left Apple Ash it was the last time I saw Karen.

As I was making no progress at Church, I asked God if I should leave,

'Please show me very clearly.'

The following Sunday the church was full as usual and I joined in the service but was concerned that even God could not do any of His work there. I asked Him to give me a scripture from the Bible to read out. We could bring whatever God laid on our hearts. I waited for my opportunity but first read to myself what He gave to see if it was appropriate. I sensed it was so being obedient, boldly stood to read the passage loudly for all to hear,

'Isaiah 42:
1 "Here is my servant, whom I uphold, my chosen one in whom I
delight; I will put my Spirit on him and he will bring justice to the
nations. 2 He will not shout or cry out, or raise his voice in the
streets. 3 A bruised reed he will not break, and a smoldering wick
he will not snuff out. In faithfulness he will bring forth justice;
4 he will not falter or be discouraged till he establishes justice
on earth. In his law the islands will put their hope... "'

I continued to read the entire chapter because all of it was important but especially so when I reached the following verses,

18 '"Hear, you deaf; look, you blind, and see! 19 Who is blind
but my servant, and deaf like the messenger I send? Who is blind
like the one committed to me, blind like the servant of the LORD?
20 You have seen many things, but have paid no attention; your
ears are open, but you hear nothing." 21 It pleased the LORD for

the sake of his righteousness to make his law great and glorious.
22 But this is a people plundered and looted, all of them trapped in pits or hidden away in prisons. They have become plunder, with no one to rescue them; they have been made loot, with no one to say, "Send them back."'

Horace interrupted, giving orders for music to be played and I was gradually drowned out with the rising volume. The remainder of the passage was left unread and unheard. *This is my sign.* I was one of those trapped in pits so I knew fully the validity of what God was telling me to read. There was no freedom from my pain offered in that church. I stood up, picked up my coat from the seat, took my time in doing up the buttons and walked out for good. I was not at all bothered or upset because God had spoken. I would find a new church.

Victory Church was one I heard the Holy Spirit moved freely in so I stepped, one Sunday, inside. The praise started and not long afterwards the pastor announced, to everybody's surprise,

'The Devil has just walked in here.'

I am not the Devil but I knew it was because of me.

'Keep praising, increase the praising,' he instructed.

As they did so I became very uneasy and soon felt extremely uncomfortable. Putting my fingers in my ears I stepped on the chair next to me then dashed for the door. Two men followed. The church's van stood just outside. Catching up with me one of them invited,

'Come and get into the van.'

I thought he may be from the leadership and climbed in thinking I would be delivered and start a brand new life but the state I was in did not allow my hopes to rise too high. The Devil had revealed what he was doing with me and the power of the Lord was present. The man who talked with me gazed at my shaking body, red face, tears and anguish and I waited in anticipation for his good news; the Good News of the Gospel to set the prisoners free and to heal the broken hearted was about to invade my destroyed life.

'We would like you to leave,' he ordered.

Horror and disbelief again assaulted my expectations. After a conversation with him I was allowed to stay in the van until I had calmed down. I did not go back to that church again. I had no idea why all this was going on in my life. *What have I done?* My life would be the same as ever and I felt a lifetime sentence of evil hanging over me. *Why does God hate me so much?* On my way back to the hostel I detoured and turned up at Laurence's house. He answered my knock and made light of the situation but I shouted,

'Laurence, you listen to me!'

He did, then gave me a hug but nothing came of the revelation and nothing was done to alleviate the presence of evil that so clearly manifested itself. Neither my pleas nor my cooperation with the Holy Spirit for freedom were acknowledged.

At the hostel Beatrice's sister, Sophie, who nobody had met before, also came to work and was well liked by everyone. She also loved people. When I first started questioning whether I had demons inside me I had bought a book from the local Christian bookshop that taught on being set free from them. My head had automatically raised itself to look at some books high up on a shelf. It was a brand new subject to me at the time and I wanted to meet the author, Louis Ritzburgh. I found out he was coming to do a conference for leaders in Derby so, grabbing my chance, I booked up. I was no leader but was given permission to attend by his staff. When Louis called people forward for salvation about two hundred responded to his altar call. *Are these leaders?* I wondered how on earth a leader of churches could not be saved and how anybody was safe in their congregations. There was an altar call also for the rest of us to which I went forward. Louis was somewhere wandering around the auditorium when I started to manifest and shout defiantly at God,

'Get me, if you can, you Son of God.'

It provoked Louis, who came marching down to the platform declaring,

'She has just never been loved.' How right he was but he also discerned the spirit behind the defiance towards God, 'I know what that is, it's adultery.'

I hardly thought adultery was the cause of all my problems as I had never committed the sin but he tried to cast it out. It may or may not have left. It certainly was not the end of my problems. However, I had been taught that demons and especially generational ones can hide and never be detected because the person has not performed any such sin. Even though I may not have been as free as I would have liked I did come away with the next step in my search for answers. Somebody who heard about my difficulties highly recommended a place that had just opened called Healing Brooks in Compaven, Yorkshire. Anything sounded better than nothing so I booked a place after the conference.

Sophie, who had become my key worker, came with me to buy the train ticket where I asked if there would be any holdups, an off the cuff question. Next morning, there was a massive crash along the line I was to take! But I still managed to get there without a problem. On arrival I was impressed by the beautiful countryside surrounding a huge mansion. Stepping into the spacious main hall and making myself known, I was shown to a dormitory. I would have preferred a room of my own. The founder, Reginald Hassenbury, led the first evening's session. He gave words of knowledge from the Holy Spirit about various people's problems and towards the end said,

'Something has happened to one of you where you have put all kinds of furniture against a door. Whatever is behind that door is so awful you never, ever, in your wildest dreams want it to be opened again. But it is the key to your healing.'

As usual I thought it was me. I left after the weekend a little disappointed that it had not been discovered there and then. The 'items of furniture' have to be removed first.

Back at the hostel, Colin announced he would be leaving. He had been a good warden but I prayed,

'Please, Lord, will you send a Christian here to be in charge.'

To my delight a Christian, named Lesley, did come. Wow, what happiness! When she arrived I told her I too was a Christian but there seemed to be no response. Even after she settled in Lesley kept herself in the office and did not mix with us as much as Janice and Colin but one day she asked the residents if they would like to go to an Ice Show in Bramington.

'Yes please, yes please,' was the excited response.

At the show something happened that I can and cannot explain. I sat next to Lesley half way up in the circle, enjoying the show. Suddenly, a gust of wind blew diagonally from the front, left hand side and swept over me, I knew it was God so answered,

‘Yes, what do You want?’

At the beginning of the next scene a skater, wearing a black gown down to his or her feet and a matching hood covering his or her head, skated onto the rink. Then another came and another, looking exactly the same. Each one held a candle. I watched as many more continued to spill out onto the rink until no patch of ice was uncovered and, after marching around for a while, left the rink. Puzzled as to what the point of the act was, I asked God,

‘What was all that about?’

‘That’s how many are in you.’

I was not surprised but a bit hopeless when I saw how many. However, I knew He had cast out legion for the demoniac in the Bible and afterwards the man sat in his right mind. But if all those demons were black it spoke to me of witchcraft and Satanism. I was not in a position to argue with God. My life was desperate. Whatever was revealed to me I accepted and tried to do something about.

A few months later my allocated time at Spearmint Street was at an end but I was far from ready and could not fathom how anybody could judge how well a person is before they are ready to leave care. It was like a sentence rather than a step of progress. The progression was to move to one of two group homes. I chose the quieter one at 16 Tapsing Lane, quite a few streets away.

Moving into the semi-detached house where three others lived I was still unable to mix and kept myself to myself. Sandy came too. In my small room and after a period of settling in, I sowed tomato plants in a tray; a taste of real freedom. There was no sign of them sprouting but one day the tray fell from the window sill. I quickly picked up the compost thinking, *now for sure they will not grow* but to my surprise the shocked seeds germinated; not one or two but many. A few weeks later I planted them outside in the huge back garden. Annabelle, another resident, kept rabbits and allowed me to feed the plants with their droppings. The tomatoes loved them and grew to be the best I had ever tasted and so prolific were they, that I gave bags full away to other people. I even took some up to my niece, Marie’s baptism *(christening)*. My dad was there so he even got a taste. Through Samantha’s celebrations I had the opportunity to see my father and talk to him about superficial things. There appeared to be no tension where that was concerned. I never confronted him about his behaviour towards us as children but longed with all my heart for him to apologize and even try to compensate for our lost lives. At Louise's baptism a couple of years before, while I was still living in the last home, I was very nervous of seeing him since Samantha's wedding. After the initial shock of his entrance into the lounge and settling to a cup of tea I knelt beside his chair and spoke of where I was living.

'Just think positive,' was all he could answer me with.

No apology for the way he had treated us was offered and therefore no reconciliation. His words were just a cover up to hide the pain and shame. I had forgiven him but how I saw it was that if Jesus forgives me and then turns around and says, 'I forgive you but you still cannot enter my house', I would have a hard time believing that He really meant what He said. As far as I was concerned my father did not forgive me for reporting him to the police or for being born. He pleaded guilty to them but never to me. I was the one who carried the crippling pain of his actions against my life which, no matter how hard I tried, I could not use to better my life or irreversible circumstances. He married Mrs Fabican three years after we all left home and she seemed never to leave his side. I scanned the atmosphere and was careful about what I said and did in a family gathering but always felt stupid and gross.

Back at Tapsing Lane there were times I lay on the bed feeling very ill. One evening, trying to make sense of the way I was feeling and convinced I was dying, I asked God,

'Am I being poisoned by evil spirits?'

I tried to break any effects of poison through prayer and did feel better afterwards so must have been right. The next day, on the way to church, a black cat lay dead at the end of the front garden path. I stepped over it realizing something supernatural was going on. I felt a huge black presence accompanying me to church as well. It was trying to keep guard on me so that I would not get set free. Later on in my room, I asked,

'God, when am I going to get free? There must be a conference coming soon.'

I waited for help and eventually a letter came through the post from Healing Brooks to say they would be holding a conference in Bramington five months later. *Five months? How am I going to survive?* I sat on my bed totally empty and in tremendous pain. *Why don't I commit suicide? I can't cope with this anymore. How am I going to get through the next five months?* I had to though, as when I turned on a Christian radio programme one evening a well known minister, Chuck Swindoll, spoke life saving words. Out of all he said I only heard,

'We need you.'

I struggled with the encouragement, not wanting to hear any of it because it was just too hard and following those words came others from a voice in my head, declaring,

'The whole of hell is against you.'

However, feeling obliged, I carried on, with that small amount of strength, to wait it out.

Thankfully, Theobald Petland's conference came to Bramington before Healing Brooks and I wanted to stay for the entire event. At the first meeting my insides were as if huge butterflies were moving around. I became agitated. Looking towards the platform from my place in the right hand section I noticed the rest of the row, about eight seats, was empty. Turning and looking around I was puzzled that it was only my row that was affected. Later on Theobald said God wanted to minister to people who had dabbled in the occult,

'Things move around in your house.'

They had in mine just that week; a photograph of Jesus was on top of my small television set. As I sat on my bed praying the photograph and an ornament suddenly slammed onto the floor and the television lurched forward, dislodging the glass of the table underneath. Initially it shocked me but, once again, I knew exactly who was doing it and remained calm. At his word of knowledge my insides took a turn for the worse. I shot out of my seat, ran at top speed down the aisle and across the front of the auditorium. Nobody had a chance to think as I sped towards the far wall. A few ushers took up their positions to stop me but I heard Theobald shout,

'Let her run.'

I wanted to run straight through the wall but stopped on approach, abruptly turned and headed for the platform, determined to push Theobald off the stage from underneath and at the same time struggled to keep myself from doing so. When I saw the height of the platform I knew I did not stand a chance. I forced myself to stop and sit down against the wall near the side door in full view of everybody and banged my head hard against it several times. A man approached but by then I was in a kind of trance. He gently coaxed me to come out of the auditorium and sit with him in the corridor. A woman came with us. As we walked through the outer corridors of the hall I knew I was in trouble. For sure I had ruined my chances of getting free. The man sat beside me and talked for quite some time. I remained in a 'trance', immobile and inactive. Eventually, he spoke about abuse and an involuntary tear fell down my cheek.

'Halleluiah!' the man exclaimed.

He reached into his pocket, pulled out his handkerchief and handed it to me. The lady prayed to break hexes, curses and such like but nothing seemed to happen. Eventually, the man let me back into the hall where I sat in a different seat to the one before and that was the end of it. Later on outside the hall one of the ushers told me,

'At the ushers prayer meeting we'd had before the service God told us that somebody would run across the front but when you did we didn't know what to do.'

God even knew what I was going to do! So it was Him who made sure my row was empty. He had it all prepared without the help of man. That was a vindication to anybody who might have judged that I was doing it for fun. I never do something like that for fun. Those types of bondages are never welcome in my life. All my existence was of wondering around aimlessly from place to place so who would do that for fun? That marked the end of that episode.

Matthew Minnerton was about to leave his church in Bramington and give his place of leadership to the worship leader but he was not as nice as Matthew. I continued to attend the Tuesday evening meetings and during one of them when I was being prayed for by Terence Libbington, one of the pastors, a quiet and gentle man, I was screaming so much that he said,

'God's not attacking you, Rachel.'

At which I laughed and was able to relax somewhat.

As I continued to wait for the Healing Brooks conference yet another Theobald Petland conference came to Bramington. I did not pass up taking every opportunity to get set free as God had told me to make the most of them all. During one of the afternoon meetings God was talking to me through Rob Velliyan, one of the speakers,

'You have only known my anger but now I want you to come right into My lap.'

Because of constant rejection I had become quite indignant. *What are You talking about? You know perfectly well You haven't got a lap. If he keeps talking like that I'm going to run out.*

'Don't go out from My Presence,' God answered unexpectedly through Rob.

My hair almost stood on end as he read my thoughts. That was it! I took off from my seat, ran across the front of the auditorium and out through the side door. No sooner had I reached the corridor than a woman appeared from behind and instructed,

'You just sit there. I can set you free. I'll go and get somebody else.'

'God told me not to go out of His presence. I want to go back in.'

She would not hear of it even though God had said it Himself and demanded that I sit there until her friend arrived. Reluctantly, despite my own convictions to the contrary, I felt obliged to follow them to a room away from the auditorium. Once inside, one of the women started to pray and then quickly suggested,

'I'll go back and get the others.'

What others? I sat patiently until the 'others' arrived. At least five entered the room. Shocked, I watched as they brought in chairs and sat in a semicircle around me. I was trapped. The lead lady started her deliverance session with the announcement that,

'You don't have one spirit of witchcraft, you have eight.'

I had seen more than eight on the ice rink. After her diagnosis she went on to cast them out. Unprepared for the bizarre way she lifted her voice like a banshee, I braced myself. So loud and high were her decibels that I cringed, shut down and was unable to cooperate any further. In no time the others were praying too but not so loudly.

'You are not cooperating,' the leader announced.

Neither would you. For a while I sat not knowing how to get out of the room and dared not show my intention to do so. I had disobeyed God, albeit under her demands, so deserved all I got but I *had* said I wanted to go back inside. Eventually, I screamed that I wanted to get out and back to the meeting but they refused to let me go. Time went on and nothing was accomplished at all. My glasses were on the small table in front of me. The door behind the helpers' chairs, with no space between them, was firmly shut. The only practice of self defense I had was with my father and that was to stay perfectly still while he abused me; that was all I could do. The horror escalated so I prayed silently and fervently that God would rescue me,

'Please, please send an usher to help me.'

I started to yell, unable to suppress the terrible encounter with the team who had not been part of Theobald Petland's ministry. During the noise we were all making with our raised voices and what seemed more than an hour, one of the team stood to leave; *now's my chance.* Eager for him to move his chair so that I could run for it, I gazed at the door. As he moved his chair, making a gap in the semi-circle, I sat on the edge of mine. Without replacing his chair he walked to the door and opened it. Instantly, and to the utter surprise of the rest of them, I fled for the door and ran two steps up the corridor when a strong arm pulled me back towards the door. I yelled with all my might in the struggle as my shirt came loose about my waist. At that moment as usher approached and, totally unmoved it seemed, wanted to know why all the fuss.

'She doesn't want to get free,' said the leader.

Oh yes I do.

'You've left your glasses in here,' said the lady who had led me there in the first place.

'I don't care,' I screamed.

I did not care if I never saw them again, sensing it was a trap to get me back inside.

'Give her her glasses and let her go,' ordered the usher.

The lady brought them from the table. I grabbed them and raced for the auditorium only to find the meeting was over. Sorely distressed I had learned one hard lesson; obey God in future, no matter what! Thankful to be free of the team and ready to stay in future meetings, I went for lunch. Fear increased in anticipation of the evening meeting. I sensed something might happen and it did. During the offering Ernest Stoutherd, the worship leader, walked up to Theobald and took the microphone. He announced to the auditorium,

'In all my sixteen years of ministry I have never had to do anything like this. There is an ice block stopping the worship getting through.'

He took off his jacket, gave it to Theobald, lay face down and prayed. I watched and waited. When he finally stood up he encouraged the people to praise the Lord. As they did so it became a major torment. I blocked my ears hard to try to reduce the agony and controlled my urge to scream because I knew if I did I might disturb what God was doing as well as more than likely get told off from those in authority but my urge to scream was so forceful I could barely contain it. At the same time I turned ice cold myself and was relieved when the praising was over. It was hard to keep it bottled up for so long and I regretted that I had suppressed my reaction as they just may have responded favourably. After the meeting I approached some counselors and told them that what Ernest had done was because of me,

'No, it wasn't.'

'Yes, it was!'

I became confused. Involuntary tears rolled down my expressionless cheeks. A couple who had been sitting behind me at the time stood beside me listening. I thought they wanted to speak to the counselors and they did, about me!

'We believe you. We were watching you the whole time and we believe you.'

I did not know what to say but thankfulness was all I felt. I loved them so much. The counselors did not back down but kept silent and left me without any kind of help. On the Saturday afternoon Theobald's wife, Rosemary, held a healing service where the congregation queued up when called forward for prayer and the laying on of hands. I joined the queue. Worship was under way and as I stepped forward coldness blanketed me. With each step I grew colder and colder. My thighs were so cold that icy waves radiated from them as I held my hands in front an inch away! When I reached Rosemary she merely laid a hand on me. After she prayed I was lying down on the floor and a little later the power of God really set to work. My hands banged on the floor with such speed and force that when they finally stopped they were bruised and injured. I had to have them bandaged by the first aid people and I was thoroughly exhausted. During a later meeting a man tried to cast out a demon as the power of God again had me lying on the floor, my head moved hard and rapidly from side to side so that my neck ached and froth oozed from my mouth. He commanded,

'I break your power in the name of Jesus.'

The demon replied from my lips,

'I break *your* power.'

The man did not know what to say next so left but eventually I calmed down and, with a very red and hot face, stood up. Nothing more was done and I returned home.

Back at Tapsing Lane and waiting for the Healing Brooks conference was tough but it finally came around. A man named David from our fellowship had taken on a few of us problem girls and gave us lifts to and from meetings. As he was driving us to Bramington to the Healing Brooks conference I heard God say,

'Don't let *anyone* stop you coming to Jesus.'

I reported it to David and added,

'Who's going to stop me?'

Louis and Mary Ritzburgh were the main guest speakers at the event and I happened to be sitting behind them. Mary, not knowing me, turned around and said,

'You are going to be set free this week.'

I was greatly encouraged but wondered how. I trusted those people and I trusted God that if He said something it would happen. When God started to move in the meetings to heal the broken, I responded to His invitations. Fear, inferiority and tension were the most prominent feelings. Something was spoken while I was sitting half way back in one of the meetings; I screamed and ran for my life down the centre aisle and out across the front of the hall to the right hand door but remembered that I was there for my promised deliverance so returned after lunch. A female member of staff met me later and asked,

'Was it you that ran along the front?'

'No.'

I had not run along the front, it must have been somebody else. After she left I realized she was talking about the front of the hall and not the seafront which was directly opposite the building! I blessed myself for misinterpreting her question. At least the lack of understanding had got me out of trouble. *I hope she doesn't ask me again.*

'Don't let them frighten you and don't scream or we'll take you out,' she advised, meaning the demons.

Demons are very powerful entities, so what she was telling me to do was not altogether helpful.

That evening, while sitting in a different place, I pleaded with the woman sitting next to me,

'Don't let them take me out.'

Reginald Hassenbury, the host of the conference, spoke from the high platform,

'God wants to heal people concerning mothers. He wants to cut the umbilical cord,'

My mother was the furthest thing from my mind at that point but I flinched slightly and my head lurched forward of its own volition. A finger appeared over my right shoulder and a vicious voice ordered,

'I told you not to fear. We are going to take you out.'

I turned towards the lady I had spoken to for protection. Thankfully, the finger pointing woman went away. I peered all around to see where she was but could not see her and breathed a sigh of relief. *I know! I'll go up to the platform and tell Reginald I want my mum back. They can't get me there.* Reginald carried on preaching about mothers and I longed more and more for the return of mine. Checking behind again I saw no sign of the lady and slipped quietly out of my seat. I had not planned to be a problem but decided to politely stand and wait for a moment when Reginald was not talking. Reaching the front I stood silently and calmly before him and there was a point where he did stop. I looked up into his face, confident that he would understand and said,

'I want my mum back.'

No sooner had I uttered the words than the lady who I thought was out of sight appeared at my right hand side, stretching towards me. I turned, wondering why she had come but her hand was already on my shoulder. Another lady came forward from the front row and they both grabbed hold of one arm each; my arms. A man also darted forward from the front but had second thoughts,

'Man handling,' he declared and immediately withdrew.

The two women pulled me, with their backs towards the double doors on the left hand side. Five thousand people looked on. The carpet in the front of the platform allowed my shoes to grip it and for a moment I thought I would be able to win against the force of the abductors. I watched as my feet neared the edge of the carpet and finally onto the floor where all my fighting ceased. The ladies had the upper hand and I slid on the polished surface towards the door but still pulling away with all my might. Speedily, they pulled me to the other side of the door. Once there the two ministers dropped me in indignation.

'We'll call an ambulance and they'll come and take you away.'

I could not understand that the conference which was meant to help people like me get out of bondage and heal the brokenhearted was causing me much more agony than anything the hosts were preaching against. They had won my trust and respect and God had won my faith. Why all the confusion? They continued to threaten me and the first lady, Harriet was her name, pointed a harsh finger in my face. By then my brain was reacting to the terror she was inflicting on me. I lived in a twenty four hour care home and the conference was my ticket to freedom but what were they doing? I stood up and backed against the wall. Harriet kept her finger pointing in my face and my body struggled to contain the terror. I was in a fight for my future survival and knew they meant what they said about the ambulance. How was I going to get out of it? In my horror I stared at her finger and did all within my power to control not biting it off, being well aware of the consequences if I did. My head almost exploded at the threat of being taken away,

'God is in there,' I said, as I pointed towards the doors.

'He's out here.'

'He's in there and I want to go back in where he can heal me and set me free.'

'You're not going.'

It was one battle they must not be allowed to win. I had to fight hard for my freedom if I wanted it so badly. Harriet was losing her strength against me. She could not control my determination to get what I needed and had been promised. She glanced at the door, opened it and entered the auditorium. Grabbing the opportunity I hooked my left arm round the huge, oblong door handle and stood inside the auditorium, the other lady still had hold of me so I could not run but she did not put up as much of a fight as Harriet. The worship music was deafening but I bellowed with all the force I could muster,

'Help me! Help me! Help me!'

Each time, my bellowing grew louder but nobody seemed to hear or care less until, suddenly, a lady ran forward and flung her arms around me! She hugged and hugged me. I broke down and sobbed uncontrollably as she took me back out into the corridor where I had come from.

'Oh, she's responding to that,' I heard Harriet say as she arrived back on the scene.

Well what do you think? I could not believe or comprehend such a comment and was shocked at the lack of help from the person who ran the conference, Reginald Hassenbury! It seemed to me that he was only interested in the event running smoothly and not at all about what might be stirred up in some people because of it. In my understanding of things God highlights areas of all who attend these events in faith; faith to be set free of whatever is binding them to whatever degree. Harriet, seeing me in such a state, disappeared through the door again while on the floor I sat sobbing unable to do or say anything. The nightmare of that event was felt only by me. I was on the receiving end of what others understood it to be. But God had warned me beforehand, had He not? Suddenly, David arrived and stood looming over me. It was as though my mother was standing there; the relief of a familiar face helped like a sedative. I thought David would defend me but he said nothing, just remained calm and submitted to the request to remove me from the building.

'You are banned from the rest of the conference,' he said later.

'But I can't because God told me not to let *anybody* stop me coming to Jesus.'

David had two other men staying with him at his bungalow for the conference and one of them, named Sid, offered,

'It's okay; we'll get you back in.'

David was concerned and took me back to stay with them that night. The men tried to minister to me but I knew God was not in that and nothing happened. God sent the men to be my bodyguards, I was sure.

'We'll go in after nine when they are started,' said Sid, 'and we'll sneak you upstairs, right up in the balcony. That way nobody will see you to get you out.'

I did not like what they were suggesting but had no choice. I felt certain that God would have protected me no matter how I got in but I allowed their help because of what was in their hearts. Next morning we arrived as planned. During the worship I stood way out of sight of the leaders with my spirit crushed and eyes and ears open for the next move on God's agenda. Louis Ritzburgh, who was leading that meeting, told the congregation somebody had a song to sing. A woman obeyed and sang a few verses but none spoke to me. When she finished singing Louis added from the platform,

'There's another verse.'

That would be for me I was sure. The lady resumed singing,

'Don't be afraid of Me, My children. Don't be afraid of Me.'

She continued with the same words over and over but her tone descended with each repetition. Tears fell as I swallowed and felt the lump in my throat. I allowed the words to penetrate my soul,

'That's not from God!' Louis shouted.

He stopped the singing that was ministering to the pain deep within and my chance of being comforted that moment was snatched away; another episode of somebody leaning on their own understanding. Soon after that a lady came over to where I was sitting and began to pray. She knelt before me and I felt like a little girl being addressed by a huge adult,

'Your dad did something to your mother while you were in the womb.'

'What did he do?'

'Was your dad perverted?'

'Yes.'

She did not continue but my curiosity had been aroused.

'What did he do, God?' I asked silently.

He did not answer so I continued with my day. By break time boldness had built into me and I walked confidently through the building. Harriet, at one point, walked straight towards me. I looked directly at her. She stared back but said nothing. My confidence was not in rebellion, it was in Jesus my Saviour. *I am going to tell Reginald about this.* That afternoon after attending a session led by Reginald I approached him and thought I had freedom to air my grievance. As I poured out the situation to him he glanced over my shoulder so I turned to see what it was he was looking at,

'It's her,' I said.

'She's the one,' Harriet told him.

That was a very tight battle.

'Reginald, don't let them ban me. God said He would set me free and told me not to let anybody stop me coming to Jesus.'

He allowed me to stay without further restrictions. I still wondered when God was going to do what He had promised through Mary. By the final session of the last day still nothing had happened so I started to worship God with all my might, reaching as far as I could up toward Heaven and prayed in tongues *(a spiritual languag*e) to get God to come. David was out in the aisle while I stayed where I was in the middle of a row, half way back on the left hand side. Suddenly, I felt a firm hand brace my forehead. It held my head for about one minute but no words were uttered. After that, all the moisture in my mouth dried up; opening and closing my mouth produce no saliva whatsoever. Louis Ritzburgh stared in my direction from the platform. I was sure he had seen something going on. David glanced at me as though from an unheard command. I motioned to him for some water which he gave from his flask.

'Did you put your hand round my forehead, David?'

'No.'

'Did you see anybody else do it?'

'No, nobody was doing anything to you.'

I explained to him what happened and wondered what God had done. How would I be later on? Was this my miracle of miracles?

Would I be absolutely one hundred percent well? That was the end of the conference so David took me back to the group home. After he left I went upstairs and entered my room feeling extremely weak. My suitcase sat on the top of the wardrobe which I pulled down. After a few minutes I was unable to stand up and knew it was a result of the hand on my forehead. God had touched me Himself. I had to pack for my next journey to Purple Heathers. I had booked into the home of healing before the conference, to arrive the day after it and to stay for a fortnight, having no idea just how much I would need it.

There was no help in the group home and if I asked Annabelle for any she would have wanted to know all about what happened; so I refrained. It took two hours to pack my case whilst sitting on the floor.

'What did my dad do while I was in the womb?' I asked God.

'He tried to take you out,' came His swift reply.

What? I could not have made it up; such was the speed of the response. *So that was why God had told me not to let anybody stop me coming to Jesus.* I came to the assumption that He had even possibly organized the taking me out scenario. Was it that He had made me relive the moment of being almost totally lost and cast out of the womb - aborted? Only He knows the truth but I thought it was more than likely the case. The horror I had felt when being dragged out during the conference could well have been akin to a foetus being sucked up by a vast hoover and cast out of the world. I thought I would never see the outside world again when Harriet said she would get an ambulance and have them take me away. My only chance of getting free was right there where Jesus was and I was being denied all hope and support from the head of the team.

When alone, and constantly so, I always managed to get to destinations even in a situation of being totally without strength. I was the only help I had and managed the journey with great difficulty, hoping nobody would notice how ill I was. Being taken to the nearest hospital where nobody would understand was an alternative I could not take.

After the two and a half hour train journey I rang the door bell of Purple Heathers. Reverend Renpole, who had replaced Lesley Ridgehurst, opened the door with a great big welcome,

'I bet you're glad to be here, aren't you?'

How does he know?

'Phyllis and Dorothy were at the conference and saw everything you went through.'

Phyllis and Dorothy were staff at Purple Heathers and knew me from previous visits. At least I had witnesses right there to the horrific goings on so I had no need to explain myself. It was as if I had fallen into the hands of angels.

'We're putting you in the balcony.'

'The balcony?'

Haven't I even got a room? Where will I put my case? I kept quiet as I followed Reverend Renpole upstairs. He unlocked one of the doors and invited me to enter. I thought we had to go through the room and onto the balcony but was told to put down my case inside the room. It was a relief to find that I did have a bed after all.

At ten to eight every morning a message came over the tannoy. I pulled the blankets over my head and refused to come out. A member of staff brought my breakfast up on a tray, as happened to all guests. She came back later to collect the tray but I had tasted nothing. No word or deed comforted me. I was told off. She was very patient though and I did try, with great struggle, to come out of my hole for her sake but did not succeed,

'One day people are going to say to me, "Oh, why can't she be miserable for once, she's always happy."' I said from under the blankets as she commented on my mood.

I recall nothing more of the time I spent there.

Not long after that I visited Samantha. The first day I was with her she emerged from the kitchen holding a holy picture. As she showed it to me I told her about the attempted abortion revelation of me in the womb experience at the conference, to which she shouted angrily,

'I *knew* you would say that!'

So God had already prepared her for my testimony but she had not realized that it was He who was speaking when she reached out for that picture of a fetus in the hands of Mary. How incredible is our God!! I did not blame her for her anger. She had not been there. That was the second time God had revealed to her something about me.

After a year at Tapsing Lane and feeling disappointed in the Christian lady who took over at Spearmint Street, a man moved into our group home. He was not at all sensitive to the needs of others around him and played his music loudly every day. It was torture to my soul so I asked him to turn it down. He did not so I reported it to the main house. They were not interested in what I had to endure but said he was entitled to play what he wanted. Unprotected again I resorted to my own defense mechanisms. One night I went down to the kitchen after begging for it to be turned down but he would not oblige so I screamed. That did not help. He did not take any notice so I screamed again; as though being murdered. The taunting went on and so I let out another high decibel scream. Lesley heard about the incident and both she and Sabina came to see me the following day.

'We've been phoning around,' Lesley said, 'and have found a twenty four hour care home for you in Ponrish *(a small town along the coast)* and you can have your cat.'

I was dumbfounded; yet another betrayal into strange hands. No love, understanding or anything. These basic commodities of life were nowhere to be found even in the Christian I had prayed for to watch over us. In a panic I took off to one of the pastor's houses near Grace Church. Desperately, I knocked on his front door.

'Hello,' said the elderly pastor.

'Excuse me, I've just been kicked out of a group home and have to go and live in Ponrish. I don't want to go. It's so unfair.'

He invited me in. I stepped into his huge hall. He then led me into the lounge to our right where I sat on an exquisite armchair. The place was a glorious mansion. *I could come here*. There was plenty of room. I could have been looked after by that family and something could have become of me. Envisioning that happening I looked, begging, into his eyes.

'You can't stay here,' he said, even having heard my entire story.

My shoulders humped over as I left his residence. *'The Son of Man has no place to lay His head.'* Matthew 8:20. The well known words in the Bible reverberated in my mind. The Holy Spirit had told me that so long ago when I lived in East Ribford; my first home after leaving Apple Ash.

I trudged back to Tapsing Lane with a feeling of great abandonment by the church I had given my life for and set to pack my belongings once again.

Chapter Five

24 hour care

Next morning Lesley and Sabina came to collect me. They told me that the staff at Ponrish were preparing an emergency room. About two hours later I arrived at the twenty four hour care rest home. I recollected that I had cried out to God for help a few months back, when still at Grace Church, as I was not coping. He gave a word of knowledge shortly afterwards, acknowledging my prayer and saying help was coming. Even though I hated what was happening I held in my heart that this could be His answer. Christians did not have such places and I was devastated. We were greeted at the front door by Jacqueline; a thin lady with long, blonde hair who was in charge and did not seem to fit such a place. Lesley and Sabina accompanied me upstairs as we followed Jacqueline to my room. The impact of the anciently placed, deep apricot emulsion painted on top of chip paper and the broken wardrobe door was unimpressive. They spoke of neglect and, as at Spearmint Street; the bed had not been prepared.

'We moved the resident out of here so you could have it. It wasn't right for you to have an attic room,' explained Jacqueline.

I did not want to be in any room. Lesley and Sabina only stayed long enough for me to put my belongings inside the room. I walked over to the huge windows with their long, dark blue, velvet curtains. At least there was a view of the large green outside.

'Please will you come and see me,' I begged.

'Yes, of course, we'll come in about two week's time.'

That seemed forever to me and it was forever because they never showed up, history repeating itself again. Was my life never going to change? I walked with them past the dining room on our right, which led to the lounge at the bottom of the stairs, to the car. After saying goodbye I was left to myself to get used to the new home, though it would never be a home. I hated the word 'home' as I never really had one and avoided using it as much as possible. Seeing the other residents made me want to vomit; one of the old men had nails so long they were curling over into the palms of his hands. He was often left to sit in his excrement during the day. The place stank. I was told one of the resident's names was Merlin. *Oh no, a wizard.* I instantly distrusted him and quickly learned that the house was occupied by twenty two residents and that most of them were men from the drug background or out of prison. There were only two other females; one an older lady who watched television all day and another much younger woman. *What am I doing here?* I had to get away, again, so leaving my things mid unpacked left the room and ran out towards the High Street. But it was no use, there was no escape. With no money and well out of my territory, I returned. Not wanting to mix with the other residents I remained in my room. That night as the noise of the downstairs television spilled up into my room I became deeply agitated. Noise coming from others and invading my living space always tormented me. Unable to come to grips with what was happening I lay on the bed and stretched my arms towards Heaven.

'Please come and get me, Lord,' I begged, 'please don't leave me here.'

There was silence from the God my hope was meant to be in.

I continued travelling by train on a Tuesday night to Bramington to attend Matthew Minnerton's meetings held in a small church. I told them what had happened. During one of his meetings whilst preaching to everybody I heard him say,

'You may be there for three days, three months...'

Yeah, I know, three years. I felt like Elijah who had been sentenced to being fed by ravens.

As soon as possible I applied to stay for three weeks at Purple Heathers. They allowed me a bursary, like they had always done, because of my situation. During one lunch time a lady asked,

'Have you ever been to Willow House?'

That led to a conversation about the place. I sensed that I should go straight away as my maximum time allowed at Purple Heathers was three weeks. As soon as I could I phoned Willow House. They booked me in and when I left Purple Heathers I went directly there. On the train while staring out of the window, my troubled mind and fear filled belly chugged along with feelings of suicide. *Should I jump from the train and kill myself?* I was used to such feelings before a major deliverance so knew I had to ride it out. Feeling quite frail on arrival I was welcomed and led to my bedroom. Breakfast was served in bed as at Purple Heathers but there was no tannoy system at Willow House. A lady knocked to bring the well laden tray in and as she opened to my answer a medium sized, black dog entered with her. I followed with my eyes the quick marching animal across the carpet where it vanished into thin air. The lady also saw it as her eyes pursued it in the same direction but we said nothing. Supernatural events as that one make a person speechless and yet both people know they have seen something that is not, yet is, actually there. It is usually a sign of heightened spiritual activity, more than likely sent as a distraction or to cause fear. A chapel service was held later on. At lunch times in the dining room, tables holding between six to eight people brought terror once again. I sat at the warden's table, even though he was away, to feel secure and protected. The day he returned he introduced himself as Mark. It came to his attention that I needed in-depth ministry and an appointment was made. In the evening I attended a chapel service and during the worship when I opened my mouth to sing no sound ventured from my throat at all. I became concerned but knew it was a demon stopping me. A certain vicar had also arrived from Manchester, by the name of Daniel Ebbworth. We began to talk and I discovered he was fasting.

'What are you fasting for?'

'You,' was his astonishing reply.

Most of my pastors, as far as I was aware, did not even do that. He was a humble and gentle person and I did not know quite how to respond. I was, however, very pleased and extremely thankful. In the art room the following afternoon I painted a watercolour of a bird and later on handed the painting to Daniel.

'This is for you.'

'That's a shrike. Did you know I am a bird watcher?'

'No.'

I had not been told and could see that God moved me to paint it without my knowledge. I loved moments like that. As Mark had been away the previous week other members of staff had attempted to minister but it was very hard going, spiritually.

When Daniel came it became easier. I went to my room after lunch to prepare for a deliverance session, during which I looked out of the window and noticed a huge, black expanse of sky. The type of cloud you would not expect to clear for an entire day. My inner senses told me the Devil was mighty angry and the hosts of hell had gathered for the battle for my soul. Fear accompanied my prayers. Ten minutes before I was due to go to chapel a single flash of lightning slit the sky but I do not remember any thunder. Hoping not to experience any more lightning I crept quickly to the chapel at half past one. Mark, the warden, Daniel and a couple of other members of staff were waiting for me. Mark dedicated the session to God and began to pray. As he prayed against ancestral curses, while sweeping a hand above my head, I ducked down automatically. Not because he might have hit me but with the impact of the curses being broken; like a rope being cut.

'Did you see that?' he asked his staff.

As the session went on Mark asked a demon its name. A tremendous amount of evil filled me and out of my mouth came,

'Lucifer.'

Pandemonium broke loose. I started writhing on the floor. At one point my left arm stretched excruciatingly along the floor above my head as if about to be pulled off from the shoulder joint by an unseen force. When the session was over I was told much about whatever else took place.

The following is Daniel's version of what happened. He paid a great price for being there:

"The following account is true and accurate, being compiled from notes taken at the time the events occurred.

I am a retired priest, ordained into the Church of England in 1971. Throughout my ministry, I have felt a real faith and commitment to Christ's healing exercised through his church.

Some years ago, I was invited to act as a locum at Willow House, Kent. I gladly accepted that invitation, and I hoped particularly to learn more while I was there about the laying-on-of hands with prayer and anointing with oil.

I arrived at Willow House late in the afternoon. The journey of 241 miles had been long and tiring. As I came through the door

at 4.00 p.m. the guests were gathered for tea. My eyes met those of a small, auburn-haired woman. As we looked at each other, I knew in my spirit, the Lord had brought me to Willow House to meet her. Later, I learned that her name was Rachel Pallitan.

Two days later the team discussed Rachel and the information she had disclosed about her life and the abuse she had suffered. We agreed that a Grieving Service needed to be held for her in the evening.

Mark Nescome, the Warden of Willow House and his wife Irene arrived back that morning from a time away.

In the evening at 8.00 p.m. the Grieving Service was held in the Chapel. This was a Rite; A Holy Communion service with readings for the Commemoration of the Faithful Departed.

During, and after Holy Communion, the presence of Christ in the Chapel grew in power, love and radiance until it was almost overwhelming, Rachel poured out her anger and bitterness about her life, the abuse and sufferings she had endured to Christ and how He had let her down. We encouraged Rachel to give all her hurt and turmoil to Jesus on the cross.

Christ's presence was blazing in the Chapel. At one point, Rachel's hand flew to her lips, she giggled and the pupils of her eyes turned upward and almost vanished under her upper eyelids. Seeing that, some instinct told me she had demons. At the end of the ministry, Rachel asked, 'Can I have a hug from all three of you?' And all of us hugged her.

Two days later I met and talked with Mark in his office about Rachel and we decided to begin deliverance ministry with her, Mark taught me the basics of this ministry (I had no previous experience). He emphasized the need for our personal purity, so I hurried to pray in the Chapel confessing as many sins as I could remember!

At 2.30 p.m. we held a Healing of the Family Tree service for Rachel in the Chapel based on Holy Communion which I celebrated. Afterwards, Mark led Rachel through personal renunciations of various occult practices – fortune telling, Ouija board, spiritualism etc. *(I, Rachel, had very little experience of these as described in my first book Is Anybody Out There?) *Later, I placed my hands on Rachel's head for healing. I noticed she was shaking her head from side to side as if refusing the* *impartation of grace. Then it occurred to me, this response was from the demons within her, rather than Rachel.*

Mark began commanding the demons to come out of Rachel and she started yawning them out. She lay writhing on the floor of the chapel emitting long shrieks, her eyes bulging, her face swollen, her hands clawed, her body contorted. Mark was kneeling beside her.

'Who is there?' he asked.

A deep 'male' voice replied from within Rachel – 'Lucifer'.

Mark responded, 'Ah, Lucifer! The Lord rebukes you Lucifer!'

The atmosphere began shaking and trembling. There was a burning smell of sulphur and a motoring energy was coming out of Rachel (unfelt by me, Rachel). *I was standing in the way. A great 'wind' blasted through me and I disappeared. I could dimly feel I was still standing, but I could no longer see myself. I did not exist! All I was aware of was the Holy Spirit still burning like a tiny flame inside me.*

Gradually, I re-emerged into visibility. I could see myself again. But the great 'wind' was still streaming out of Rachel. I was aware of this energy rushing like an invisible river between me and a woman member of staff standing opposite me.

I looked to my right and saw the curtains of an open window of the chapel being blown out horizontally by this power pouring through the window-space. The bush outside was being shaken and tossed about as if possessed. A clap of thunder rang out from the dark sky and there was a sudden, sharp rainfall. This was my introduction to the deliverance ministry!

Next day we gathered again in the chapel for the second deliverance ministry session held between 2.30 – 3.30 p.m. It still smelled of the sulphur, rather like the smell in a crematorium.

While Mark was laying on hands, Rachel kept shaking her head and saying, 'No'.

At one point during ministry, Rachel's left arm was pulled out to full length towards the window through which Satan had left. She was screaming with pain and yelled,

'I am the one who has come up from the great abyss'.

It looked as if some invisible demonic being was trying to tear off her arm.

At another point, Rachel held up her violently shaking left hand, her face congested, her eyes darting about.

'There's a ring!' she cried.

The wedding finger of her left hand was icy cold. The blood vessels had broken and we saw the black circle of a ring imprinted in her finger. We realized Rachel had been wedded to Satan.

Gently, Mark took Rachel's left hand in his hands and stroked it. He declared,

'She no longer belongs to you (Satan). We bring Rachel's hand into the Church. She is no longer yours. She belongs to Christ now'.

Mark continued commanding out the demons. On one occasion, Mark was standing a few feet in front of Rachel. His finger was raised rebuking the spirits. I saw Rachel's neck swell and a demon come up into her face. Her eyes filled with the demon and I saw a flash of malice spark from her eyes as the demon gave a long, squinted, hate-filled stare at Mark.

Then I saw the demon swiveling Rachel's eyes to look round the chapel to see who else was there. And her eyes were slowly turned to stare at me. I was looking at a creature from another realm glaring at me in and through the eyes of Rachel. That stare is burned forever in my memory.

During another violent period in the ministry, when the demons were being particularly threatening, and I was frightened, I felt the holy Spirit being poured down vertically through the top of my head, then jetting out horizontally from my midriff, hitting Rachel and almost knocking her off her feet.

At the end of this deliverance ministry session, I could smell a lovely fragrance in my nostrils and sinuses. I told Rachel about this scent and she replied,

'You have been given a special anointing from the Lord for this ministry'.

The fragrance persisted in my head for about a month.

Two days later Rachel gave me a picture of a great grey shrike she had painted for me in the Art Room. I have kept her painting ever since.

Two ministry sessions were held during this day between 11.00am and 12.45 p.m. and 4.45 p.m. and 5.45 p.m.

The following day I left Willow House at 9.00 a.m. I knew my world and understanding of spiritual realities had been changed forever by my meeting with Rachel and all that had happened in that chapel.

When I arrived in church on the following Sunday, members of my congregation asked me about my experiences at Willow House, I replied that I would need about a month to ponder and assimilate what I had experienced.

My meeting with Rachel Pallitan at Willow House, which was wholly in God's purpose and our times of ministry together, were life changing hours for me. The anointing I had received there from the Lord for deliverance ministry and spiritual warfare completely changed the whole direction of my future ministry into paths and experiences I could not have possibly foreseen.

Extracts from my journal with names changed to protect the identities of place and people.

Reverend. D. Ebbworth. 17 April, 2014".

Somebody from Grace Church happened to be at Willow House at the same time and informed Laurence, my ex pastor, that I was there. He, in turn, felt it his duty to have a word with Mark about me, even though I was no longer in his church, telling him that I was looking for attention. Mark's attitude changed for the worse towards me after that. At one point after ministering to me, Mark declared,

'I don't like doing this.'

He meant casting out demons. I was not too keen on it myself but I knew at that point he may not offer me much more. That evening whilst he was ministering to me I felt exposed and vulnerable. The feelings of being so alone stood stark in my heart. In my desperation for some affection I crawled over to where Mark was sitting in the chapel and, in front of everyone, rested my head in his lap. The following day a couple took me into Teekbush where we bought a cake from a baker's shop. When I closed the door behind us on the way out a notice stuck on the door read,

'***** ban'

I sensed God was speaking to me and not long afterwards Mark banned me from going back to Willow House. He told me what

Laurence had said and I was devastated. At these points I knew the Devil was at work doing his best to bring total destruction to any form of deliverance. I could not blame my pastors but did expect them to know about such things and be able to deal with them. When the Devil had informed me a year or two previously that the whole of hell was against me God had also told me one day while at a service at Grace Church,

'I will move the heavens to save you!' and He had indeed.

Ministers were only instruments that God was using but I was the victim and, as such, knew slightly more than they did in the way I felt, acted, was tormented, etc. Nobody can feel those things for somebody else so I found communication was vital. I described my situation as clearly as I could but still was not comprehended the way I had hoped. I was angry with both Mark and Laurence; with Mark because he had witnessed everything that had gone on. How could he agree with Laurence that I was looking for attention? How could Laurence judge when he was not even there? I loved Laurence, he was approachable and I wrote to him later on from Thornbush House asking how he could say such a thing and informing him how it turned Mark against me. Mark, who had been so fruitful in my deliverance, became totally useless. By now I was getting used to the raging battle. Physical pain never left me. My eyes very often became half closed when I needed to be delivered and I found it hard to keep them open. Placing slices of cool cucumber on them was soothing. It was always a sign to me about what was going on in the spiritual realm.

I returned to Willow House some months after that, despite the ban, when a locum preacher stood in for Mark. He was a small, thin man and good fun. Mark had also been very funny at times and that was what was needed in places of healing and deliverance as laughter is a good medicine. Mostly, though, I could not laugh even when I found things hilariously funny. My mouth and heart stayed in neutral.

During the coffee break on one of those days a man and his wife were in the lounge. They were there for somebody else but spared me some time. The man said he had a hugging ministry and asked if he could hug me,

'Yes,' I said.

He hugged me but it felt like a sharp knife ripping through me. How hard I was in receiving affection! I thought maybe they could help me on a more regular basis but that door did not open up. Another morning at coffee a man sat beside me. I had never before set eyes on him but he started to tell me that his wife had had similar ministry to mine.

'Oh,' I said.

He went on to describe the battle she had with her pastors believing her. I was not quite sure why he was telling me and felt slightly uncomfortable. I told him I would be going to London to another conference where Arthur Leemaker, a prophet from the USA, would be preaching. Perhaps that was not so wise, as at the conference one of the speakers spoke about fathers and I went wild. My anger flared and I started to shout as pain and a longing to be heard and loved was released. A man came over to minister the love of God but no sooner had he reached me than he was called away. I turned to see who had called him. *How did he get here and how on earth does he know where I am sitting?* It was the man who had been sitting with me, in his black suit, when we were at coffee in Willow House. I came to the conclusion that he must have been a wizard and was lying to me about his wife. I thought she must be a witch and he a plant from the Devil to stop further ministry. It seemed with every step I put forward somebody or something was there to stop the progress. The man who was praying for me never returned. How come people did not listen to me? They only wanted to listen to the sophisticated but never the victim. From then on, despite much opposition from the Devil and ignorant people, I sought to attend every conference I could find as they seemed to be the places to go to for a powerful miracle or touch from God. I became known as the 'Conference Queen' to some. My life depended on them. At one Theobald Petland conference one of the speakers gave a word of knowledge saying,

'Your father would have killed you but you didn't know how to pray. I protected you…'

I went forward when invited for prayer for healing that day but somebody interfered with it and I lost what could have been a great release of pain. I often wondered if somebody might see my need and offer to help on a more permanent basis but they never did. I had to fight my circumstances alone and that also meant taking myself to certain Christian establishments who ministered short term to people, say for a weekend and afterwards appointments of one day in length.

During ministry one day at a place called Blossom House, a Healing Brooks establishment. The first evening meal brought all the insecurities to the surface. I could not face the people. My insides screamed to get away. I abruptly stood up, shouted that I wanted to get out of there and left the room. Two members of staff followed, one of whom told the other,

'It shouldn't be like this.'

'Well, it is like this!' I responded.

I found neither their training nor the spontaneity of the Holy Spirit covered people like me. What an absolutely hopeless case. Was there nobody on the face of the earth who could cope with me or who understood, even though they were the most top ranking establishment who 'knew it all'? I was taken to a caravan in the garden. When ministry prayer began and the staff were coming against some of the demons and strongholds the wind churned up and the caravan rocked from side to side. We all knew it was not a phenomenon of the weather but a visitation of the enemy of God. As the wind howled I expected the result would be heightened prayer but the session was soon calmed down and I was faced with yet more disappointment.

'We bind you in the name of Jesus. Go right down,' they ordered the demons.

The spirits they had been commanding out of me had to go right down again into my insides to nestle there until it was 'time' for them to leave. I felt that that moment was the time and my thinking went wild; even in the panic I had to submit but not without some resistance. *How can they leave those awful things in my life? What's the matter with them? Would they like to have evil stuffed deep down on the inside and live with it?* I protested aloud and their response to my distress was,

'They are bound so can't do any harm.'

Oh no? I knew better and that their very presence filled so much of my life with hell itself. A terrible place to be and to have to live in the company of hellish beings was not my view of being saved. I went home feeling they had become scared because of what had happened to the caravan.

Some time later, one Tuesday night, during one of Matthew Minnerton's meetings, I longed for Matthew and his wife to take me in and love me like one of their own children. Well, I knew I could never take anybody's child's place but I wanted to be loved like they were and not feel so forsaken all the time so my next plan hatched; I would tell his wife what I needed. At an appropriate time I left the hall and once outside turned right towards the nearest Off-license. I had enough money for a cheap bottle of wine. I picked up a bottle, making sure it was not apricot; remembering the episode in Mackton, and that it had a twist top as opposed to a cork which I would not be able to open without a corkscrew. With my head held high, so as not to arouse suspicion, I took the bottle to the counter, paid for it then hurried back to drink it before the meeting finished. I sat round the side of the hall before going back in and unscrewed the top, put the neck of the bottle to my lips and swallowed gulps of alcohol till almost none was left. *Hurry up and take effect. Come on.* Once I was sure I no longer had full control of myself and that I would be freer to tell them what I needed, I went back inside. Desperation grew and when Matthew's wife came to pray for me I stopped her and asked for what I needed but again was turned down. *Right!* I grabbed my Bible, marched to the back of the church towards the dark outside and hurled it through the open doors into the walkway which was about six feet from the step.

'And You can have Your Bible back!' I screamed at God.

My only concern was for the bright red and other autumn coloured leaves I had placed inside to keep fresh. *Not to worry.* But my heart grieved over them. They were my only friends. One of the men went out to rescue the Book and brought it back inside. Meanwhile, I was approached by Benjamin Tocking who hugged me, 'till you stopped shaking', as he put it. He and his wife were kind and loving but I could not respond to love of any sort. All I could do was yearn for it. He led me to a room where someone stayed with me until I was calmer and finally went home.

Around that time the Fellowship was about to go to Fording Mills in Wales for a conference but the pastor forbade me to go. I could not see why and began to pray. At one of the Tuesday night meetings another pastor was preaching. I listened for God to speak to me about the conference. During his message the pastor said,

'It doesn't matter what Fred Bloggs says, you follow Me.'

God wanted me to go but fear caused me to ask Him over and over whether it was indeed Him telling me to.

The day after I had arrived at Thornbush House I found two Christian men, one was a member of staff and the other, a resident. They lived in the owner's other house located round the back in another road. I went to pray with the two of them. After telling them about my situation, David, the member of staff, prayed and said,

'God is going to send two angels before you.'

I wondered if he was talking from the top of his head so pursued further confirmation from God Himself. The following day I sat praying in my room with the Bible open on my lap. It slipped off onto the floor and picking it up I glanced down at the page it had opened at,

'Go away for three days and then come back to Me.' 1 Kings 12:5.

God was telling me all over the place that I should go but I was going against the wishes of those in authority. Was that right? I asked the Holy Spirit,

'What will I take? Should I take a cardboard box or a suitcase?'

He did not answer so I made my own mind up. *Even if I take a suitcase I can still live on the street.* I packed my small, red case. The following morning I turned on the radio. It was not usual for me to do so. The second I tuned in a voice from Thought for the Day proclaimed,

'There's somebody,' a slight pause and then, 'going to do something new and difficult today. Don't worry if everything seems to be going wrong…'

Totally amazed that, even after deciding to take the step, God confirmed with yet another sign. I turned off the radio wondering what was going to go wrong, or seem to, so I carried my suitcase, early in the day to Ponrish Station where I took my seat on the train; so far so good. Once reaching Apsing Station, not too far from Ponrish, I was fairly happy but nervous about what I was doing. *What am I going to do about my accommodation?* After the train had been sitting at Apsing for about twenty minutes an instruction came over the tannoy telling us to get off as the train had broken down. At first I became angry and then heard,

'Thank Me, Rachel'

'Okay, thank You, Lord.'

Once onto the platform I stood beside a smartly dressed lady and, putting on a posh voice, mentioned,

'I'm going to a conference today but haven't booked any accommodation yet.'

'Why don't you ring them now and ask if they can fix you up?'

If only you knew.

'That's a good idea.'

Swallowing fear I made a call from the call box on the platform. The receptionist kindly said,

'I'm sure I can arrange somewhere. I know a couple you could stay with but if they can't have you, you can sleep at my place on the floor.'

After putting the phone down I hoped my pastor had not been standing beside the receptionist, listening. As far as I was concerned he may have been right there to stop my request from going any further.

'How long are we going to be?' I asked the railway worker about the train.

'Could be an hour or two.'

God was holding the train up just for me. I wondered how He was coping with all the other people who had been put out of their day's routine because of this. *Not to worry.* Eventually, we were on our way to Noffold where I was to change trains again. I was due in to Fording Mills at four o'clock. Once at Noffold I was out of my depth in knowing what to do. At Fording Mills there would be the lighthouse where the meetings were to take place. *How can two hundred people fit into a lighthouse?* I had been told Fording Mills was just one street so reasoned it would not be hard to find. Walking across the foyer of Noffold Station I headed towards a woman I did not know and spontaneously told her I was on my way to a conference at Fording Mills and was really held up.

'Oh, I'm going there too.' Chances of that happening were remote but God had been with me so far in an amazing way. We walked to the train together and waited forty minutes before it took off; another Godly holdup! The lady I was with explained that we would need a taxi. I became confused. *A taxi for one street?* 'We get off in the countryside,' she continued.

How come the countryside? I said nothing about my predicament so as not to arouse suspicion and let her lead the way from then on. I would have been hopelessly lost without her. What would she think of my behaviour once I got there? *Never mind.* We finally arrived at Fording Mills in the dark at ten past seven. I hated being late for anything. Feeling shaky, I entered the main doors of the large white building called The Lighthouse! People were registering for the conference and finding their well spaced seats, not the packed sardines I had envisioned in a narrow, concrete cylinder. I noticed a lady from our fellowship in the doorway that led to the main hall beyond the foyer. She was twice the size of me and a good hiding place from the pastors. I stood in front of her.

'Hide me, Ellie,' I joked, seriously.

I double backed to the desk to my right and queued to register. False confidence gave me a hand. I smiled at the receptionist and introduced myself.

'Oh, you phoned this afternoon from the train. Just go and sit over there and when your hosts arrive I'll point you out.'

I hurried to the safety of the corner of the foyer and sat down. While looking straight ahead a man emerged from the centre doors that led to the hall. My heart flipped as I recognized Matthew Minnerton. He looked directly at me. I felt nothing but compassion as in obeying God I had to disobey him. He was a good pastor but only God is God. I smiled.

Finally, my hosts were introduced and I joined them to enter the hall. Carrying my carrier bag with my Bible and notebook inside I strode down the centre aisle with Mr and Mrs Warsing, blissfully unaware of my nightmare, leading the way. I did not get very far down the narrow aisle before I set eyes on my advancing pastor, the one who had replaced Matthew.

'You! We want you outside,' he said rather sternly.

Was he looking for a fight? I thought of pub brawls cowboys had after a few whiskeys.

'Please can you put my bag on my seat?' I asked the Warsings, 'I'll be right back.'

They took the bag so my arms were free for the ensuing confrontation. Once outside my pastor cast the first blow,

'If we knew you were coming we would have made sure you wouldn't have had any accommodation and I have told the ministers not to minister to you.'

'Well, I have asked God to take me up to the ceiling if He wants to minister to me,' fully expecting Him to do so.

'You are not to move,' he continued in his threatening tone.

I blanked out and then thought, *Here goes yet another chance to get set free. Why don't these people want me well? Why won't they let God do what He wants to do with me?* They were quite happy to keep telling me off. Why did they not want to see the results of what they wanted; my freedom? My gaze was on Jesus not on them and their religious methods and commandments. I now understood why God held up the trains the way He had. They would have turned me back if I arrived at the scheduled time of four o'clock. They were not in the slightest aware of what their God and my God was saying to, or doing with me. I went back to my seat with a heavy load on my shoulders, not the hope I could have had nor the support of loving people who would not have wanted their own children to go through half the pain I was suffering. I sat through the meeting wondering what my hosts would do if they found out I should not have been there. Would they throw me out? *I better not say anything.*

After a static meeting, at least for me, I was taken to my accommodation and was in for a wonderful surprise. Stepping from the car, carefully avoiding the mud, I was led into the house. My hosts showed me to my room which had a camp bed already prepared. The following morning I sheepishly entered the kitchen. Mrs Warsing proceeded with me into the dining room where a river, framed by their lounge windows and long, crimson curtains, gently flowed by. She showed me my seat at the well laid out table and, hesitating, I quickly pointed out,

'I shouldn't be at the head.'

'You are a guest,' she equally pointed out.

That kind of honour had never been part of my life and I felt as though I was sitting on a hedgehog. Not because the seat was prickly but for the novelty of sitting in an inappropriate place for Rachel Pallitan. After breakfast we all went off to the conference. I had to leave them to sit where I had been ordered by the pastor; way towards the back. Whilst everybody else worshipped and praised the Lord I sat with my mouth shut and heart caged. How I longed to be like them without a trouble in the world. During the morning break I spoke to some of the other girls from my fellowship and they described their accommodation. God had looked after me Himself. I had been treated like a queen. I thought, *God has taken my plight and 'set a table before me in front of my enemies.'* Psalm 23:5. At least in that much I was blessed. The meetings, however, were not such a pretty table. What was set out for me there caused enormous pain. The top part of my chest near my throat constantly ached. At the end of that day I still had not spoken to the Warsings.

In the morning one of the pastors from America led the meeting. As he led worship he sang a new song which broke my silent grief,

'If You don't want me to sing, I won't sing
If You don't want me to dance, I won't dance
If You don't want me to smile, I won't smile
I only want to do Your will.'

The Holy Spirit moved upon me as the minister continued to sing so that I started to sob. I tried to keep as motionless as possible but could not; if I as much as showed my heaving shoulders I was ruined and they would send me home, or something equally drastic. I felt thoroughly let down by the pastor who had sung the song. Had he not heard what my pastor ordered the ministers? Part of me wondered if he was showing compassion in an underhanded way. Why could he not stand up openly, refuse to give in to my pastor and protect me? But then, he may simply have been obeying God. So many queries raced through my mind. Nothing came of it and the conference moved on eventless for me until home time. On the way back to the Warsings I could not hold onto my secret any longer so told them everything. To my surprise they listened, understood completely and did not judge me. They were, I felt, friends. Throughout the experience my father's presence hovered like a great canopy, making sure the events tormented my soul. His training held me captive in all situations.

I had obediently stood still for three days and the conference was coming to an end. Matthew Minnerton led the meeting in the morning and at the end of his message spoke about people needing to have an umbilical cord cut from their mother *(spiritually)*; the very thing Reginald Hassenbury had mentioned at his conference but never got around to accomplishing. I felt an uncomfortable tugging at my belly button so knew I needed what he was saying. So far I had felt the callings of God throughout the service and ignored them for the reasons stated but if I did not respond at all I would regret not having received anything from the Lord for the sacrifice I had made in attending the conference. Matthew continued calling people forward for prayer. If I went forward I could hide in the crowd and not be spotted by any of the ministers so when Matthew gave one more invitation I plucked my feet off the ground and ran. Disregarding anybody else I pushed my way to a safe place at the front, right hand side. Surrounded by the crowd, that had also come forward, I was certain no pastor would see me. A gentle man approached me and said,

'You need the love of God.'

I was expecting a healing but before I could open up to receive, a man tapped the person praying for me on the shoulder. I am sure his inaudible words were,

'We are not supposed to be praying for her.'

The man came back to reiterate what the orders were concerning me.

'We are not supposed to be praying for you.'

In desperation I told the man,

'I am frightened of my pastor.'

Then turning, my eyes unexpectedly beheld the familiar shirt of my pastor. I had not realized how short I was in comparison to him. Slowly lifting my head towards his serious looking face, compassion filled my soul and I loved him; just like I had done to my father when I sensed his vulnerability. The man beside him told him what I had said, to which he replied,

‘Oh, everybody’s scared of me.’

So he knew! I felt a sudden relief. There was my vindication; a confession from his own lips. His cover had been blown. That, I felt, was the reason God wanted me to attend and not really for any other. God is not mocked; He wants shepherds after His own heart to care for, feed and love the ‘sheep’. I certainly had to do without on so many occasions just because I was a wounded scrap that nobody wanted. I travelled home unhealed and undelivered in the way I longed for, yet strangely delivered in another.

Some weeks passed and back in Bramington Matthew Minnerton held some meetings in a hall where a man came forwards to tell of a picture he had of a dog being called for his dinner. Each time the dog ran to eat from his dish he found it empty. The owner repeated this many times until the dog realized he would never get any food and so stopped answering the call. I felt like that dog. There was also a word about false loyalty and that we were not obliged to stay where were being let down so much.

Back at the rest home everything was taken care of. The cooking and washing were carried out by the staff. All I had to do was eat and rest. I remained in my room for ten months without venturing outside, except to buy essential things and go to church. Sandy, my cat, entertained the residents with his beauty and character and was company for me.

Church was my only escape from the hostel but a place where I had violent reactions when being ministered to. I prayed all week for God to come and speak to, heal and deliver me. Every Sunday He faithfully came but I could not receive Him in a calm way. As soon as He came I took off. As somebody once prophesied to me,

‘Like most people who are coming to Jesus walking forwards you are walking backwards so when He reaches out to touch you, you are ready to run.

Children sat on the floor in the hall and even though I was greatly distressed, I made sure I did not stand on any of them whilst running for the door. In all my disturbed state I tried not to hurt anybody. Mostly, I was withdrawn and timid except for those moments of deep anguish. I still desperately wanted to be loved and be part of a family but all my voicing and pleas still landed on deaf ears. I needed much time spent on me in order to reach the pain hidden deep within. The only thing that touched that was if I banged my head on a concrete wall. The vibrations of the impact rippled through my body, dislodging the agony for a brief moment. Anything out of my internal territory caused my personality to short circuit. The effect was immediate and unrelenting. Then one sunny day I decided I would like to go to the library and find a good book to read. As I walked through the doors I marched directly to a section straight ahead and did not have to search for the book for anything longer than a few seconds. God does not always move by announcing His presence, at times we are unaware that we are even being led by His Holy Spirit. I reached towards the book entitled, 'Nobody Nowhere,' by Donna Williams. I took the book home without further ado and started to read. This girl was autistic and immediately I knew.

'God, am I autistic?'

A lump surfaces in my throat even as I write. I collapsed onto the floor under that conviction and cried in total and utter despair. After a long time, I gathered my strength and read the book to completion. My life story is completely different to hers but the symptoms of being so isolated, unable to be loved, being different, etc and so so frightened, people invading my space, being taken out of my territory and the resulting disturbance in my behaviour often of a violent nature of hitting myself on the head hard in total frustration, rocking backwards and forwards, all boiled down to this. So often I found it hard to express myself, my brain would go numb and I could not think. The inability to take people's advice because of that fear and threat of having to come out of my territory and blamed and persecuted for my 'rebellion' when nothing inside of me could function was sheer torture and they walked away. Once I realized there was a label to my condition and that nobody had ever diagnosed it because of my lucidity I knew I would not be believed should I tell anyone so I kept the discovery and shame of it to myself.

One day Jacqueline came into my room and asked if I would like a job for twenty pounds a week,

'Think about it,' she said.

I did think about it and agreed. I cleaned the other house in Ordin Street but no amount of work eased the pain. My energy levels were nil and often I lay on the wooden breakfast benches to get some relief and rest. The owner of the house, Angus Pitbridge, became a father figure in my eyes. Not because he was the type of father I would have chosen but simply because he was in charge of the institution. The only time we saw him properly was when he visited on a Tuesday to give us our pocket money of twelve pounds per week. We also had the pleasure of seeing both him and his girlfriend on Christmas Day. I gravitated to him in my need for a father but as always it was met with misunderstanding. How could I respond to the constant grown up stuff when I was just a child inside? But he was normal and backed away. No amount of reasoning or church could correct my longing to be in a safe and secure environment.

Staff at the home came and went. Jacqueline enjoyed the sunshine and often lay under its heat for hours. She was softly spoken but I was afraid of her for no reason. The day I heard that she committed suicide I was dumbfounded. How and why?

As for visitors to the home the only member of my family to visit was Peggy and that, quite rare. It was I who usually cycled many miles to visit her in her flat. On one of her visits we went to the beach. She had brought a friend. Not wanting to sit on the beach we all lay down near a hedge on the grass. An hour or two later I walked them to the station. Peggy was wheeling some kind of trolley and asked,

'Did you see that lady hang her dustpan and brush on the hedge?'

'What dustpan and brush? I didn't see one,' I said,

'You know, when she was getting changed. What's that you wear on the beach to sunbathe?'

'Oh, you mean the suitcase?' I offered, knowing what she meant but also had caught her misrepresentation of thoughts.

'No,' she answered, becoming quite frustrated at not being able to get the words out.

'The.. the.. the bikini.'

We laughed. I wondered if that kind of thing happens when people are severely traumatized. The brain has a job to function correctly.

I eventually left Bramington church and started to attend Ponrish Christian Fellowship. There, I stood against a wall instead of mixing with the people. I had not intended to become an object of close inspection but mostly that is what I ended up as. A woman volunteered to help me but I could not be comforted. One morning as I entered the hall I caught sight of her from afar with a flower in her hand and wondered if it was for me but brushed the idea away. When she finished talking with somebody she approached and handed me the rose. In fact, it was four roses in one. She explained,

'When I came out of my house and was walking down the path, God stopped me.' He said,

'That rose there, pick it.'

She was shocked but He repeated the instruction.

'Rachel. Pick it.'

She pointed out the parts of the rose just as He explained them to her.

'This is the part I have broken off.' She pointed to a small stub.

'This is how she used to feel.' She pointed to a crumpled up and torn petal.

'Used to?' I said, stunned, 'I still feel like that.'

'This is how she is now.' She pointed to a closed bud.

'And this is how she is going to be.' She pointed to a rose in full bloom, bursting with colour and display.

All of those aspects were on one stem. I stood amazed but could not see the slightest possibility of becoming like that open rose. Even she wondered how on earth God could change a person so closed. I was not in a position to openly appreciate the help of others. Her words only embedded themselves in a part of my heart. I was not instantly healed by the revelation but God had spoken and I had somehow to believe the unbelievable.

'Do you know I went out during the week to buy some reds?' I asked.

That is, red watercolour paints. I did not have any. God must have moved me to buy them but I had not been aware that it was Him. It was just a realization that I had no reds. I bought about three shades so when she gave me the rose I was able to paint it that Sunday afternoon. Next morning the flowers were dead and completely shriveled! Later, while studying the painting I realized nothing was said about the leaves so asked,

'What about the leaves, God?'

He explained straight away,

'You see those leaves leading to the buds? They are huge. That's because the developing buds need lots of food in order to grow. The buds are dependant on the leaves being so big. Look at the tiny leaf on the hugest flower, that is because once bloomed not much food is needed any more. I understood perfectly that when I opened up I would need little food, little dependency on others and God for my growth process. But as for then my need was great.

As I struggled with my situation I started a twenty one day fast. One of the members of staff at the hostel kept trying to discourage me but I was determined to finish it as I was about to attend a weekend retreat at Blossom House. I had to get a breakthrough into my healing. I could not complete the fast, however, and abandoned it with only a few days to spare; more to please the discouraging member of staff than myself. At the healing weekend a man said, as he preached,

'You didn't finish the fast.'

Another member of the team saw a cork trapping a lot of water underneath concrete. That tied in with another word I had had at a Nicholas Barwin conference where a man had told me,

'There is a wire and it's beginning to fray because of your willingness to be made whole. The wire is attached to a cork. There will be a violent shaking and the cork will come out. There is lots and lots of water.'

I had wondered if the water was tears but I also thought perhaps it was the Holy Spirit and living water ready to be unleashed. I did not get a breakthrough at Blossom House and became convinced it was because I did not finish the fast. After that event I heard that Nicholas Barwin was coming to Bramington again and I wanted to go but had no money. At the time I was seeing a psychiatric nurse who offered to buy a watercolour painting if I painted one for her.

'Yes, what do you want it of?' afraid I would make a mess of it.

'Whatever you would like to do.'

'What about a waterfall?'

So it was decided and I set to work. When finished I did not think it looked like a waterfall but she bought it for seventy pounds and I went to the conference. My accommodation was arranged by a woman from one of the churches in Bramington so I knew I would be in a safe place.

Martha, the lady I stayed with, noticed I had problems and during my stay said,

'I could do with having you for about six weeks.'

I thought she said that so she could sort me out but it could not be done.

My constant prayers to God bombarded Heaven. He was delivering me bit by bit and teaching me along the way but I felt the bondage acutely and tried to cooperate with Him the best way I knew how. He would often tell me what was about to happen and He told me things would happen in that conference. I wondered what He would do so asked,

'When will it happen, God?'

'Thursday,' answered His still, small Voice.

On Tuesday I panicked because He had not done it yet. During lunch I wandered to the shops in the centre of town and, such was my anxiety, He had even gone to the trouble to use somebody to plaster huge posters on an entire shop window that read, 'DON'T PANIC'. So I lived the rest of that day and Wednesday in a slightly calmer mood. At lunch time on Thursday, the final day of the conference, I rested on the beach quietly and saw a vision of myself hoisted above the congregation towards the ceiling with my arms outstretched; as though being crucified before the five thousand people in attendance. Hamish Depson led the worship. During that last meeting he prepared for us to leave as 'God's army'. God had still not come and I was by then really distressed.

'God You said You would come. Where are You?'

For some reason the departure message took its time and I felt the keen inability to go with the others and join the army of the Lord.

'Come on, God,' I pleaded under my breath, 'don't leave me, don't leave me.'

As I stood waiting, trying to find His presence, a mighty gust of wind blew across from the left and caught my breath. I gasped, then let out an enormous cry that filled the arena,

‘God, I can’t come with You. Don’t leave me, don’t leave me!’

With my eyes closed I stepped onto a chair and raised my arms towards Heaven. I wanted my Heavenly Father to take hold of my hands and hoist me upwards. I continued to cry out in a loud voice when somebody’s hands grasped my ankles. *Oh, they understand.* Convinced they were trying to lift me higher I stretched my arms even further heavenwards. It was not long before I realized they were not of the same faith as me; they were trying to get me down. Once on the floor I was left feeling the whole mission of finding God aborted. Why do people have to interfere with other people’s faith? That was that! I left with everybody else. A couple of ladies from my fellowship told me later,

‘When you did what you did, we knew it was the Holy Spirit. You could hear a pin drop.’

When Nicholas Barwin came back to Bramington the following year the first thing he mentioned was what happened at the end of the last conference,

‘Did you feel the Holy Spirit?’ he asked in total awe.

I sat staring at him and mused, *I’m sitting right here.* My eyes narrowed towards him wondering if he would even acknowledge that I too had been there. Other than that nothing happened in the way of healing or deliverance.

Back in Ponrish the local Baptist church was just opposite where I lived so I attended that from time to time. One of the elders took his son to a church in Sharpington, called Life Ministries, every Tuesday evening. They volunteered to take me with them. For months I walked through the doors without a smile. Neville Hartingford, the minister, commented one evening on a certain person who always entered with a miserable face,

‘Here comes Miss Glum,’ he announced, for all to hear.

Not realizing that no matter how much I tried I could not find a smile. There was no way of dredging one up. Then one particular Tuesday evening as I waited for God to speak a woman started to prophesy. I looked over to my right. She was sitting on the far side of the hall directly parallel to me.

‘Can you take the mockery? Can you take the rejection?’ she asked.

My mind switched off at the thought of even more helpings of what I had suffered all my life. I heard nothing else even though she spoke on for quite a while. Her finishing sentence woke me,

'I am the Resurrection and the Life.'

As I continued to watch, the lady lifted her hands and an extremely pained expression covered her upturned face. Her body tensed. I wondered what was about to happen. The following week as I tried to get some attention from Angus Pitbridge, he mocked me whilst in the other house's office. Diane, the youngest female resident, sat on a bench in the dining area. He started to make a fuss of her. I knew it was to taunt me. The more he did it the more anger surfaced until I could take no more. I hit the wall as hard as I could with the flat of my hands until they smashed through the glass of a picture. Blood flowed freely and profusely through my badly sliced fingers. Angus angrily shouted,

'Now you've got my attention!'

He took me over to the kitchen sink after they dripped blood onto the carpet and kitchen floor, ran cold water over them then drove me to the local hospital for a dressing. As I sat in my room later I recalled the prophecy and the image of the girl who had given it. I understood the painful look on her face with the raising of her hands. My fingers are scarred as a result of the tormenting attitude of somebody who should have known better than to mock emotional illness. Not just somebody but the head of the rest home and one who we residents had to trust would do us no harm. One time when in his car he goaded me with misunderstandings. I could not take it and while he was driving I opened the door and stepped into the road. Needless to say he was not very happy about it and so life went on in Thornbush House.

Another Healing Brooks conference came to Bramington and God ministered to me again but the staff were messing it up by interfering; using their rules, rules made by man. One male member of staff told me to stop manifesting and I felt he was trying to stop the process of deliverance. I screamed as loud as I could,

'I'm in hell!'

‘I know you are,’ he sneered.

I understood he was thinking a demon had spoken but how wrong he was. Anybody with demons in them, especially occult ones, is living in hell on earth. During the conference Reginald Hassenbury was in control of all the Holy Spirit was doing. What he ordered was what his staff had to do which included not delivering certain people like me. I pled for my life,

‘Look! I have to live with these things,’ I shouted.

He then nodded towards his helpers, giving them the go ahead to get me free. That caused me great anxiety and I was in a place of tension instead of relaxation but as they prayed fluid oozed from my mouth and people stared. Someone put a stop to it and that was that. I lost trust and again went home dejected. It was another case of ‘getting to know your leaders’. I wondered if there were any good ones at all. I dreamt one night that I was aboard a bus and had somehow got upstairs with my bicycle. In dreams you can often do the impossible. At a certain stop I got off the bus, bike included and right opposite was a public toilets. I was desperate to go but once inside I found them all full to the brim, all blocked! When I awoke later God explained the dream without words. I could find no church where I could dispose of the waste products of my life; the things from the past that had impacted me so badly. Nobody would listen long enough to hear me out and prayers were not powerful enough to flush it all away.

I could not cope anymore with life in Thornbush House, especially when I sensed one member of staff was on drugs and another, Walter, told me that that certain member had a drug plant in her house. Naturally, being gullible, I swallowed every word. Something had to be done. I started to talk to him. He invited me to a café and over a coffee I told him I was going to report the manageress of the home for the drugs I believed she had. Next day I made my way to the social services department. There I reported what I feared.

‘Go to the area supervisor,’ they advised.

I told Walter what I had done. The next thing, he was on his way to the social services himself but blocked my way when I wanted to follow. I felt I had been set up and that he had gone to say all kinds of things about me that I could not defend myself over. I wrote to the area supervisor, Mr Stoweson. He replied shortly afterwards offering me a private appointment. Petrified, I made my way to his office and there spilled out my complaints, including Angus using residents to work instead of employing proper staff. I had been a resident at Thornbush House for three years. My face and neck were redder than red and I was shaking. Mr Stoweson was a good person, I thought, and said he would write to Angus. Feeling just like I had after I reported my father I waited for the resulting consequences. Not long after that I received a letter from Angus giving me a fortnight's notice to leave the rest home. The manageress came to me one day while I was in bed refusing to get on with life and told me,

'There's a big world out there.'

I was hardly prepared for it so pulled the covers over my head. What good could I do or be out there? No education, just a mat of problems. I made up my mind for the first time never ever to enter a hostel, rest home, institution or anything like them ever again in my life. I told God I did not care if it was His will. I never wanted to see one again then phoned Martha in Bramington, who had put me up during Nicholas Barwin's conference.

'You know you told me you could have me for six weeks? Well, can you have me now?'

And so I was on my way to a new life. The upheaval, though welcome, did not come easy. All the emotional turmoil came with it.

Angus Pitbridge found out I had a place to move to in Bramington and was quite taken aback,

'I thought you would go to another hostel.'

No way.

Chapter Six

Life in the real world

A man I met at a Christian meeting in Ribford, close to where I used to live, invited me to rent a place back there. It sounded good but I declined, being afraid of men anywhere near me. Feeling safe was not whether a place was safe but a feeling of safety. If I sensed any amount of threat severe physical pain and unsettling was the result and even panic. I had no choice but to deny those feelings and veer away from them. They could well have been an internal warning system. Their strength could overwhelm me and I had to follow the signals if the situation was not to deteriorate. I gave the cold shoulder to people if they showed any sign of wanting to be near me. I did not want them to suffer the disadvantages of my bondages. On the other hand my true self, the yearning and pining innocent, vulnerable child only wanted to be picked up and cared for. But that could not happen, especially when there was so much grief and feelings of abandonment to prevent it. I told the man I had a place in Bramington but had no way of getting my belongings there. He offered to take me and my bike but not Sandy because Martha could not have him. He would have to remain at Thornbush House where the staff volunteered to care for him until I could collect him. Sandy often sat on the stairs looking through the gaps in the dark wooden banisters at those who passed by. That was the image I was left with the whole time we were separated.

I arrived at Martha's house, knowing I would only be there for six weeks. She had a lovely big house and huge, well kept garden. I knew it was not my home and behaved just as well as anyone would expect me to. Martha's kindness could not be thanked enough. I painted her a watercolour of boats floating on water. The brownish mount that complemented and surrounded it went well in the room overlooking her back garden. The day after I arrived I phoned Mr Stoweson who, sounding genuine, wished me all the best for my future. Why did he not do something about my complaint? I wondered what more I could have done so as not to be rejected yet again. Those in authority are always at an advantage over the ones who depend on them but then again they are equally responsible for how they treat them and will be judged accordingly, if not by man, by God Himself one day. I settled at Martha's where she looked after me well. We chatted a lot. My time allocated of six weeks turned out to be longer but eventually she introduced me to a couple called Nellie and Oliver from her church who had a 'granny' flat where I could live and I was to move again. They came to Martha's house where I met them for the first time and after that I prepared to leave. On arrival at their home I heard God say,

'Take them as you find them.'

Nellie and Oliver were a kind couple about my age and had been married for two years. They showed me the flat they were preparing for me which was the basement of their semi detached house. I slept upstairs in another room until it was ready; God had provided a place of security as a second step to a more independent life. I felt far from ready. Nellie and Oliver shared their meals with me for a few weeks. The time came when I moved downstairs and, after sorting out my social benefits, I started cooking for myself. After about six weeks with them I asked if I could have my cat, to which they agreed. We went to collect him but he was far from well, though definitely happy to see me again. I watched as he mounted the steps of my split level flat. He was barely moving. After a visit to the vet and a dose of antibiotics to fix his high temperature he fully recovered. I felt let down that Thornbush House had not notified me of his condition and caused him to suffer needlessly.

Whilst at the flat my stomach started to burn quite a bit. I doubled up on occasions and wondered whether I had cancer. After a visit to the doctor, who prescribed antacids, I had to make another visit a few weeks later because I was not responding to them. *Good, I've got cancer.* The doctor spoke of giving me a barium meal but I thought it better to leave me. I wanted to die without all the tests and probing. I had been visiting a local church during that time and one Sunday evening someone gave a word of knowledge that,

'Somebody has trouble with their stomach; you know what it is and are just about to go for tests.'

With that, the power of God hit me and I was instantly healed. I lay on the floor while He ministered to me but was angry that He had done so. *Why couldn't you just leave me to die?*

Some time later a foreign man started to pastor a church at a hotel in Bramington. He, Pastor Leonard Frambert, was an answer to the longing of what I had been crying out for; the raw power of God creating miracles in people's lives. When he and his family arrived I thought it quite a coincidence that they should come over the very year I was hurled from Thornbush House. Was the desire I had expressed to Queenie in Mackton *(Jesus presence all the time, not just on rare occasions)* about to be fulfilled? Had God brought me out because He was able to get me healed at last? A hotel on the seafront was the new church's meeting place for a few months. I sat at the back in my sullen way but went forward for salvation whenever the call was given. I never felt saved at all, then one day after going forward for the umpteenth time somebody told me I should not keep going but to believe by faith that I was saved. I could not do that with conviction but obeyed and never answered the call again but I still needed something more than just going forward to accept Jesus Christ as my Saviour.

During one meeting a lady who usually sat on the floor at the back, behind the chairs quite near me, started to talk to me and we became friends. She, whose name was Christine, had a rather tall boyfriend called Donald who wore a black wooly hat and long camel coloured coat. It was winter. I walked with them as far as my home. Christine lived a few doors up from me and Donald, with his mother, not too far away. Christine chatted a great deal which gave me a, 'somebody is interested in me', feeling. I soon got to know that she too had been in a psychiatric hospital. Her family had put her there thinking she was mentally ill following her conversion and subsequent behaviour in always talking about God.

Donald was a level headed studious type with a degree. Christine had known him since her youth.

I continued to go to the church at the hotel with all my emotional problems. Often people call that 'baggage' but I thought that a callous way of describing pain and trauma of such a life as mine.

When Mothering Sunday came around in June I wondered what it was like to have one *(nothing new to me but I still felt it keenly).* I hated that day, never knowing what to do with myself. As I approached the hotel hundreds of primroses awaited the mothers. I would not get one because I was not a mother nor would I give one because I did not have a mother but I never missed a service through suffering. I sat alone towards the back on the right hand side of the hall. During the service the pastor instructed,

'Mothers, go and find your daughters. Daughters, go and find your mothers.' I stood absolutely still. Then he directed the rest of us, 'Go and see if anybody is standing on their own and go to them like a mother or child.'

I could not. As the subject became more pronounced my stomach felt like every drop of life was being pressed out. Pain in my head and chest escalated to such a point that I could no longer stay in my place. Another instruction was given for mothers to find their children or equivalent and, with that, I quickly left my seat. Adrenalin pumped as I picked up speed and ran round the hall aflame with fury. Once at the other side I ploughed into a row of chairs, knocking them flying and hurting my leg. Several people came over to see what I had done; helpless faces peered down at me. I belonged to nobody. Who could understand such a pitiful person? Not much was said about the incident but at home time I ran along the road by the seafront, next to the traffic, hoping to be sucked under a car. Eventually, the church moved to Ampring, a village nearby. I walked for at least forty minutes from my home and, once there, continued to seek God for healing and deliverance. It did not matter what the pastor had arranged for the service, I knew God would come to me. He always did when I asked. Does it not say in the Bible that He is close to the brokenhearted, a father of the fatherless, the orphan, the widow and the stranger? Such was the anointing on the minister that people would be lying on the floor laughing under the power of the Holy Spirit. I never laughed but was extremely hungry for God and once heard the minister say of me as I lay on the floor,

'She's been destroyed. One day she'll get up well.'

I thought that qualified me for being loved by humans and started to follow him around after the services but his wife soon put a stop to it. I needed the love of a father but there was not the place. I went home and pined for the kind of love I saw in the church; the stuff only for families. Anybody outside was left outside, except when coming for prayer. I was baffled but church was the place to be because of the presence of God. The longer I stayed the more into a rut I got. Making friends was out of the question. Christine was the only person who talked to me on my level. We had something in common.

At one of the evening meetings the minister touched my right arm with his elbow. I hit the wooden floor backwards in a split second; snapped to it like a ruler. Nobody was there to catch me and I was not hurt in the slightest. It so surprised us that we could not speak. The following week the minister elbowed me again but nothing at all happened. I did not quite see the reasoning behind why God did that.

I have found that God finds a way to relay news of what has happened to people, especially ministers who have treated me wrongly, when we have parted suddenly. A girl I had known in Mackton started to attend the meetings. She had moved into the area; not one of the members of the fellowship who had caused me such grief but a vulnerable, innocent person who was placed in Mackton for her own protection. I said hello and she informed me that Roy Herpson had died and that his wife Brenda had also died some time before him. I was a little shocked to say the least but did not God foretell it in the scripture when I first arrived there? *(See page 74)*.

Even though the presence of God was still available He was not welcome by others to do as he pleased in my life, merely because I screamed and sometimes at a high pitch. Christine and I discovered a certain Pastor Zangy from Africa who had a powerful deliverance ministry in London. Off we went and stayed at a friend's house there. We attended some wonderful services. Those days shifted my circumstances up a notch. I was getting very little money to live on and could not even afford one Christian book on sale; many books contained techniques on how to get free.

Pastor Zangy took an offering one day and I asked God how much He wanted me to give. Tears ran down my cheeks as I gave Him the three pence He asked for. The pastor asked us to write down our prayer requests on a piece of paper. I asked for a bungalow that was well maintained by the landlord, was secure, had double glazing, and a garden. With my request firmly in the Lord's hands I returned to my flat and waited for His response.

Living beneath Nellie and Oliver became a torment as Oliver loved to play his classical music loud which I did like but as there was no soundproofing I was greatly disturbed by the noise. I had to find a way out yet again. While at the post office collecting my benefit money one Tuesday morning I glimpsed a leaflet offering Disability Living Allowance. I applied for it and was awarded the payment for life.

I had been suffering suicidal thoughts and tendencies all my life often banging my head hard on walls trying to knock myself out in frustration but I never cut myself as many others did. I did attempt it once but my scissors were far too blunt so I gave up on that idea. *If only I wasn't like this.* One lady from church, in compassion, tried to help and made an appointment to take me to see the pastor *(Leonard).* When the day arrived she knocked at my door and greeted me with,

'Hello sausage.'

I'm not a sausage.

Once outside I ran from her as fast as possible, reaching the pastor's house well in advance of her. During the meeting in the lounge the pastor's wife observed,

'You're a fighter. You would be dead by now if you weren't.'

I took the compliment and thought I would get further help but they passed me on to somebody else; another stranger to get used to! Delia, the new stranger, used to be the secretary of Matthew Minnerton's church. I had done a few drawings for their newsletter; pen and ink sketches to cheer people up but, even so, it did not help me make friends. My mind flashed back to the day I went on a picnic at that church. I had, as usual, been unable to help myself to food and sat alone on the grass against a tree with the lump in my throat. Not one person, and there was many, came to help or even to say hello.

When Pastor Leonard came to this country, people who had been hurt by their previous churches joined the new move of the Holy Spirit he brought. Delia became secretary there also. During her visits to me she sat on my bed in the flat as there was no room for a chair and my cat settled into the presence of God as we prayed together.

After a year living at Nellie and Oliver's they were not happy when I was awarded a back payment of three thousand pounds DLA money and with it decided to move out because of his loud music. Some months back I had been to a meeting at a church in London where Bert Ardingson, a prophet from America, had been preaching. During his prophesying he saw in his spirit that there were people crying out to God,

'No home, no home…,' he faltered slightly then added, 'homes are being built.'

In my search for a suitable home I discovered a 'To Let' sign outside a new looking, purpose built block of flats and pursued it because I thought it would be quiet and secure but unable to cope with making a decision to take it I asked a key worker from Mind *(a charity that helps emotionally and mentally ill people)* to help me. We made an appointment to see the place. The two bedroom accommodation with a large lounge impressed me. The most important things were the security and space it offered. Hidden away down some steps, hardly seen from the road, it suited me down to the ground. I asked the estate agent,

'Is it quiet here?'

He shrugged his shoulders and then, as though given sudden revelation, assured me,

'It's just like this.'

Absolute silence - I presumed it was soundproof. *Great, just what I need.* I had enough money for the five hundred pound deposit, which would be returned when I left in a year's time but I was tired of constantly moving around and hoped to stay.

Christine and I continued travelling to London where Pastor Zangy was conducting deliverance on a weekly basis. He kept a kind of surgery at a house and often arrived five hours later than our appointments. On reaching the house, where a diagnosis would be made, there was a packed queue stretching into the garden but it was worth the wait. When called I knelt in front of him for a few seconds as was the custom. He prescribed on a piece of paper how many days deliverance and how many days prayer following the deliverance I should receive. I was prescribed three days deliverance and seven days prayer. *Surely I need more than that.*

'I'm in charge,' God quickly told me.

Christine and I stayed overnight at a friend's place for the duration. The following evening Pastor Zangy held another meeting. Christine and I prayed beforehand in our friend's house for a sevenfold anointing; that meant seven times more power to set us free. During the meeting Pastor said,

'I don't know where all this power is coming from.'

Deliverance happened to be carried out in a building not quite opposite a police station. As we waited for our turn to enter the hall, songs and prayers were performed. Christine and I were often called in together in addition to between seven and ten others. Deliverance was carried out en masse. The pastors involved took one of us each and turned us around while commanding evil spirits to come out of us. It was not until my prayer days were due, however, that I was delivered. Pastor Ebenezer, who was in charge of the deliverance sessions, was sitting in a chair when I approached him. He prayed and I 'went down' in the Holy Spirit. As I lay there, clear fluid, thicker than water, oozed out of my mouth. I coughed and more fluid oozed out onto the wooden floorboards. Kitchen towels were imperative and were laid under my mouth. I lay for hours while my system poured out whatever bondage had got hold of me. The floor was awash and the pastors kept replacing the sodden paper towels until it was time to leave the building. That went on for seven days, though not continuously. By the end of the first day I was freezing and shivering and on the underground train, while travelling home, my face had turned ashen white. When the train reached our stop I could not get up from my seat, depleted of all energy. Christine helped me off.

'We'll have to get a doctor. I can't go on.'

It was not like me not to be tough but that I could not do. As I stood on the platform leaning against the wall, a woman produced smelling salts from her bag, which I refused. The railway guard called for an ambulance and I was whisked away in a wheelchair to the local hospital's casualty department. At the hospital, screened off from view, a nurse gave me a bowl and I continued to bring up the thick, clear fluid. Christine explained to the nurse that I was being delivered. Rather dismayed that she had told her I rested back until discharged. *I wondered how a nurse could understand that.*

As I continued to go to Pastor Leonard's church in Bramington the Holy Spirit carried on with the deliverance but when I continued to bring up the clear, thick fluid I was told by Leonard,

'Don't keep doing that, it's dirty.'

I knew that but I was being delivered. He also ordered me to stop screaming.

'Lord,' I begged, 'You are going to have to stop delivering me. The pastor doesn't like it, I'll just have to be bound up and not get free.'

God heard my request that evening as nothing like it happened again. Occasionally, God did come to set me free but the power to do so was greatly diminished. If they had supported me I would have been free in a much shorter time but I would have to stay as I was. In hell! The battle was ferocious and the Devil had won, for now.

Back at the flat I wondered how I would manage. The first thing I did was buy a washing machine. There was a dishwasher provided so I did not have to do too much. If I had not been awarded the DLA I would still not be able to look after myself so all of that provision helped me enormously to be more independent for which I was and am very thankful.

I became used to Pastor Leonard's church not allowing me to respond to God the way I had been doing. They permitted people to laugh and cry loudly but that was as far as they went. Any screaming or other deeper manifestations were forbidden. I heard God say to me one day as I lay on the floor,

'If my people would cast these things out they would go.'

I had been twitching slightly but nothing was leaving. The congregation followed the leader for the rest of the meeting while I struggled alone to concentrate on what God was doing with me. During worship the power increased and the manifestations escalated but nothing of any significance happened. *Please worship more, much more*, I implored silently. God was showing me an important principle. For Him to work He needed to be thanked, praised, worshipped, honoured and glorified. When a pastor took over, God took second place. I became more and more frustrated and His presence weakened.

Christine and I continued for a while to go to London but she eventually stopped going. I, at one session, felt so battered and unable to make the journey home that I walked into the police station opposite and asked for a lift; an over fifty mile away lift. The church did not think to help in practical matters so I staggered towards the only help I thought may be available.

'We need all the cars we have to do our job around here,' I was told.

'Okay, I'll just have to rest a bit and then go but I don't know how I'm going to make it.'

I wondered how I had made it anyway most times; using what little strength I had to get from A to B but was continuously prepared to pay the price for my freedom.

On occasions I visited Samantha and, being an aunty, sometimes had the job of taking her children to the park. When I left her house and carried the children's toy bikes along the road I felt so dizzy that I could barely walk. How I acted normally I will never know but I managed not to show the children how much it was an effort to look after them. When Samantha's first child, Louise, was only two years of age she had responded rapidly when I asked for a hug; jumping up in her blue dress and tidy, long white hair and running towards me replied with a huge,

'Yes.'

Her little arms wrapped around me and her simple, nonjudgmental touch embraced my brokenness. For that I will always remember her with such fondness and gratitude. I had not made it obvious to her that I was really begging.

One day she will know all about me. What will she think of me then?

Chapter Seven

My First home and Seeking More Help

The space and newness of my new home left me in complete awe. I had never lived in such a place on my own. Sandy came along with me and as I had researched how to look after cats during a move to new territory I locked him into his white, mesh cage for two weeks until he got used to the place. He did not like it much and stared at me with his huge, green eyes.

I bought some second hand furniture. A three piece suite was advertised in the local paper and Peggy came with me to see it.

'I'm changing my name back to Margaret, what it was when I was born,' she announced.

'Okay.'

I did not know how I was going to call her Margaret after so long. We had no idea how she became Peggy in the first place and kept slipping up for the first week or so.

Not long into my stay I had a nightmare about my cat being a huge draft excluder the other side of my bedroom door preventing me from getting out. I wondered if God was telling me I should never have moved but it was too late. Many nights I lay in bed crying out loud and found the place was not as soundproof as the agent made out. The resident upstairs was kept awake by the noise I made. I also found that living in the flat was not as secure as I had hoped either. One Monday evening I said hello to a man as we passed each other whilst walking down the communal path which ran alongside my kitchen window. He did not answer. When I left my lounge through the patio door the following evening I was confronted by him as he stood just inside the communal bins' wooden enclosure, not too far away. He looked as though he was emptying rubbish so I thought nothing of it. However, as I wandered past, en route to church *(which had moved again from the hotel to a warehouse about five minutes walk away)* the man was standing behind the enclosure watching me and shouted,

'What's your name?'

I turned to him,

'Pardon?'

'What's your name?'

'Rachel.'

'Come here.'

I quickened my pace to get away.

'Come here!' he repeated a little louder.

An evil silence descended as I turned towards the road. Flagging down a car I told the driver who said he would look out for him. I continued to the church prayer meeting where I told a couple of people what happened. One man phoned the police and returned with me to my home. The police arrived and reassured me of their presence should anything else happen.

'Just phone us.'

The following night whilst on my knees praying I glanced at my clock. It was exactly ten o'clock. As soon as I mentioned 'murder' a knock on my inner front door caused me to spring to my feet and walk rapidly along the hall to face the closed door. I took a deep breath. For some unknown reason I always ran towards danger rather than away from it.

'Hello, what do you want?' I asked, shaking violently while imagining him with an axe.

He began,

'I was outside your door yesterday night and saw a woman trying to get into your flat.'

'Did you?'

'Yes, she had a torch.'

'Oh.'

My mind raced. It occurred to me that I was that woman and had been unmistakably leaving my flat, not trying to get in.

'I've come down to see if you need any help.'

'No, I'm fine.'

'Are you sure?'

'Yes, positive.'

I left him, horrified. Still shaking violently I grabbed the phone and called the police. When they answered I was shaking so much that the insides of the phone almost came loose with the rattling. A policeman arrived alone shortly afterwards and sat to interview me. A rapid knock on my patio door caused me to leap across to the other side of the room where I stood rigid against the wall.

'Don't let him see me.'

Not that he could from there.

'I won't.'

He strode to the door and ordered the man to go round the front of the building where he would interview him. On his return he repeated what the man had said,

'He said he was with his girlfriend and they wanted to help you.'

'He was on his own.'

I was so traumatized by the event that he asked,

'Do you know anyone you can stay with overnight?'

I suggested Delia, who had found herself out of her depth some time before and had finally given up.

He phoned her and explained what had happened. I watched his face grow deadly serious but was left to guess what she was telling him.

'She won't have you,' he said, putting the phone down.

So even when I'm confronted with a would be murderer the church will still not help! He left after reassuring me he had told the man I did not want to be bothered by him. After closing the door I turned and, as the hall mirror faced me, I could not help noticing the deep redness of my face and neck. When getting ready for bed I was shocked to see the redness had spread right down my arms to my waist!

Even so I continued to attend the church. After one evening meeting I mentioned something about the pastor to someone. His daughter happened to be listening. I hoped my comment would bring about more understanding when she repeated to her father what I said but it led to my being disciplined instead. My behaviour deteriorated as I found I was less and less acceptable in my manifestations during ministry times until, one day, a letter came through the post commanding me not to go back until I could 'produce fruit in repentance'. I knew that was impossible and was astounded that I should get such a notice. So I remained at home for many months; often staying in bed until three in the afternoon reading the Bible. Then one day an advertisement on the television led me to the next step in my spiritual walk. The Messianic Rabbi featured was preparing to celebrate the Jewish feast of Hanukkah at Cantrin Community Centre. I went along to the celebration with Christine. Songs I had never heard were played to Jewish tunes and I felt right at home. After the service we spoke to the Rabbi and later traditional doughnuts were given with a coffee. The evening was amazing. *This must be it, I must be Jewish. No wonder I've been wondering around all my life and not belonging anywhere.*

As I was churchless I visited a small church I had attended at times when I lived in the group home at Ribford. One of those occasions, which was announced as a healing meeting, I received a powerful deliverance where I had been lying on the floor and clinging to chair legs for dear life. It thoroughly exhausted me and when it was over a lady said,

'You are going to have such a love that others will be envious.'

The church was fairly local and it was a Saturday morning. Voices could be heard inside and a notice on the wall declared that a Messianic fellowship was meeting there. Rabbi Samuel Mushi who had been at Cantrin Community Centre came out. From that day on I attended the services every Saturday but for six months I constantly prayed for guidance as to whether I should be there. A few of us helped with the internal decorating of the church. Old floor tiles were pulled up one by one, even the Rabbi's two year old son took up a scraper; helping in his own sweet way. After that the office staff needed help so I volunteered to stuff and address envelopes with the Rabbi's newsletters. Someone else was building a database. Months later the Rabbi bought a franking machine which made sticking stamps onto the envelopes a thing of the past.

I still could not help myself to food in public without great difficulty. Samuel, unlike the other pastors, sat and ate food with us after the services. He soon got to know about my difficulty when he said,

'Go and help yourself to the food.'

'I can't.'

He immediately told someone to help me. There were chicken drumsticks and all kinds of other food his wife had prepared at home. People helped themselves with ease but I could not until I got used, with the assistance of others, to helping myself without feelings of guilt and shame. It did take quite a few weeks to get to that point. Nobody from anywhere had ever helped me get over the problems my father caused. Christians were mostly spiritual and rarely helped in practical matters. It seemed less important to them.

As I became used to Samuel, my feelings of wanting to be in a family resurfaced. One day two of his sons were sitting on his lap. I struggled with the old childhood pain and left the room. Once inside the meeting hall I curled up tightly underneath one of the chairs. There was nowhere else to go. The messages I was sending out only served to get me a telling off and massive frowns from Samuel and others. Regardless, I liked the fellowship and, though it was hard to integrate, Samuel made it easier by being involved and my being able to help in the office gave me meaning in life. I felt secure in spite of everything.

God, through the government, had given me disability payments when I could not possibly hope to earn. I had not been able to work for nine years and saw the Synagogue as a rehabilitation place where I could gain some confidence and ease my way into a better life. Not too long into my stay I made an appointment with Samuel and his wife and wondered how I would get on with this new couple as I walked up the stairs to the counseling room.

'You must give up your benefits,' I was told.

'No, God gave me them.'

I could not live or cope on nothing. If Samuel wanted me to give them up he would have to provide for me. My faith, not somebody else's, would have to be as solid as a rock for me to survive.

As time went by I received news that a couple with a healing ministry, Celia Pankerton and her husband, would be ministering in Cheshire. Samantha knew a couple I could stay with so I prayed in my lounge about whether to go or not. I took the wind of the Holy Spirit blowing over me as confirmation. After preparing my things and taking a long train journey, the couple picked me up. I discovered I had met the man before at Ponrish Baptist Church! They had recently married and moved away. I was up early next morning to attend the conference. When it was time for ministry Celia taught us how to measure our arms.

'Stand with your heels together, preferably against a wall, pull your arms straight out in front of you and put your hands together as though praying. Now lift your hands without moving them and look at the tips of your fingers.'

One of my arms was about a quarter of an inch shorter than the other. Celia prayed. As my arm began to grow it trembled slightly and I cried, being shocked as God's power permeated it. As soon as my arms were healed I leapt in asking for my hands, feet and all the rest of my body to be healed as well but that was not to be. The frown on my forehead and hunched shoulders told of the confusion. I had not known that my arms were of unequal length so had never asked God to heal them and yet He did. All the things I did know about and asked for went without.

The following afternoon's meeting I went up onto the platform to receive ministry where I writhed about on the floor. Nothing much happened then but later that evening at another service I went forward to answer an 'altar' call. As I lay under the power of the Holy Spirit my head suddenly started to hurt; my temples especially. I pressed and pressed against them remembering all the pain I had suffered in my younger days at St Chad's Hospital. The pain increased to such a level that my eyes closed tight and when I could stand it no longer, I yelled,

'Stop hurting me, stop hurting me, stop hurting me!'

My face grimaced as I screamed at invisible tormenters; those who caused me such anguish throughout my life. I wondered if the release would be the end of all the pain I suffered at the hands of some Christians and anybody else. Had God at last come to the end of setting me free? A woman came rushing in answer to my screams. I heard her praying as she touched my head, then an almighty voice shouted, sending shock waves through the auditorium,

'Don't you ever *dare* interfere with what the Holy Spirit is doing!'

It was Celia, she, during the years of her ministry had seen the importance of letting God do what He wanted. I understood the urgency in her voice plus how the woman and everyone else must have been feeling after being shouted at like that. At the same time I was grateful for the concern at the urgency of seeing me set free. God was doing a vital deeper work that no eye could see. When the pain eventually subsided I lay on the floor completely exhausted and unable to move. At lock up time I was still lying there. A pastor and his wife offered to take me to their house. The wife helped me up and led me to the front passenger seat of their car. We drove off slowly at first. I watched the street lights passing in the dark outside, then announced,

'I feel like I'm going to be sick.'

'Roll the window down and stick your head out.'

I did as the driver instructed as we hurtled a roundabout at about twenty five miles per hour and threw up but it was not 'threw', it was froth. A whole load of white stuff belched out of me and about turned in mid air to paint the side of the car as the rush of wind plastered it there. I thought there would be more ministry at their home but instead the pastor instructed me to wash my face before giving me a lift back to the house I was staying in. I felt like the most vulnerable, lonely girl in the world.

Once back at the Synagogue a healing meeting was also held. I prayed for somebody else's arm that was shorter than the other and, much to our excitement, it grew.

As time went by Samuel started teaching sessions on a weekday afternoon but all I wanted was to get set free some more so became a little disruptive. I yearned for the power of God above anything else. One such afternoon on my way to the Synagogue I was passing a newsagent and by chance noticed the headlines about a notorious occultic man and what he had done to certain people. His gruesome killings sparked a plug in my brain. *Did somebody attempt to do something similar to me?* Grabbing the paper I paid for it and carried it to the meeting where another teaching was underway. I needed Samuel to look into what may have happened to me and became more agitated as time went by; finding it hard to concentrate on the teaching. One of the girls noticed and spoke up for me but Samuel wanted to pursue his course. The torment increased so I stood and with the back of my knees pushed my seat away from the circle of chairs, turned around and opened the doors that led into the sanctuary. It was pitch black in there and though I felt around for a light switch, I found none. Knowing roughly where the rear doors were I slowly made my way towards the back of the Synagogue, being careful not to bump into anything. When sure I had reached the doors I turned and, with my back to them, deliberately bashed my head hard against what I thought was the wooden frame. An almighty crash sounded as my head sank back further than anticipated; clean through a small glass panel. I suddenly had their full attention and was in great trouble.

'It's okay, I'll clear it up.'

Fetching the dustpan and brush I set to work then walked back into the hall. Unable to settle I stated coldly,

'I'm going.'

Reluctantly, I walked towards the rear, side exit door of the hall fully intending to leave but just inside the door, leaning against the wall, stood a chair. As I did not really want to leave I climbed onto it. While watching the rest of them one of the girls looked up and stared in my direction. Samuel noticed where she was looking and turned. His face lit up the hall with his surprised expression. I laughed.

'Well, it was the furthest I could go.'

Jumping down I left the hall and made my way out to a cash machine. Withdrawing ten pounds I took it back to Samuel to pay for the broken window. I thought all would be well, after all I had done my best in trying to get myself and the window sorted out. Later in the office he discussed me with his leaders and then called me in,

'You are banned from coming here for three weeks.'

I had no choice but to obey. There went yet another chance to get free. The Gospel had flown out of the broken window and had become ineffective that instant or maybe it had not been there at all.

The following Shabbat I held the service alone in bed, after which I dressed and watched Part One of 'Jesus of Nazareth' in the lounge. My comfortable Saturday afternoon was spent with the curtain closed and the door pushed to. As I watched the film a noise in the hall startled me. *There's somebody in here.* I turned towards the closed door. *It's probably an old man who's got lost in the communal hallway outside.* I settled back to watch the film but only seconds later there was a much closer sound. *There is somebody in here!* I felt the blood rush to my feet and stood up to investigate. Opening the door with a yank I beheld a thin, six feet tall, youngish man staring transfixed into the mirror on the wall just outside my bedroom. Slamming the door shut I put my foot against it, picked up the phone to my right and phoned the police who held me on the phone until somebody arrived but I screamed,

'Don't come in the front way, come in the back. He's here now. Quick!'

It took them a good few minutes to arrive and I was frightened to let go of the door in case the intruder barged in. When they arrived I let a policeman and policewoman in through my lounge patio door. The man had fled back through the six inch window in my bedroom.

'He probably thought you were talking to Butch,' suggested the policeman.

As we walked through the hall the policewoman noticed the hall light on and I was confused as to whether I had put it on or not. My bedroom door was ajar and when we tried to get in we found the man had flung a chair against it. The curtains had been painstakingly loosened from the hooks and draped on the floor and he had left a huge, black footmark on the dressing table. He was never caught but just that week I had watched Benny Hinn, a television pastor, reading a Psalm from the Bible. I had cried hard as God quickened it to me, warning me that something would happen but everything would be alright.

When my three weeks were up I returned to the Synagogue. After settling back I joined the Israeli dance group led by a fourteen year old girl on Saturdays after the service. That had been what I really needed; to be taught step by step. I soon gained confidence and learned all the dances off by heart. The young teacher sadly contracted meningitis and could no longer lead the group. I automatically stepped into her shoes and took over the teaching. It helped me communicate with the rest of the people and I felt safe doing something that kept me slightly distant in my relationships. People complimented my style of teaching with the accompanied gentleness. My aim was to have a dance group with a difference; that through the dance God would give dignity to us who were downtrodden and heal us. I was prepared to spend hours on somebody to help them get their steps right than for them to make a mess of things in public and suffer the embarrassment. As time went by our little team consisted of about six as a core group. We travelled to various places with Samuel to lead the worship with dancing at the beginning of the meetings. I felt at home.

Samuel taught the Jewish roots of our faith and that if we left the Synagogue we would be in the wilderness and lost. I knew that to be true because I felt found.

Roughly two years passed since the Synagogue opened when the fellowship who owned the building approached Samuel and told him they wanted the building back on Saturdays. We prayed and believed God would turn the decision around but we did not have a hope and had to leave. I placed a notice on the entrance door stating that we had gone east not west and remained with the Synagogue fellowship as they moved out. From then on the meetings were held in Samuel's home. All the office equipment was set up in his lounge which was big enough to cope.

As we settled into our new abode for the fellowship I continued to work in the 'office' fixing up the database. I had taken a computer course at college while we were in the last building so I could be more helpful and proficient. As my skills increased I produced monthly newsletters and helped produce conference brochures. Those of us in the office prepared for entire conferences, after Samuel said what he wanted done. While we were preparing for one I worked on the acetates; the wording for the meetings and all the songs that needed to be typed up for showing on a screen. I could touch type quite fast but did make a few mistakes so always used the spell checker. On checking the acetates for a conference to be held in Maple Meadows, Wales, I noticed the computer had suggested a replacement word for a particular mistake and showed it to the member of staff sitting beside me. Jokingly I asked,

'Shall I put that word in instead?'

We laughed.

'No, better not.'

On the first day of the conference about two hundred people in the hall were happily reading the V'ahavta; a portion of the book of Deuteronomy. I could not believe my senses when they read word for word what was written on the acetate. Raucous laughter swiftly followed, including Samuel's! I glanced towards the staff member who had sat beside me in the office. Nonplussed as to how the mistake made its way onto the screen I reckoned God must have overruled my decision. The correct ending of the V'ahavta reads:

'...and you shall write them (the commandments of the Lord) *on the doorposts of your house.'*

The congregation read,

'...and you shall write them on the droopiest of your house!'

It certainly did break the ice and from then on the people were more relaxed but I stood in my place during the entire meeting stock still, afraid to move an inch out of place.

During one of the afternoon's sessions at a time of ministry God, through one of the leaders, was quoting John 14:2, from the Bible, *'In my house are many mansions. I am going to prepare a place for you and then I will come and take you to Myself.'* Halfway through the power of God hit me. I screamed so long and so loud with the terror of going to His house that it pulsated through the roof and across the Welsh countryside. Why I was so afraid of God was a mystery because I was constantly looking for Him and loved Him.

After the conference our Shabbat meetings moved from Samuel's house into a local school hall. For a year or two we ferried our service equipment back and forth from Samuel's house then one day I heard that a certain Jewish lady, called Phoebe, would be moving down to take over management in the office. Professionalism, in my opinion, would put God right out of the equation. He would be confined to rules and regulations made by man instead of being free to do as He pleased. On the first morning of Phoebe's new rulership I explained to her,

'I am rehabilitating my life here.'

I hoped she would understand and help but instead of improving, things changed for the worse. Samuel had disciplined me a lot in the past but when Phoebe came he became even worse towards me and one day when I knocked on his front door he yelled,

'Get out of my house!'

I left straightaway as his mood was not one to be trifled with that day. However, later he reinstated me. As Phoebe became used to her role I became more uneasy. We had always made prayer a priority before the day began and I wanted to continue doing so but Phoebe was against it saying we were 'too busy'.

One day when Samuel came into the office I told him,

'When I was praying at home I had a picture of a train that has gone off the tracks and lots of people were hurt.'

As I was concerned about things, I invited Samuel to an event held by Norman Flickwick but he declined the invitation. I trusted Norman as miracles happened during his services. I went along to it by myself, feeling vulnerable. People could only go to the platform after his preaching if they had received a miracle, not simply for prayer in order to receive one. I had not but Norman's assistant said she would get me up there. I wrote out for her my life history and all my hopes were up for a great release of God's power over my life. However, though I had stood in the line to go onto the platform the lady refused point blank to let me go up. Time pressed on and if I did not leave soon my last train would depart from the station. I had to get away but would not leave until I had all I could from God and thus, Norman's prayers. I did not stand for the betrayal and pushed forward; explaining and shouting to the ushers at the injustice until the lady finally let me up. Once on the platform, at the very last minute, the lady said to Norman,

'She has been abused in every way.'

His response was to simply wave a hand over my head. My arms flew into the air then collapsed at my sides like hanging ropes as I 'went down' like a 'rag doll', as somebody who knew me mentioned next time I saw her. I was quickly carried by two men and dumped around the side of the platform behind some long curtains and left. Lying for a while in silence with an eerie presence I opened my eyes. Totally deserted I stood to my feet and made my way back to my seat. The hall was practically empty. I gathered my belongings and made my way to the station. The last train to my destination had already left so I got the next best train which stopped at the station before mine. By the time I had walked home from there it was three o'clock in the morning. I told Samuel's wife later what had happened. Did she care? And

Samuel had missed a great opportunity to be ministered to, and I, the support and care I needed. Perhaps I should have taken his decision not to go as my own but how does one know when one expects such great a change in his or her life?

Other people warned Samuel about the way he was taking.

As the office at his home became too small Samuel was constantly looking for a building to purchase. We all kept our eyes peeled for a suitable place. He who seeks finds and soon Samuel discovered a building locally. On the quiet of Christmas Day, which no longer existed for us, we all, suffering from flu, moved into our new 'Synagogue'. The building was tall and possessed enough room for everyone to have their own office. At the opening prayer meeting, while waiting on the Lord, I heard a still, quiet voice in my mind say,

'Original.'

I mentioned it to Samuel and as I did so my hands pounded up and down inside my deep jacket pockets so much that my keys jumped out onto the floor. Up to then I was not aware of a particular unfolding problem. Samuel remained silent.

New people arrived from outside the area, mostly women who we had met whilst touring. I found it hard to get used to them but continued to work despite all the pain I was experiencing. What Samuel asked me to do I was happy to carry out but had the habit of challenging him in public when I felt he was saying wrong things in the meetings. The office was gradually taken over by the new people. As time went by things deteriorated. Samuel came into the office one day and started telling me off about something, probably my feelings of constant rejection. At the confrontation I became fearful and called loudly,

'Yeshua, Yeshua, Yeshua.'

That is Hebrew for Jesus, hoping it would deter him from getting worse. He stared at me then left and went back downstairs where he had been building *(he was a builder before he was a Rabbi)* to enlarge the sanctuary. As he worked a beam fell and broke his finger. I could not help wondering if it had something to do with how he was treating me. I had done my best to help him get the Messianic movement running in the area but obviously it was not good enough. All I wanted was for God to feel right at home.

During all the trouble with the Synagogue I occasionally went to one of the local churches on Sundays and thought to mention the trouble and get some advice so made an appointment to see Nathan Stonemuir, one of the pastors. After telling him the awful things that were going on, he responded,

'Go back and submit to him.'

What? I hardly thought that appropriate but, nevertheless, I returned.

Messianic Judaism, as opposed to Orthodox which strictly adheres to the whole law, or Progressive *(Reform)* which leaves room for man's judgment of the law, meaning, was it solely of God for all time or was it for the period of time the Jews were living in? Messianic Jews believe in neither but in the sovereignty of the Man, Yeshua, who claimed to be Divine and was crucified for the sins of mankind. They believe He rose from the dead, ascended to Heaven and is the Messiah to come and that He is seated at the right hand side of God until He comes a second time to redeem His righteous ones *(those who believe by faith that this is the case)* and to judge the world. However, in the eyes of the other Jewish communities that view is considered blasphemy. Messianic Jews wait on Him alone for guidance as to how to live according to the scriptures, including the New Testament. They believe the blood that was shed by Him on the cross cleanses people from the sin that separates them from God Almighty and that they can be filled with the Ruach HaKodesh *(the Holy Spirit – being born again)* or they cannot live for God as He intended them to. It was too hard without the Holy Spirit who also marks those who believe in Yeshua as His own.

Eventually, Samuel opened a shop where a lot of Messianic literature and other items could be purchased. There was opposition from the non Messianic Rabbis and some thought he was taking advantage of the unfortunate in society, or so he told us. Of course I did not agree with them at the time. If the Synagogue was not of God then what was left?

I became aware that Phoebe and Samuel were not altogether 'Kosher' in their relationship and one Saturday morning during worship I had a picture in my mind of the ten commandment tablets that Moses had written but with one difference; the

Hebrew letters were all broken up. At first I had no idea what it meant but prayed and the interpretation came as clear as day. Simply, the commandments had been broken. I went to the microphone and shared my picture with the congregation, to which Phoebe shouted,

'Amen.'

How can you shout 'Amen'? I was shocked by her answering in that way and she took nothing to heart.

Time there was running out for me as the situation became even worse. I continued to pray at home. God seemed to be telling me to go to Phoebe and give her a word from the Bible. It told of her end and, being petrified of giving it to her, I gingerly approached the shop. I certainly did not want to give such a word but a man was standing outside wondering whether to go in or not and after chatting with me for a while came in with me. I did not mention why I was there. After he spoke with Phoebe I tried to give her the word God had given as gently as possible; as though I might be wrong. She took it humbly, it seemed, and I left. I returned by way of the Synagogue where some of the others were helping out with the building work, walked down into the sanctuary, lay on the floor and cried. What had happened to God's house? *Why don't people love Him and why won't they let Him in?*

Samuel's next idea was to create a school for the children in the Synagogue. It was a good idea to educate children away from a potentially harmful society but he was ill equipped with staff.

Samuel showed more kindness to those who had taken over and, being human, I longed for kindness too but did not get it anymore. Now and again he was in a good mood with me but mostly his discipline was excruciating. One time in the service I sat with my tallit *(prayer shawl)* over my head, teardrops fell from my eyes and after landing on the floor were the size of two pence pieces.

At home, when the feast of Purim was due, I prayed to God to send rain so hard that everyone would know it was from Him. I had read in the Bible in Ezekiel 47 where the waters come up underneath the threshold of the temple, and how He answered! It rained so heavily that water gushed from the ceiling at the front and flooded the Synagogue. A river ran down the right hand side and out towards the back door. I tried to be positive by bringing reference to the chapter in Ezekiel, hoping Samuel would turn around in his ways and save the Synagogue from its present situation. However, I got some hard looks from the intercessors. We filled many buckets of rainwater mopping up that day!

That, my fifth year at the Synagogue, was by far the most painful. When Samuel's eldest son took his Bar Mitzvah I sat at the front, right hand side to put the acetates up so people could read the words on the screen. The Synagogue was filled with both regular attendants and invited guests. With my tallit over my shoulders and round, black rimmed, Jewish hat I turned around to see sitting behind me was the pastor who had thrown me out of the last church I was in and beside him sat his associate pastor. I sat with my back leaning against the wall without a trace of a smile and wondered what they thought of me then.

A week or so later and feeling unhappy both with the Synagogue and myself I went off to London to see a black pastor who I had seen on Christian TV. He was a very kind man and bought me fish and chips for dinner every time I went but I did not get any deliverance. One afternoon he listened to my entire story from end to end until sinking in his chair with exhaustion but his exhaustion was nothing in comparison to my situation. Any consideration I had towards him took second place and had to. After all, I had been seeking for so long to find a solution. Pastor Fimkoko, as was his name, came down to the Synagogue one time to taste of our services which were pretty good really with Jewish worship songs, Jewish dancing, a meaty message from Samuel, prayer ministry for individuals and a hearty meal that we all contributed to, to end with. I was no longer the dance leader. Behind my back the leaders had put an older lady in my place and I only became aware of it when, during another ban from the Synagogue, Samuel told me of the results of their scheme. After putting the phone down I collapsed onto the floor, fragmenting some more but ever so slowly, I was aware of God's arms lowering me to the ground. A few weeks later the new dance leader broke out into a severe eczema rash and wondered what she had done to deserve it. When the Devil is out to destroy you he will use anybody and anything in his power to do so. Something not many people going about their daily business have ever developed is discerning the spiritual world around them and why so many nasty things happen to them. In the New Testament 1 Peter 5:8 says to stay alert because the Devil prowls around like a roaring lion seeking whom he may devour. We must resist him and so I did not retaliate with that leader or take revenge even in my prayers but talked about the problem gently with her though nothing was resolved. I left it at that.

The highlight of any meeting I attended, be it Synagogue or church, was when the Presence of God came to meet us. I could never quite understand why He was given so little time at the end to heal and deliver His people. I do know it grieved Him. He wanted full opportunity to serve His miraculous power in restoring us but man was reluctant to step aside and let Him take what rightfully belonged to Him. He had bought us with His blood and entered us into His New Covenant, had He not?

The latter day trouble increased to such an extent that every day was filled with fear for me. Samuel told me to get a job outside of the Synagogue and I found one at the end of the road, cleaning in an office. The owners happened to be Jewish and as we had been taught that Jewish people outside of the Messianic Movement were our enemies I was petrified of my employers. *Better not say anything to them about anything.* I did open up though and told a little of my life story to the wife of the owner. I mentioned I had been to college to try to rehabilitate myself and she invited me to teach her how to prepare spreadsheets. My stomach flipped around inside and I screamed silently. I had to run away, again. *What if they find out I am Messianic?* Even though we were meant to support the Jewish people we were terrified of them. What craziness! I had even been attending the local Jewish community centre learning Israeli dancing and loved it and had even taken part in a Chanukah show they put on for the Jewish community. Our team at the community centre was made up of wonderful people but I had so many questions about my identity. Who am I? What am I? I had to find out if I had Jewish blood and not just guess so started to research my family tree and ancestral history. There was no immediate Jewish blood but I did find a woman by the name of Elizabeth Jacob *(her real name)* and if I have traced her correctly, she was my fifth great-grandmother. So who knows we, as a family, could have drifted from our Jewish roots hundreds of years ago.

What was happening to the Synagogue? One Shabbat morning two men came into the sanctuary bringing with them a bowl, water and towel, offering to wash Samuel's feet. Samuel held a lot of resentment towards Gentile churches.

'We have come to wash your feet and ask for your forgiveness as Gentiles for our part in persecuting the Jews,' said one of them.

'No, I will never forgive,' answered Samuel.

The men left and the room was filled with an air of uncertainty and bewilderment.

After that Samuel started to preach for five hours at a time and we had to sit and listen. He demanded more and more commitment and more and more of our time. The frustration in him grew and various people warned him about his divergence into sin with Phoebe, words they believed were from God. At times I left the room to go upstairs to the toilet and on my return listened at the bottom of the stairs to what he was saying. The swearing and shouting reverberated with his seething comments to the very walls. If the building could have upped and fled, I am sure it would have done. I continued with my work for as long as I could then one day at an intercessors' prayer meeting concerning those events I was sitting at the back of the sanctuary. I only wanted to hear what God was telling me to pray so sat silently waiting while the others prayed. Suddenly and without warning my head flung upwards towards Heaven and I cried out,

'Oh God, possess us!'

That was all.

Phoebe and the other women Samuel liked ganged up on me more and more until Phoebe stripped all my work off the walls and cupboard doors. Every trace was completely destroyed by them. They told me about their takeover and I could not handle the injustice or rejection. All my work over the past five years was suddenly unacceptable. I had bought the computer I worked on, on hire purchase out of my own money. One of the women from outside the area had taken it over. Broken yet again I could barely come to terms with what was happening. I had brought hundreds of envelopes home to get ready for mailing and they were still there because I was not wanted in the office. Soon enough Samuel and Phoebe told me to take my computer and go.

I asked a friend to come with me to collect it. Later, I rang Phoebe to ask what to do with the envelopes,

'Leave them on the steps outside the Synagogue.'

So that's what I did but in my heart I could not let go of the Synagogue, not for a long, long time. Many other people chose to leave, broken to the core; many of whom had sold their houses to be part of the movement. I wondered what would become of the word I had given to Phoebe. For a year or so the Synagogue went on as usual but there was trouble for Samuel. He and the ones who remained with him ended up running charity shops to raise funds. Eventually the Synagogue closed. Samuel had taken seven of the women as wives/concubines, though not legally and moved to another part of the country with them. He was convinced he was chosen by God to be a king, as in the Old Testament. The non Messianic Rabbis had been right all along but I felt that I would be persecuted by them if I were ever to join them. If God was love then where was His love for me?

The first Passover after I left was creeping up and I wondered if God would be pleased if I celebrated it. One morning as I was going out of my house I spotted something lying in the road. *Should I go and get it?* Feeling conspicuous and awkward I crossed over to take a look. *It's a frozen leg of lamb.* I picked it up and took it home. *God must have done that to cheer me up.* I prepared a Passover meal and invited some other people who had left the Synagogue to my home. We enjoyed a superb evening.

A little while later I returned to the church I had been thrown out of knowing that by then the pastor knew what had been going on and would be more sympathetic.

Away from the Synagogue I decided to get on with the life I was going to live many years before; get an education. I applied to study a GCSE in Law, reasoning that I would not be as vulnerable out in the world but I felt like I had died. Every morning I lay with a heavy heart and arms outstretched towards imaginative parents who never arrived. Even God remained silent.

Chapter Eight

The United States of America

Many months later somebody informed me about a small local church called Healing Balms where the pastor had words of knowledge and an inner healing ministry. I went there for a while. A lady told me she had designed a website for the fellowship so I came home and did a search for it on the internet but instead I came across Healing Balms Bible Center in Forkhampton, USA. Very cautiously I read about the ministry and prayed as to whether I should get involved in the course Pastor Tierney *(head of the Bible Center)* was offering. He had written his autobiography which I downloaded from the internet and read from cover to cover. He loved Jesus and served him wholeheartedly. Satisfied that he was genuine I applied for his tape course for a diploma in Christian studies. He loved his family and over time I got used to him as a dad. He even allowed me to call him Dad and that was a lifeline for me. For the first time I had a godly pastor and dad to help me come closer to Jesus. The correspondence course was the best I had come across in any church I had attended. When the study on the 'family' came through the post I hugged it for a long while and cried at my loss. I told Pastor Tierney of my tormented life and shared many poems via email with him that I had written over the years. I prayed for him and his family often. As I prayed one day, after about two years of knowing him, I sensed he was physically ill and asked him if that was true. He replied that it was correct and to keep praying. When I had not heard from him for a while I phoned his office out of concern and somebody at the other end also confirmed that there was something wrong with him. When he was able he wrote that he had a virus and was coughing a lot but that,

'Our faithful Lord will come through.'

I trusted him.

'What if he dies?' Samantha asked, during my next visit to her.

'I'll just have to take it as it comes.'

He was sixty six years old. I thought he would live into his eighties but his e-mails were asking me to pray for him. He described how weak he was and sleeping a lot. Never did I read a negative word from his emails as he pastored me. I loved Pastor Tierney so much because he accepted me unquestioningly. When his emails stopped coming in I waited for days on end whilst praying for his recovery and asking God to tell me what was happening. I sensed it was the end. A few weeks passed and eventually I received news that he was in hospital. I bought him a get well card and wished I could have been there in Forkhampton. During the long wait for communication I went to stay with Samantha and her family where God told me,

'This is my provision for you.'

I cried daily as I checked my emails for news of his health; nothing.

Not long after I returned home the telephone rang and I happened to have a visitor in my home at the time. Picking up the phone I greeted the caller,

'Hello.'

'Hi,' said a strange American voice, 'is that Rachel?'

'Yes.'

'This is just to say that Pastor Tierney passed away last night.'

As Cybil *(his eldest daughter)* tried to stay cheerful I could not comprehend why God had taken him. The song of a blackbird snatches the pain away as the tears fall. I did not think the same grief I felt then would be experienced again as I write six years later. *Every time I love anybody they are always taken away.* It must have been my fault.

'Can I come to the funeral?' I asked Cybil.

'Yes.'

That Sunday, ironically, a guest speaker who had been raised from the dead came to a local church to speak. What great timing! Unfortunately, he was hurried away after the meeting and I had no chance to ask him to pray for Pastor Tierney's resurrection. I asked another pastor to pray with me but he sent me to somebody else and with each passing on my faith diminished. I had told Cybil only to believe and he would come back but he did not.

I thought I would qualify for bereavement money from the government but I discovered nobody gets benefits for bereavement abroad so I used my credit card to pay for the air fare. The Tierney's had become my family and now I was faced with yet another separation. Many times my head swung back and rested against my shoulders as I sobbed. Pastor Tierney loved Jesus so much. If he did not I would never have taken to him in such a way. I rarely felt the love of God that most Christians told me about and so having a flesh and blood 'dad' and pastor who really cared began to open me up to Him. Jesus sometimes compensated for my not being able to feel His love on the inside by making His presence felt as wind or breeze but He was not human; there was a great void in my heart. I booked the flight on my birthday, 15th September, only two days before the flight to the United States, asking for special assistance because of my condition *(that is, my usual one).* Who could have imagined such an event and especially in such circumstances. I phoned Cybil to confirm the booking. She had already made arrangements for my arrival,

'You will be staying with me on the first night and then with Mom. Marcus and I will meet you at the airport.'

Many times I dreamed of being greeted by parents at a railway station or an airport; that of flinging my arms round somebody who loved me and to whom I belonged without question, to be welcomed with enthusiasm. I tried many times to give that kind of welcome to others but they just stood there outside of my world. Here I was with another dream devastated. The dream that one day Pastor Tierney and Mabel, his wife, as a mum would meet me with smiling faces and arms outstretched, take me to their home where I would be healed of all my pain, but it was not to be. *Why is God so cruel to me?* I suffered diarrhea for two days, such was the grief of losing somebody so full of the love of God. I tried to reason with myself in all sorts of ways but the grief did not abate. The flight took thirteen hours with one change. I did not cry on the plane, just sat and stared, pushing the grief back into my soul. I had been given a special fare reduction for the flight because of the bereavement and one stewardess approached me gently, squatted beside me and all at once I was a little vulnerable child again. She handed me a small, navy blue case filled with toiletries, courtesy of American Airlines.

I changed planes at Dallas for a smaller one to Ontario. The seat next to me was occupied by a young lady.

'Are you getting off at Ontario?' I asked, numbly.

'Oh, no, I'm dropping off over the Arizona desert.'

'I'm sorry; I'm so used to travelling by train and stopping at stations.'

My thoughts began to run wild. *What if this is all a trap and I'm left stranded at the airport?* On and on, like an endless rolling river, they pursued me till the journey's end. Cybil and Marcus *were* there, recognizing me from a photograph I had sent to Pastor Tierney. They introduced themselves cheerfully, not showing an ounce of grief. We stepped into the heat and sunshine of my first visit to Forkhampton. The forty minute journey away from the palm trees of Ontario's airport seemed longer and the nearer we drove to Cybil's mother's house the more tired I became. Jet lag was a new experience for me. It was early evening when Marcus helped me out of the car and down to the front door of Mabel's house. I felt a sudden weakening at the knees, my legs giving way at the anticipation of entering Pastor Tierney's home. *Would he be angry with me for coming?* The home was vibrant with activity, not like a mourner's home. Lots of food had been prepared by Cybil's sister, Nadine. Everybody was smiling and full of life, very different from the English, I thought. I was shown a chair, sat down and was then invited to help myself to food but that was difficult. I tried to act as normally as possible but felt sure Pastor Tierney had told them about me. Mostly, I observed them, not wanting to take any steps out of character or say anything wrong. My arms hung by my sides as I struggled to sit upright. The family kept talking to me. I wondered if they were trying to keep me awake until bedtime.

'I had diarrhea for two weeks,' Nadine explained.

I told them about my experience with it. I had never heard of grief bringing that kind of reaction before. As Cybil and Marcus opened the door to leave a chorus of loud cricket song filled the air. They lived in a single story bungalow about ten minutes drive away with their two year old son, Luke. I looked forward to a good night's sleep. Lying in bed exhausted I heard unusual sounds of an animal howling in the night. It was a long night lying in the dark but I managed to sleep a little until Cybil knocked on my door. She had finished in the bathroom.

'I'll iron your dress,' Marcus offered.

He liked ironing so I let him. He made a perfect job of it too and that pale blue dress was long. We all dressed for a hot day but respectfully for the occasion. Nobody wore black. Pastor Tierney had gone to the most glorious place imaginable so only cheerful clothes would do.

'I haven't got any flowers,' I told Marcus.

'We'll call into a small shop on the way,' he assured me.

Once down the garden path Marcus opened the car door for me to climb in. On arrival opposite the shop I got out of the car and looked right for oncoming traffic. Marcus suddenly put his arm in front of me, making me stop. I should, after all, have been looking left in America. Marcus pulled the shop door open but I was disappointed to find barely any flowers to choose from. What I did see was a small white bear, about nine inches in height, sitting on its own with flowers attached to its back. My face lit up as I thought of Roly Poly, a stuffed polar bear with its cub I had bought from a chemist shop at home. I had mentioned him to Pastor Tierney who wrote a hearty hello back to him over email. He was not at all like other pastors. He simply loved people and accepted them as they were. If I said anything negative about God though, he was quick to correct me. Words cannot express my admiration for the person God had provided for me at such a time of tragedy; having been thrust from the only fellowship I thought was the right one.

'I'll take him.'

'Are you sure?' asked Marcus.

'Yes.'

Pastor Tierney would understand and welcome the bear.

I stepped from the shop happy to find that little bit of treasure. We carried on to the cemetery where Marcus parked the car. Cybil travelled separately ahead of us with her mother and son. In sandaled feet we stepped into the blistering sunshine and walked up a long, wide pathway towards the place where the coffin would be brought. Quite a few people were active preparing the audio equipment. I clung to my bear until Cybil asked where I would like to put him. Not letting go I sat him with the other flowers on the ground. When the coffin arrived I placed him on top and took some photographs then, glancing to my left, I caught sight of Mabel in her cheerful flowery dress and wondered what kind of character she was. I had not wanted to offend the family but needed a bit of space for myself to express my own love for the pastor who let me call him 'Daddy' too and who helped me to trust again. I tried not to overstep my position as an orphan but it proved a very difficult thing to do. Mabel did not know who had bought the bear and I was careful to keep myself in the background as much as possible. A lady organizing the coffin and grave approached and asked who the bear belonged to. When she found out she asked gently,

'Where should I put it? Do you want to take it home with you or should I put it in the coffin by his head?'

My heart sank and I wondered what the correct thing to decide should be, but even to surprise myself I said boldly, yet a little guiltily,

'No, put it next to his heart.'

I meant no harm; it was what I really wanted to do and expected a massive amount of trouble and accusations but did not get them. Whether they did or did not know what I asked for, the family did not seem to mind. The confusion and difficulty with accepting what I had done myself was enough to cause me never to do that again. The unworthiness I felt was almost intolerable but God, who walked alongside me in all my pain, was still there and not condemning me for that small act of love.

After the funeral Mabel drove me back to her house where I settled for the rest of the week. I cried every night in the garage that had been converted into a bedroom. Mabel and her family did cry but on the whole took the death of Pastor Tierney with great fortitude and belief that God did as He pleased and trusted Him with all their hearts.

Mabel's house was simple but it opened up a whole new world for me. She kept three parrots on the platform in the yard. Two grey ones mimicked phone calls including the ringtones and made a lot of noise. Hank, a white one, had a yellow tuft on his head and there was Skippy the Alsatian, a gentle and quiet dog.

The morning after the funeral Mabel sat across the breakfast table watching me pensively,

'Have you ever been to the Crystal Cathedral?' she eventually asked.

'No, but I've seen their services on television.'

She arranged that we would go on the long drive to Anaheim, Orange County, for a visit. After we had taken our tour of the sparkling cathedral with its many statues and other interesting features Mabel wanted to take me to a particular restaurant but we found it closed so I suggested something that was very important,

'I noticed Disneyworld just opposite the cathedral, can we go there?'

I had always wanted to see the place so it was decided upon and we turned up at the kiosk to pay.

'Do you give any discounts?' I asked the receptionist.

'No, we don't.'

'Oh, I'll have two halves then.'

I thought I might get arrested seeing the expression on the lady's face. Mabel and I stared at each other.

'Oh yeah, I'm a half,' she said.

I did have in mind that Mabel was grieving but did not know what to do so carried on as normal. We stopped at the restaurant in the grounds and I was delighted to be presented with a kind of hot pot stew served with bread on top shaped like Mickey Mouse, ears and all. The trip up the river later was exhilarating and I took photographs to make sure when I returned home it was not just a dream. Later on we took a ride through an underground wonderland where 'A Small, Small World' was being sung by a familiar sounding children's choir. I wondered if it was St John's, my junior School. At the end of the day we enjoyed a carnival but I kept my eye on Mabel wondering how she was doing. I was not quite sure what to say or how to bring comfort as I felt that as I was not a close relative it would have been a bit of a liberty to intrude. The Seven Dwarfs marched past followed by Snow White who sat regally in a huge swan. It was altogether a superb day.

It was not often I had a day out with a 'mum' and I wondered what it was like to be a real daughter. I thought about my mother being the same size as me and how I would deal with it but out of respect kept my thoughts private. I felt disjointed. *Why was I not allowed to have a mother and why such a cruel sadistic father?* Being an orphan was not a thought in the mind but a dark place in my character and personality I could never get used to. If the church had not condemned me so much for trying to get close to couples I would have grown out of it a lot earlier. I have never grown out of it, it had become a trap and the key to the lock could never be found.

The week was short and I would not have missed it for anything. To say goodbye to Pastor Tierney was a great necessity. Mabel drove me to the airport where we said our goodbyes too. She told me I would be welcome to come again the following year.

'Phone me when you get home. It doesn't matter what time it is,' she said as we parted company.

Once home I phoned her. She answered to my expressed surprise at her offer that she would keep the phone beside her pillow.

I continued to finish the course Pastor Tierney had been taking me through. He had been marking my work as we posted back and forth. Mabel was quite happy to carry on marking it until completed. I found it hard to carry on listening to his voice when he was not there anymore. I cried every day for a year and kept in touch with Mabel by email but getting on with life was impossible. One day as I trudged along on the pavement with a heavy heart I felt Pastor Tierney's presence sweep alongside, put an arm round my shoulder, march me at a faster pace and say, quite energetically as in one of his lessons,

'Pep in your step, right?'

I smiled and he was gone. The experience lasted me quite a few weeks.

I started to attend the Healing Balms church I had left to do his course. The pastor there fell into sin and moved on, another took his place. I tried to join in but did not feel quite at home anywhere anymore.

When I recovered slightly from the grief I enrolled on English and Maths GCSE courses and passed them both with A and C grades respectively. That made three altogether, something I never dreamed possible but trembled through all the exams. I recalled that after the Law exam I had vowed never to take another GCSE as my hands had turned ice cold and white with shock. When the Law result arrived I had been sitting by the sea in the bright sunshine at ten in the morning. I mused about opening it to kill time while waiting for an appointment. Not a soul was in sight, just God and I. Holding the envelope I wondered whether to wait until I phoned Samantha or to open it there and then. The sun wanted to see so I opened the envelope and scanned the page. B was the only letter on it. I let out a hearty laugh, knowing it would never act as a cure for me.

After the GCSEs I wanted to try an A level. Having already studied Human Biology during my nurse training I was sure to pass so applied, was accepted and prepared to start that September but my next trip to visit Mabel in Forkhampton was almost upon me which meant missing a week or two of the course.

The airport was only a forty minute train journey from my home. A friend met me there to see me off. We both sauntered to the spectators' gallery so I would know where to wave once I took off. In the ladies later on I choked back tears. Sometimes crying was a warning that something was not quite right, in other words a prophetic weeping.

At Ontario I disembarked. After two uneventful flights and collecting my luggage I could not see Mabel at first but finally a friendly arm waved. We walked in the hot sun towards her car. I reached it just ahead of her and stood waiting for her to open the door. Mabel's voice spoke out behind me,

'You need to go round the other side.'

Oops, we're in America again. On reaching her house I was greeted at the door by what looked like a miniature Doberman whose name was Bobby, a new addition to the family.

When a little settled I handed the finished course to Mabel who marked it the following day and awarded my diploma without a ceremony. In a few days it would be my birthday and Mabel planned to take me to SeaWorld in San Diego for the day. Before that at the Sunday morning church meeting, where Mabel had taken Pastor Tierney's place as pastor, God decided to show up unexpectedly. During the meeting Nadine announced something about God's love. I experienced piercing pain as the love of God tried to penetrate my heart, making my eyes water considerably. *I mustn't let them see it.* Because I had been so mishandled in churches I was afraid of being torn apart but the pain was unbearable. I held on until after the service and as soon as it was over went to the toilet to have a good cry. On my way back to the main hall, through a small kitchen, there was a full length mirror. Looking back at me was a perfectly normal, well dressed, pain free looking woman; the vastness of pain hidden beneath the surface of my skin. *Nobody would even think I'm in any pain.* I told myself, shocked and disappointed. *How then can I get the help I need?*

'We're going to the restaurant for a meal afterwards,' announced Cybil.

What? How could I possibly go there in my condition? Then I remembered, to them I looked quite normal as I had seen for myself. *Just behave then.* The restaurant became a threat and I had no money to buy a meal with anyway.

'I'll pay for it,' offered Cybil, as if to read my thoughts.

The lump in my throat grew exponentially. The pain had to come out, relief would not come otherwise. I sat opposite Cybil but my flooded eyes forbad me to read the menu.

'What do you want, Rachel?' asked Cybil.

It came easily for her and the others to choose but for me the difficulty was so great that I suddenly stood up and with the back of my knees pushed my chair away causing all eyes to penetrate me and I stood shocked as Mabel approached and stared into my face. I wondered what she thought of me. Fear accompanied my returning gaze.

'Please can I go back into the church and let go of the pain.'

'No.'

So what was I to do? I left the restaurant and wandered through the hot streets sobbing. A few people stared but I was used to it so ignored them. I thought of disappearing into the distance but that would only make matters worse so turned back and sat on a bench round the corner from the restaurant until Mabel and the others walked by, a long time later. Mabel announced they were going home but not to me. By then I felt I deserved the treatment I was getting but on the other hand all I needed was to communicate, to talk it out. There was no invitation to do so. I denied all inclination to remain where I was and followed Mabel to the car. As she drove home we did not speak. I went to my room and lay down.

Cybil had invited me to a jewelry party held later in the afternoon but the day was already ruined and as I could not mix, nor did I have any money, I felt extremely vulnerable. Mabel did not call me to go and left the house. At five o'clock I ventured upstairs. Mabel still had not returned home. I longed for a touch of motherly comfort as I peered through the lounge window. Her car was not there so I sat on the floor at the base of the radiator. After half an hour I was still sitting there when I heard her car engine and a few seconds later the key turned in the lock. She peered into the room then carried on down the hall. *She's completely ignored me*. I remained sitting there until she came back and saw me.

'Are you coming to the meeting?'

'Yes.'

I jumped up to get ready but the problem was still ignored. If she had addressed it, it would be all over by then. I was in a mood and could not shake it off. At the meeting I sat quietly and went straight to bed once we returned home.

The following day was my birthday and I wondered if the trip to San Diego would be called off. I could not imagine her doing such a thing. Mabel did call me in the morning to get up but was on the telephone for most of my valuable time. Cybil had left a present and card on the table with my breakfast. I will never forget her kindness. At about eleven o'clock Mabel decided to take me and we had a good chat driving along the Forkhampton highway. I paid for the entire trip, not only for myself but also for Mabel. What made it hard was that she could not relate to my situation. She insisted on bringing Cybil's youngest son, Elliot, who was just a baby, with her. I felt she had done that because she needed a distraction from me but it really was not necessary. When we arrived at SeaWorld I mostly wandered around on my own while she stayed somewhere close by with her grandson. How my heart ached for some of her time. We had lunch together but in a tense atmosphere and afterwards walked by an oyster stand together and, stopping there, I bought an oyster she had chosen for herself. Inside was a beautiful golden pearl which pleased her greatly. Next, the pool of whales was the highlight of my day.

'If you don't want to get splashed by the whales avoid the first ten rows,' shouted a voice from the loud speaker.

I sat where I could get soaked to cool down in the intense heat and for the fun of it. Mabel sat at the top of the bleachers with Elliot. When the show was over a lady asked,

'Would you like your picture taken with a dolphin?'

'Yes, please, I love dolphins.'

So it was arranged. The first dolphin was reluctant to come out so another took his place and I was sorry to learn that we were not allowed to touch them. I bought the photograph she had taken and displayed it with pride in my room later; if only I could have gone swimming with one.

When it was time to leave Mabel saw how wet I was from the splash of the whales and taking a towel from the car, wrapped it round me in such a motherly manner that it made every part of my day shine. She had not had the bad day she feared and never had to fear in the first place. It was only when I felt condemned, ignored and rejected that my behaviour deteriorated to that of someone starving to death – in my case, total shutdown.

A couple of days later Mabel and Cybil invited me shopping to a huge mall in the outskirts of the town. Luke came along with us. I cannot recall Elliot being there. As usual I felt like an outsider, not because they made me feel that way but just because of my customization to the fact. I kept quiet and became moodier. We stepped from the car into the forty degree Celsius heat which I welcomed like I would a bath when filthy. I prayed that we in England would experience such wonderful temperatures during our summer times. Whilst walking towards the entrance of the mall and watching the slabs of concrete pass beneath my feet a small coin beckoned my attention. I picked it up, inspected it, then called to Luke,

'Here you are, Luke, would you like a penny?'

He accepted it with Mabel's encouragement. What would he do with an English penny and what was an English penny doing outside a shopping mall in Forkhampton, the United States of America? I followed Mabel, Cybil and Luke into the mall from behind; moodiness still adding pain to my day. I needed reassurance but dared not tell them I was in trouble. It would spoil everything but were not things already spoiled? Mabel and Cybil chatted between themselves then Cybil turned to face me. She spoke some encouraging words that did not ease the pain. I needed to tell them what was wrong, thinking it would bring relief and more support. The pain worsened and I lagged further and further behind. Most people would say I was having a sulk but it was a far greater problem than a mere sulk. My body racked with unexpressed grief as I watched the closeness of the family walking ahead of me. *I shouldn't be here. I don't belong with them. I wasn't born to them. They don't even know me.* They did not turn around for a long time and so I decided it would be best if they carried on without me and hid myself round a corner. *I'll stay here till they've well gone,* but I panicked. *What if I get lost?* By then I was sure they would not notice my absence. After all, they had not turned to see if I was still with them, except for Cybil's once. Coming out of hiding, when feeling sure they were far enough away, I turned the corner. Knowing where they were headed I headed that way myself but stopped short; they were nowhere in sight. I had not expected them to vanish altogether. The mall was much bigger than I anticipated. We had arranged to have a coffee in the café area so I headed for that but they were not there. *Should I wait? No, I'll go right outside. They are bound to have noticed I'm missing and will be very angry by now; can't face that on top of all this.* I approached the outer door just beyond the café.

'Rachel!' I heard from somewhere behind me.

My stomach somersaulted but I carried on straight for the outer doors, pretending not to hear.

'Rachel!' two year old Luke bellowed from his tiny lungs.

I turned to see where they were but could see no sign of them. When a two year old calls who can resist? *Oh my goodness, I've really done it now. Why didn't I turn round the first time?* I carried on outside and stood for quite a while on some rocks, gazing at carefully placed plants. *What if they go home without me?* I made my way back inside, glanced all around but again saw no sign of them. My sandaled feet headed up one path towards the entrance. I would wait there for them till five o'clock.

It took at least fifteen minutes to get there but, once there, I found it was nothing like the entrance. *This isn't it!* None of us had a mobile phone so I had to rely on my instincts. I asked a member of staff,

'Excuse me, please can you tell me where the entrance is?'

'Sure, it's way up there at the bottom and turn right, you go the length of this path then you're there.'

Now I'm really in trouble. I hurried as fast as possible and after thirty minutes reached the reception area. Once there, I asked for an announcement to be placed over the tannoy system, letting Mabel and Cybil know where I was. While waiting I told the receptionist,

'I'm going to have a look in the car park to see if their car is still there. I'll be straight back.'

In the still blistering heat I ventured to where I remembered the car had been parked. Relieved that it was still there and that they must be still in the mall, as there was no sign of them inside, I turned back towards the reception area. When almost at the doors a voice behind me shouted,

'Rachel,' I stopped, 'get your butt back in the car!'

How on earth did they get into the car so quickly?

'You saw us in the car and just walked off.'

'I didn't see you there. I came out to see if you *were* there. It must be the high seats that hid you all from me.'

I wished I was Luke. Both Mabel and I had left announcements but neither of us heard the other's. Again, the feeling of having run away from home was upon me and that terrifying feeling of doom that always accompanied it. Once in the car both Mabel and Cybil showed how angry they were. I had lost their friendship. They had no idea of the emotional turmoil I had been through in the beginning. Mabel said,

'I'll be up early in the morning and driving you straight to the airport.'

Oh my goodness. Surely she would not do such a thing. God was the only witness who truly knew my condition so I turned to Him. He was never far from my cry. I stared out of the window and in the ever familiar atmosphere asked,

'Will she keep me, Lord?'

My head nodded slowly and hopefully imperceptibly. I knew everything would be alright in the end. Once back at Mabel's house and we were alone, I asked,

'Can't you wait till Thursday? I've made that appointment with that minister called Roland Bothkins at his church on Wednesday? He might help me.'

I had met Roland in England through a Freedom from Bondages conference where he was ministering. When I discovered he was only a forty minute drive from Mabel's I thought it a good idea to see him. Mabel had offered to take me.

'No,' she said but then softened as I knew she would.

As I stood in the kitchen she approached me with her arms opened wide and gave me the longest hug I ever had. I felt nothing. Such was the trauma of my day, and theirs to a degree. If only people could understand each other but perhaps it was a kind of internal Babel where nobody would understand the foreign life of another and with each misunderstanding we are scattered further apart.

At Roland Bothkins' nothing significant happened. I expected a great deliverance but he resorted to teaching instead. That was no good to me. Mabel and I deliberated whether I should move to Roland's clinic for a few months but I had no money and Mabel could not possibly be expected to keep an eye on me from where she lived. I let go of the idea. On Thursday Mabel drove me to the airport.

Once at home and after recovering from jet lag I gave Mabel a ring but she was not at all pleased to hear from me,

'I want you out of my life! Read the Word!! Read the Word!!' she growled, ousting me just like everybody else.

How come nobody reads in the Bible what it says about the orphan, the stranger, the outcast and the brokenhearted? My spirit rose up and in a tone unheard from me before, I firmly demanded,

'No, you are not going to get rid of me. I won't be rejected by you.'

Determined not to receive any more rejection or injustice because of pain I sought compassion and lots of it; what was alright for families had to be alright for me too. How could I behave in a manner the same as they did when I was treated with such disdain? What chance had I ever been given to feel the loving warmth of anybody close to me? For me it was the unforgiveable sin to be treated with love and favour but, just like my father, it was okay for them to be loved and favoured. I would not allow any more because I simply could not take any more. Mabel softened again and allowed me to stay in contact after that. I admired them even from the depth of my pit. Just like a beggar on the street reaching out to passersby for a few pence I recognized there was something in them that I needed but did not have the remotest chance of obtaining, unless they had a generous hand reaching back.

I had been attending the church that I was thrown out of prior to my Synagogue experience and asked for an appointment with one of the leaders. During the appointment she prayed that I would be given a fresh slate with Mabel and that week it was granted. I rang Mabel and she recounted how she had put Bobby, the little dog, out in the yard but distinctly heard God say,

'Bring Bobby in.'

She did not bring him in and God repeated His command but still she did not obey. Later on that evening she arrived back from church where Bobby was sitting on the doorstep in a pool of blood. An animal had attacked him and bitten right through a bone in his leg.

'God also told Cybil to put him into the house later but she did not have the time.'

When Mabel saw the dog God spoke to her again,

'You don't leave *anybody* out!'

From then on we were in contact from time to time and I thank God for His intervention. I was sad to hear about lively, young Bobby but God performed a miraculous cure and sealed up the hole in the bone. The following day I tried to contact the leader who had spoken to me about the clean slate but she ignored my many attempts to contact her. I could not comprehend why. For a while I continued to attend the same church. The Holy Spirit continued to come on me and during one service, whilst deeply resting under the power of the Holy Spirit, a couple of ushers came along to pick me up. It disturbed a very deep work the Holy Spirit was doing and I cried like a child who had just been woken up.

'The girls want to do a dance,' one of them said.

I was dumbfounded. *Is the Gospel all about entertainment now?* No two ways about it the church seemed to be changing in favour of performance rather than getting people healed and delivered. I needed far more healing and deliverance than anybody else. Although I had won a battle with Mabel I had not won the battle with them.

I gave up church for a while until a friend told me about Bondage Buster Ministries which dealt with setting people free from the effects of Freemasonry. God ministered to me on occasions through them and I came to believe that I had been ritually abused somewhere in my history or through the generational bloodline of my ancestry. When certain things were mentioned in the meetings like, 'being sacrificed on an altar', I would suddenly scream, shake and thrash about then receive ministry from members of the team but knew the prayers were not strong or long enough to get me completely free. There was also certain gossip going about within the ministry and generally I felt it quite disturbing.

I decided to read the Bible in forty days entirely alone and asked God to stop me everywhere that the Word applied to me and I would write it down. In the morning I read fourteen chapters of the Old Testament and in the evening fourteen chapters of the New Testament. I wrote my diary from the tenth of July to the eighteenth of August. On the first of August I read Jeremiah 30:12 onwards for the day:

12 *'This is what the LORD says:*
"Your wound is incurable,
your injury beyond healing.
13 *There is no one to plead your cause,*
no remedy for your sore,
no healing for you.
14 *All your allies have forgotten you;*
they care nothing for you.
I have struck you as an enemy would
and punished you as would the cruel,
because your guilt is so great
and your sins so many.

[15] Why do you cry out over your wound,
your pain that has no cure?
Because of your great guilt and many sins
I have done these things to you.
[16] But all who devour you will be devoured;
all your enemies will go into exile.
Those who plunder you will be plundered;
all who make spoil of you I will despoil.
[17] But I will restore you to health
and heal your wounds,"
declares the LORD,
"because you are called an outcast,
Zion (Rachel) for whom no one cares."'

How would He do this? As I pondered, His presence as a gentle breeze wafted over me. *What conference will I be going to?* But, that very night this is what happened. I quote from my diary:

'I dreamt I was in a horror film but didn't know at the time that it was a film.

I and a friend tried to escape in her open top car. I told my friend to close the roof as we sped off, glad to get away. We encountered a very steep hill and because of this the car kept slipping backwards. It couldn't make it and slipped right back down to the bottom of the hill. It was as though it landed in a deep sided, slippery basin. Our enemies were right behind us with massive rifles and guns as if to guard us. We were captured again. There were black bullets everywhere and we were made to drink them till we were full. When we were back inside a shed I told the captor that I didn't want to be in the film. He thrust money into my hand and made some understanding sympathetic remarks then went away. Another man came out and wanted an explanation. The atmosphere by now was extremely horrible and very frightening. Another guy came in and went over to the electricity plug for some reason. It was as though they were panicking that I wanted to leave. I left one part of the shed and went into another part where there was a huge vat with clear, thick fluid in it. My right hand dipped into it and came out dripping and then I woke up at about two thirty in the morning with the same thick fluid coming out of my mouth.'

I was certain I had been delivered of something. God had ministered to me during the night again. I woke on my side in a comfortable position so the fluid drained freely onto my pillow or I would have drowned. God thought of everything! When I got up later I rang Norman Flickwick Ministries for prayer. A nice sounding lady answered and interpreted my dream as the bullets being demons and that the money was the Devil trying to buy me.

While I was in Forkhampton I had told Mabel I thought it would be good for me to keep reading the Bible every forty days as God was setting me free but she suggested I needed to get an education and not be too serious about it. My own reasoning was that first things should be first but, as always, I allowed another person to decide the best thing for me. I took her advice and was also wide open to a friend's suggestion of University and attended an open day for further adult education at Cantrin. The rain was pouring down as I approached the marquee they held it in. As I turned into the opening of the canvas structure I wondered if I should pick up a University brochure to see what was on offer. A BA in Creative Writing attracted my attention. I had gathered quite a bit of education over the past few years. Dare I take a step further and go way out of my league? And so in my first year at University I did well, though nervous and shaky most of the time. I had also contracted an underactive thyroid which affected my health in quite a big way.

I left church altogether and made trips to a certain museum in London instead on Sundays. *From now on this is my church.* My legs, however, were so weak that I could barely stand at times. I was slowly dying so decided to make another one off visit to a well known church in London not far from the museum. During the evening service one of the songs, the words of which I cannot recall, filled me with fear. God was beckoning me. He knew I had had enough of life on earth and wanted desperately for it to be over. But I was so scared of Him that I screamed silently,

'Nooo!'

Being confused about His love and tangled up in my own dread of Him I backed away from His invitation, feeling sure that if I died I would go to hell, having refused to come to Him. Continuing through my health battle I wondered how I would get through the degree, part of which was an invitation to see the opera, La Boheme. I made enquiries about how to reach the opera house and when the day arrived, caught the train to the closest station. Making my way down the country lanes towards the venue a red mini turned in the road. I flagged the lady driver down and asked directions which she kindly gave.

'It's between half an hour to a forty minute walk,' she said and drove on.

I wondered how I would make it but as I usually made everything through great difficulty it was an automatic thing to keep going. Two seconds later the same car drew up alongside me and offered a lift all the way to my destination. Again I acted as normal as possible. I did not want to end up being taken to hospital. After meeting up with others from my class and finding our seats I watched the story line unfold and became deeply identified with the star, a broken hearted lady who wanted nothing more but to die. After the interval I could barely make it up the stairs. My body felt like a sack of lead and my heart palpitated. *Should I tell someone?* I sat back in my place and not long into the second part I heard the friends of the star reciting,

'She can hardly make it up the stairs.'

Involuntary tears ran down my face. Still later, as the star lay dying and I too sat feeling my life ebbing away, I heard the friends pray,

'Don't put this candle out.'

Again tears ran down my face as I braced myself for the inevitable 'putting out'. I longed to be cared for as the star was but I had nobody to pray such a prayer for me. Over the years I had come to feel that I was a nuisance to everybody, especially when needing extra help. But then thought about my looks and understood that people would be put off first because of those. An object of scorn I managed to maintain some dignity throughout the evening and fooled everyone to think I was just like them.

A few days later, while on a train to Bramington, I met a girl who I had known since Matthew Minnerton's days,

'I've been praying for you for two years,' she announced.

My head spun. *Me? You prayed for me?* She announced that Evelyn Perristaff of a certain Ministries in Australia was coming to England. As I was at a standstill in my life I felt that might well be an invitation from the Holy Spirit. Using my credit card I paid for the conference she was to hold in Somerset. Evelyn has a ministry to set people free from all kinds of occult bondages. I could not cry out enough to God for His intervention. *This must be my big breakthrough.*

A few days after being informed about Evelyn Christine informed me of a local, though not that local, church which seemed to be the hope of my dreams. The Holy Spirit was moving powerfully and they loved people, she said. Those two combinations were a great attraction but I was hesitant and asked God if I should go. I thought maybe it was my last chance, that God was about to lose all patience and cast me from the earth. I had not been to any church for about a year and a half. *Can I trust it this time? Is this really the church for me?* I did not go immediately but eventually went along.

Chapter Nine

Back to Church

My first Sunday at the new fellowship was hosted by a lay preacher, a member of the congregation, while the main pastor, Raymond Carlison, was away at a leader's conference. On his return the following week I was introduced to him. I sat in the front with Scarlet, a lady who had taken me and a friend of Christine's, and thoroughly enjoyed the meeting. When it was time for prayer the Holy Spirit came on me powerfully as was usual at other churches and afterwards Raymond came over to talk to me. I opened up and chatted quite a bit but refrained from telling him too much about myself. I told Christine I would never tell a leader again about myself as it only ended in heartache. It was not long, however, that I learned I was in safe hands. God reopened my heart with the love found in that beautiful church, revealing its emptiness once more.

The church held meetings at ten o'clock on Sunday mornings and again in the evenings at six. Worship, a message and then a call forward for prayer was the only structure. The Holy Spirit could do what He pleased. Raymond, standing on the doorstep, welcomed people at the door with a hug and sometimes a kiss. As I was starved of affection it was a great welcome and jogged the memory of my mother standing on our front garden path with her hand over her eyes welcoming us home from school, though I never realized that was why she was there at the time. I told the pastor about the conference with Evelyn and he seemed uneasy about it but as I had already booked I went along. Once at the venue I felt extremely uncomfortable at the style of preaching. The discomfort was at such a pitch that I phoned Raymond. He put the decision to remain or leave firmly into my hands. Perhaps my thoughts were sparked by the Devil trying to stop me getting a miracle. At the end of that first meeting I made my way to Evelyn's husband, Scott, and told him how I was feeling. He seemed resigned to it and I could not understand why he said nothing to encourage me to stay but because of that I stayed and tolerated the forceful preaching. However, I sat up and took notice when Evelyn spoke about guards watching over us, making sure we would not get free. I recognized my nightmare of the year before. After prayer ministry as I lay on the floor under God's power the familiar thick fluid oozed out of my mouth. I wondered if it would ever stop being a way of healing for me. The shame I felt at not having a normal life was ever present. At testimony time I shared my dream and later one of the team invited me to Australia, a school Evelyn held of ten days duration. The school was held at their headquarters every year but I thought it hardly likely that I would accept. The thought of travelling such a great distance alone was way out of my imagination.

Every conference, not only Evelyn's, was a battle. Despite everything, I always made my own travel plans and because of insecurity made sure I got up extra early to be first in the queue in order to avoid suffering intense agony. Very rarely did anybody come with me to the queue. If they did they would often come later on because I offered to save them a place but they never offered to get up and pay the same price in return. I had tried asking ministries for reserved seating to avoid the sheer stress of having to always be in the front of the queue but it was not granted. Only people in wheelchairs were granted that but not the emotionally damaged.

Norman Flickwick, who had held miracle services, came to a town in Cheshire one year. My eldest brother and his wife lived in a village not too far away and allowed me to stay with them. As usual I was in the queue extra early. The first night of two I entered the venue with the others and had to sit in the bleachers. Suddenly, I recognized one of the ushers and asked if I could come down to sit at floor level which was reserved for pastors,

'Jump over, Rachel,' he said.

I did and sat, with the permission of the Norman Flickwick team, calmer and felt looked after.

'Please will you remember me tomorrow and let me sit here again,' I begged one of the team.

'Yes, we will.'

I stared, trying to detect her honesty. Unsure of whether I could trust her or not, I still got up early next morning. Usually I took so much baggage with me but that morning I purposely extracted many items from my bag. However, while clasping my lilac address book I became confused. *Should I take it or leave it?* It hovered in my hand for a moment and finally I decided to take it. Removing my keys also I left for a miraculous day. God would heal me then my brother and sister-in-law would be healed too. Disappointingly, though, nothing happened, so it must happen on the second and final night.

I arrived at the venue doors at eleven in the morning. By three o'clock crowds had gathered and it became difficult to move. When the doors finally opened I asked one of the ushers where I should go and that I had been reassured by Norman Flickwick's team that I could sit at floor level with the pastors.

'You go up to door sixteen.'

It was a long way round and I soon discovered I had been directed to the back of the auditorium. A queue of pastors was in front of me and when I finally got to the ushers who were directing the pastors to their seats I was confronted,

'Have you got a letter?'

'No.'

'Sorry, we can't let you in.'

I jolted and stared across to the grey haired lady at the front of the auditorium.

'That lady said I could sit down there with the pastors.'

I showed my disability rail card.

'Sorry, we can't let you in without a letter.'

Everything inside me went into a whirl of activity.

'*You* can ask her!' I screamed, as though on my death bed.

The stress on me trying to get a secure seat was overwhelming. Tears surged through my body into my red face and escaped through bulging eyes as I stood stock still. The usher suggested,

'You can go and ask her but you have to go right round the outside of the auditorium.'

'I can't, there's so many people filling the seats,' the words bellowed from my ever tightening throat.

I abruptly turned only to find the stairs behind me blocked with more pastors streaming in; it was almost impossible to get back up. They stared at me as though they had only just woken up and were unmoved at my outburst. I pushed my way through in desperation, still screaming in panic and pain, until an usher with a sympathetic face asked what was wrong. He pointed a finger to a shortcut through the auditorium,

'Look, go round the seats this way.'

By then I felt totally humiliated. I had been there since eleven and all my plans for a peaceful and secure entry were totally demolished. Hurriedly, I passed the chairs skirting the auditorium which felt like a ten minute journey. Finally, I reached my destination only to find massive confusion. An usher stopped me as I approached the way in to the pastors' area.

'You can't go there,' she said.

'Yes, I can. That lady with the grey hair said she would let me in. She knows me from last night.'

The grey haired, well built, lady kept as low a profile as possible and refused to come to my aid. I looked to my side at the bleachers. I could only go into the third row by then. A couple of ladies invited me to join them there but I was no longer secure and would not be able to get out of the centre of the row quickly or easily. Totally trapped, I refused the offer and continued to make my way towards the pastors' section on the floor. Eventually, a chair was placed for me to sit near the platform to wait until all the pastors had taken their seats. It was useless but still I had hopes that they would find me a suitable chair where I would feel safe and looked after. Sobs racked my body. Norman Flickwick's doctor friend headed my way, patted me on the head, said nothing and walked right on by. A lady usher also approached and asked,

'Would you like to sit with me at the back?'

'No, I can't. I have to sit at the front.'

How could I make anybody understand? Finally, I was tended to and told,

'Follow that usher.'

The usher took me across the main floor and led me to about fifteen or so rows back on the left hand side. He had found a row of three chairs and that is where I sat for the rest of the meeting. *I should have just been normal and gone in the first entrance. Now look at it. It's so cruel and unfair.* At least I was on the floor. A young couple sat on the inner two chairs. I asked them to mind my seat while I went off to buy some things then joked about having to use my credit card. When I returned the meeting got under way as normal and I chatted to the couple sitting beside me informing them of my awful experience. Finally, I calmed down. As was my habit before the worship I took my glasses off, put them in their case and was determined not to put them back on because I wanted my eyes healed. However, an urge came over me to put them back on. *Why put them back on when I want them healed?* I left them off no matter how strong the continuing urge was to put them on. People were joining the line to go up to the stage because they had received a healing and had a testimony to tell, I followed. I wanted to be prayed for by Norman Flickwick for my healing. While still in the queue I overheard one female usher say to another,

'He's going to do a call for salvation.'

Oh no! I sensed they were saying it to get me out of the way so stayed put. Suddenly, I felt the urge to go back to my seat; it persisted more strongly than the time I felt to put my glasses on. *How can I go back now when there's so many ushers always getting at me*. I had had enough by that time and could not face any more so remained where I was. Another urge came but I ignored it. *Perhaps it was the Devil trying to stop me getting a healing?* The urge did not come again. The call for salvation did though and I went forward to the front of the stage to get a 'touch from the Lord'. It did not come but I was hemmed into the front by the crowd and could not return to my seat until they had all dispersed; a long time later. The crowd finally eased and I made my way back to my seat only to discover all my belongings had vanished. I became frantic. An usher directed me to the control room to see if any lost property had been handed in but it had not. The police were called and thankfully I knew my brother's phone number off by heart. The staff phoned him. He got out of bed to drive the forty minute journey to the venue. I waited but informed my sister-in-law that my keys were in my suitcase with a tag on them.

'Okay, I'll phone your credit card protection to let them know.'

I understood why I had been led to empty so much stuff in the morning but could not understand why I decided to take the address book. All my contacts were missing. *If only I had put that back!* The thief or thieves would have noticed my disability rail card in my purse. I understood then that God was the one who was trying to warn me, by urging me to keep my glasses on and go back to my seat. Why I did not receive a healing at the healing service I did not know and came away confused. Why had Norman Flickwick not been given a word of knowledge that a thief was about to strike? Next day my sister-in-law helped me buy a coat from a charity shop. I loved the black, shiny PVC jacket they had stolen. After I returned home I needed to deal with the repercussions of the theft – something thieves never think about regarding their victims. I left my brother and sister-in-law without a good impression of Norman Flickwick's ministry.

Back at church that Sunday I stood waiting for a hug hello and a hug goodbye at the end of the service. Everybody in the small congregation loved each other and they loved us new ones too, at least, it looked and felt like love. I thought they understood me but as time went by I learned I was wrong.

Around that time I traced Len Bradwith using the internet *(the man who had taken Margaret and me out at weekends as children)* and ventured to make contact by letter, not knowing if after all these years he still lived at the same address. I thought it highly unlikely but to my surprise I received a welcoming reply so visited him once or twice. Each visit was filled with fear but prayer helped me face the visits with trust in God that Len would not advance towards me. *After all he is eighty.* He was healthy and helped his niece with her business from his home. She lived abroad. I arrived at his house one day out of the blue on a very wet, rainy day, wearing my rain gear and carrying a cross to put on my mother's grave. My socks were soaked. He kindly cooked me an egg on toast and dried my socks over the fire. When they were dry I left to place the cross on my mother's grave and then returned. A few minutes before it was time to leave I rang National Rail to check on train times. The whole of London had a blackout and the trains were few and far between. I did not mention it to Len, deciding instead to risk the journey home, fearing he may invite me to stay overnight. I could never defend myself in case I hurt the other person's feelings. If there was a way out of a situation quietly I would take it quickly.

In my letters I had asked Len if I could have copies of slides he had taken of us as children but he said only if I would go over and stay for a day or two. Of course it petrified me so I quietly refused. He led me to the door, stepped outside and with his back turned to the houses opposite tried to give me a long, open mouthed kiss. So my misgivings were confirmed. Stunned and disgusted I turned my face away but, as usual, did not put up a fuss for his sake.

'That's not love,' he said.

I left him and the slides hoping to be able to get them at a safer time. A month or so later Samantha phoned to say she would like to come down.

'Will you come to Kent? We can see Uncle Len together.'

She had met him on a couple of occasions as a child and stayed with him and Aunty Mo for a couple of weeks, separately from Peggy and me, so agreed to come. The day after she arrived we made our way, with some chocolate for him, towards his home.

'He's in, there's a car outside.'

We knocked on the door and unexpectedly his niece Cynthia opened it. Len was in hospital. After greeting Cynthia she took us to see him. He was dying and could no longer fight for a life he felt he had no more use for. He tried to make me smile but failed and told Samantha he had invited me to stay with neighbours so we could sort out the slides but that was not true. I could not have stayed with strangers even if he had invited me. We left knowing his remaining time may be short on the earth. At home I waited for Cynthia's reports on his condition. At church the following Tuesday night I became upset during the prayer meeting which was led by Brian *(the only elder at the time).* The Holy Spirit was touching me but nobody took any notice. At the end Brian announced,

'We'll close now.'

I quickly stood and declared,

'The Holy Spirit is on me and you want to close the meeting. And you don't care.'

I paced the floor but Raymond came over and gently chided me,

'Does he deserve that?'

'No.'

Raymond put his arm round my shoulder and I felt all at once protected and equally considered. That kind of discipline was the best for a broken person. I was crying and draped my right arm over Raymond's nearest shoulder. It was the same position I had been in once with Uncle Len's shoulder when I was nineteen, ready for a photograph. Raymond gently prized me away and sat me on a chair to the side of the room. It was the following day that I fully understood what had happened. Cynthia phoned to say Uncle Len died and it happened to be the exact time I cried at the meeting. Neither Raymond nor Brian could have known but the Holy Spirit did.

Uncle Len's funeral was arranged by Cynthia and I asked Raymond if he could take me. He replied that he would see what he could do. He told me later a couple would take me over there. He would be visiting somebody in Bedford and would not be phoning until after eleven o'clock that night so I waited up until the phone rang.

'I will be there with Brendon at seven thirty in the morning to pick you up.'

Brendon was Raymond's only son and a nice lad of eighteen. I praised and thanked God that I had not been let down. They both turned up as arranged and the funeral went well. Later, we went to Cynthia's *(Uncle Len's house)* for something to eat. When we left I told Raymond my mother's grave was only round the corner and asked if he could take me but he refused. He and Brendon wanted to get back to the football but I was grateful for what they had done and always will be.

At church God was still setting me free. During the services I manifested and fluid continued to ooze out of my mouth. Sometimes I hit out during the ministry, not knowing if anybody was nearby. The tenderness of the ministry team began a deep healing. Raymond prayed for me and the team would take over but sometimes when I got too violent Raymond put a stop to it. I could not help it as I so easily welcomed the Holy Spirit to do as He pleased. *I should be totally free soon.* A few weeks later the Devil got wind of the move of the Holy Spirit and how people were getting set free. One day as I lay crying, screaming or thrashing about in pain or demonic manifestation Raymond came over and knelt beside my head,

'If you don't stop I'll put you outside.'

I was shocked to hear such a comment. Surely God was doing as He pleased with me so He should be allowed.

'You mean you would put me out in the road,' I asked him afterwards.

'Yes, well out on the doorstep till you calmed down.'

Before going home I mentioned to Raymond that the music was a nice level, not too loud but not long after the comment they turned up the volume. Being unable to bear it I went outside for the rest of the worship and sang on my own from the doorstep. One of the ministry team followed me out. She was called Roberta and was the wife of Oswald who had just been appointed as a deputy pastor by Raymond from a church a couple of towns away. I opened up to her explaining that I wanted Jesus to come, adding,

'You know, in Isaiah 54:2 in the Bible where God says, *"Stretch your tent curtains wide",* I believe He is saying you should include people like me who you don't know how to help.'

When the preaching started I returned inside and on it went week after week. The congregation, in the tiny red bricked church, grew in numbers because of the moving of the Holy Spirit. Pastor Raymond accumulated quite a few leaders from those who had not been leaders when they arrived and none of whom he knew very well. I had been in fellowships where hastily promoted and unqualified leaders could not stay the course, some falling into sin.

One Wednesday, while a team of us were cleaning out the church, Raymond turned to me and said,

'Nobody likes me.'

'Why?'

He merely stared at me. I could not see how anybody could not like him. He was down to earth, confident and well in control in the meetings. At one Sunday morning meeting as I waited for God to come and minister Raymond said,

'I can see warrior angels getting ready to do battle.'

Yes, they are coming to set me free. They did come and I received the power of their deliverance with the usual thrashing and fluid pouring from my mouth. However, Raymond was becoming more uncomfortable with it. After one such meeting, knowing this, I asked him,

'Why don't you get people who need deliverance together outside of the main meeting, say, a meeting during the week? Just let God come during worship and you just be there to help us.'

'Yes, we are organizing that.'

My hopes were up and I was prepared to wait and I did - forever. However, I had made progress and was beginning to express myself freely during worship and wondered about making flags but every decision I made was a real upheaval. Tentatively, I managed to make both large and small flags which I and others waved during worship. Was it right to be making flags? While continuing to make them in my lounge, producing many vibrant coloured ones, I asked,

'Lord, do you like these? They are not healing the sick, raising the dead or anything,'

His answer came as a gentle breeze and I cried.

However, I was not sure whether it was a 'yes' or 'no' and because it was not clear I carried on.

Sometimes, if I was feeling too much pain in a meeting and knew I would be totally ignored I waved a flag around a bit hard until the stick snapped in two.

'I'm sorry,' I said, addressing Raymond.

'It's okay, it's gone,' he said while waving a hand over his head which meant he forgave me.

A year and a half went by of the wonderful presence of God and He ministered to us every time we met. Every day was a new day as the logo read on the wall at the front of the church. I loved the fellowship but knew I had to stay at a distance which was very hard because being with them was opening me up. When Raymond prayed for me I was able to receive from God very easily because of the love in him. I lay on the floor under the power of God feeling unthreatened and listened to his wife singing beautifully in worship. As I listened to the words God's presence swept over me again and again but sometimes if the words hit a sore place or some demonic entity, a manifestation was the result. Eventually, Raymond became impatient. Was I not warned about the impatience of people before I went to

Mackton? At one meeting I was lying on the floor crying or in some kind of state when he came, picked me up and slammed me into a chair. I continued to concentrate on what God was doing and held on to it with all my strength. It seemed obvious to me that we were up against a demonic brick wall in my life that was not about to shift. Because of the manifestation I came under strong discipline and eventually my behaviour changed for the worse. I prayed for hours pouring out my heart to God and begging for His help. When He came it was always in church, which meant even more manifestations and more trouble. Would trouble ever end? Another day after the service Raymond told me he was going on an outing with his daughter; I needed some good memories to combat the bad ones so asked,

'Can I come for the drive?'

'No!'

They wanted to be alone and my hopes of an outing or having a 'father' figure to enjoy for a few hours were dashed. I never asked again but I did ask,

'Can we have an orphan's day?'

'Yes,' he replied and walked away.

They often took the youth to places but us older ones, I felt, were kept at arms length and, even though my begging was a desperate plea, I was ignored.

Raymond tried to move me on to Oswald and Roberta. He also wanted me to respond to other people praying for me but I was too insecure and afraid of being damaged all over again. If Raymond kept praying for me and allowed me to get the stability I needed I would eventually heal and open up to others naturally instead of being forced. I could not do what he said so withdrew into God and tried to get my touch from Him alone.

When I finally succumbed to Oswald and Roberta they took me to their house after church one Sunday. At first I felt uneasy but later came to life a bit. They had rabbits and snakes. I thought it unusual for a pastor to own snakes as they signified the devil but I liked the down to earth way the couple had about them. Perhaps I would get used to them in time but when Raymond was around I only wanted to go to him. For me it was a natural thing to do. In my early days he said I could phone him at any time of the day or night. Of course night times, I reasoned, would only be for emergencies and my emotional condition was a state of emergency at times. He would describe events out of his life experiences which helped more than any sermon. The time he took to talk to me was a lifesaver. His wife, however, never spoke to me.

One week Raymond invited a guest speaker, named David, who none of the congregation had met, to the fellowship and he got into conversation with me,

'You are a princess. As with John, Jesus wants to take you on a tour of Heaven.'

I already knew that sometime God would do something special in my case. As time went by I became sure it must have been wishful thinking but he was the second person to say something like that, albeit years apart.

Because of the influx of people, mainly from other churches, our little building was bursting at the seams. Raymond decided larger premises were vital but some of us did not agree – *'better a crust of bread and love than... ',* Proverbs 17:1. I prayed earnestly that God would speak to Raymond about his plans to move to a new building and not long afterwards Raymond's father died. While visiting him in Bedford just before he died the Holy Spirit asked him,

'What are you doing?'

When Raymond arrived back from Bedford and told us what the Holy Spirit said. I leapt for joy *(statically and silently).* Raymond, though, ignored the Voice and went ahead with his plans. Many opposed him but he found a church to rent for a while which he later bought through the Movement's headquarters' finances.

'There's a bus right up to the door,' he informed me.

My stomach turned over as I envisioned the lifts he had been giving me to church and back home threatened and therefore my continued healing and sense of security. I discovered the bus did not go from anywhere near my home so made the hour's walk to the church every Sunday. If Raymond drove past he often picked me up, after picking up others. That meant I did not get greeted at the door so after finding my seat I came out again for my greeting and hug. I chatted with him and he tolerated it but sometimes acted like he did not want to talk. However, he made me feel welcome so I stayed to talk, not realizing that deep down in his heart he loathed my coming. It was clear to me that God was using him to heal me but he did not want to be used in that way anymore.

I often helped clean the church; decorating and sorting things out when needed. Later on I cared for the two small flower beds at the front of the church, outside. I bought plants with my own money thinking that if people saw flowers they would forget their problems and enter the church with joy.

Raymond made regular visits to David in Wales for mentoring and David came to speak more regularly in the new building. After one such service I asked Raymond to pray for me as I was in much physical pain. He refused. Before we left the old building people gossiped about me, constantly criticizing my going up to Raymond after the meetings for a chat. His reason for saying no to ministering to me was to put a stop to all that and also the reason why he pushed me over to others but I could not possibly trust others! I knew what I needed and when he walked away I followed. Nobody can make a broken person behave in a certain way, like act normally, because they are not normal. They only have the capacity to act according to their brokenness. Not accepting his 'no' for an answer I stood nearby waiting and when I finally gained his attention, told him,

'When you pray for me I always receive from the Lord. It is the Holy Spirit; He only comes on me when you pray. '

'It isn't the Holy Spirit.'

He put his hands on my shoulders and my knees buckled slightly at the Holy Spirit's power and I went down under the power but not to the floor.

'You see, it *is* Him.'

'No, it isn't.'

I was sure his behaviour was for the benefit of David but it had a devastating affect on me. My stomach turned as I panicked at having to spend the rest of the day alone at home, stirred up emotionally and left with the pain. Turning to David I started to explain what was going on and ended up shouting with frustration at being misunderstood. Outside later I told Raymond,

'I'm so hungry. It's my food.'

'It's not your food.'

'Yes, it is.'

Later that week I phoned Oswald, afraid of what they may be saying and doing behind my back,

'Is everything okay with me?'

'Well, seeing as you ask, no, it isn't. You made such a scene on Sunday and your going after Raymond has to stop. His people know him. You are not to send him any texts or speak to him and if he doesn't do something we are going to go over his head.'

'I'm going to Australia soon to try to get help.'

'Well, we'll leave it till you come back from Australia and then…'

On putting the phone down I texted Raymond to inform him of what Oswald had said. My whole world collapsed. I was left with nothing. A family is with each other every day but I was only with them for one morning and two evenings per week. *How would they like it if they were me?* That night I lay worried about my whole life and again its history was on the surface of my mind. I cried out to God.

'Have mercy on me, Lord, have mercy on me.'

I went deeper and deeper into a place with God beseeching mercy from Him until He answered by giving me a picture. I suddenly saw Oswald in my mind, that tiny pastor, walking towards me carrying a huge chain as thick as any I ever saw and almost twice as long as he was tall. God had shown me what was about to happen and with a determination in my spirit I prayed,

'Oh no, you don't! I break that chain, in the name of Jesus.'

I said nothing to anybody about the vision but that Tuesday I walked to the prayer meeting. The orange chairs from the old building had been brought in to replace the pews which Raymond had us strip out when we moved but there were a couple of pews at the back of the church. I lay under one of them and buried my head underneath my cap but still joined in the meeting as much as I could, worshipping God and crying. Oswald was favoured above me; though he had been told a few times that he was being too hard with the Bible on us. Raymond, over the past year or so had stood up for me when the other leaders wanted to throw me out and I valued it highly. After all, it was all I knew – being thrown out and rejected.

'We never throw anybody out,' he told the congregation.

As I lay under the pew Raymond spoke a word of knowledge, 'Some of you have had chains of restriction put on you.'

My ears pricked up. A great sense of relief swept over me and I wanted to go forward and ask for prayer but dared not budge and nobody bothered to come to my aid. They only wanted Raymond themselves. In my observation Oswald was always talking to Raymond at the door and nobody said anything about that. At the end of the meeting I gathered my flags and left but they were too heavy so I turned back. Raymond was sitting at the front on the edge of the platform and welcomed me to sit by him. I did so eagerly and some of my burden lifted. That night he gave me a lift home. Later in the week he came to see me at home with his wife, Gail. As he talked I listened to his telling me off for constantly texting and phoning him. I could not speak so he got up from his seat shouting at me as he left the flat. Gail stood next to me and I knew her support was for him and rightly so I suppose. I was never against Raymond no matter what he did to me. I loved him and his family a lot.

'I have something to tell you,' I said, panicking but in a calm way. No, he was going to leave. I continued, 'It's about you.'

Gail, still standing beside me, said nothing then Raymond returned. I proceeded to tell him about the word of knowledge he had on the Tuesday and the picture I had of Oswald carrying that huge chain and wanting to take any decision over his head. He seemed to take it to heart.

Raymond had succumbed to other people's complaints about my going to him after the meetings. Not one of them knew why I did what I did. He still allowed me to talk to him but reluctantly and sometimes walked away in the middle of a conversation. I would be left waiting to finish it later. If we had finished the first time I would not have waited but gone home. It caused him to accuse me of hanging around after him but I wanted to finish the conversation and so on it went every week. I had always encouraged Raymond concerning his gifting in the Holy Spirit but he always tore himself down.

In the early days when Raymond gave me a lift home he would jump out of the car to give me a hug. He always brought others in the car with him and, though that was welcome in my eyes, I felt that I was not trusted. He did not have to do that with his daughters and I certainly was not going to do anything out of the ordinary but he explained,

'It isn't you; it's what others may think.'

It was hard because of that but it was okay too as he did give me quite a few lifts and when he did I was healed a little more. Like a starving beggar I had to extract what goodness I could find from those in authority and many times I would hear that people who do such things are a drain and a nuisance. Being accepted by the person in authority was like a valuable jewel, a much needed balm for my soul, but the idea of being a parasite drove me to many thoughts of suicide.

One evening as I was chatting with Roberta at the back of the church and simply trusting her with my soul, our conversation came round to Gail who had had an illness for many years. It was getting worse and put down to my going to Raymond all the time.

'You mean I am making Gail ill?'

'Yes.'

'She's a pastor's wife. I'm not even touching her and if she loved me too that would really help. If she cannot cope with people with problems like mine then why is she a pastor's wife? I'm going to write her a letter.'

The accusation left me stunned. Gail was making herself ill with her own assumptions and insecurities. As soon as I finished speaking to Roberta, being unable to wait to write the letter, I marched straight up to Gail at the front of the church.

'Gail, am I making you ill?'

With that she lost her temper.

'I know you've had a hard life but stop going up to Raymond after the services or you will lose him altogether. You've chosen the wrong one there.'

'Gail, I would never hurt you, I love you. Besides which, this is a house of God.'

Why would I go about looking to sin when I was seeking the Lord? It did not make sense and she did not make sense but made up her mind to cast me off. The only words she had ever spoken to me when she did accompany Raymond were,

'You're judging.'

'I'm not judging. I'm just telling what happened.'

My mind swam as I saw yet more opportunity for healing going down the drain. Tears ran down my face at her lack of trust and that, despite my terrible history, her helping hand was nowhere to be found. I left the hall. Raymond was standing at the door as I exited where he have me a much needed hug.

Gail's worship to Jesus was something I always looked forward to. God always met with me when she sang. My disturbed behaviour negated any love I felt towards them and remained a problem. They misinterpreted everything I did, causing me to cry to God for deliverance even more than usual but Raymond no longer wanted deliverance in his church as he said it was,

'Too dangerous.'

Then the Kingdom of God is not welcome here either. My heart sank as I saw the Gospel of Jesus Christ yet again being turned away. I knew there were ways He could deliver us but Raymond was not allowing even private sessions with individuals. I came to the conclusion that he did not really want people to be set free because that is the bottom line and it matters deeply to God. He put his own safety before the bound up flock he was supposed to care for. Because I loved them and had seen so many times what happened to pastors who turned away from the suffering of others I was afraid for him and the fellowship. Despite it all I continued to attend the meetings and wave my flags during the worship and God continued to meet with me but He no longer came with the same power. The Holy Spirit began to be limited only to happy people and not sad ones. Some of us were no longer tolerated. During one meeting when the power of the Holy Spirit came on me I was completely neglected and Raymond spoke to the congregation as I lay looking dead on the floor,

'You might think we are being hard on her and treating her badly. Well, we are.'

I lay vulnerably swallowing the words as though drinking poison. He had just betrayed himself. He had already put guards to watch over me. If I was a 'disturbance' in the meeting somebody would come and either sit or stand by me. I did not feel loved anymore but like a prisoner. There was not an ounce of compassion in them that I could detect and I had no idea how to handle it. One woman with long blonde hair and always chewing gum (*Georgina, Brian's daughter)* stood in front of me blocking my view. They were thinking that when I looked at Raymond I was fixed on him but I was not. I concentrated all my thoughts on Jesus and hoped Raymond would be compassionate enough to allow Him to come to me. After all he was the pastor at the front so how could I not look at him? The whole situation caused so much pain.

One time a man who does a miming act was invited to the church. I sat at the front with my flags. The talented man mimed a piece called, 'The Father'. He placed a chair on the stage and welcomed the Father. Father issues always tore me apart and that day was no exception. As he mimed to a CD my heart began to tear. I turned towards the back of the church where Raymond was because my behaviour was about to crumble as I tried to cooperate with the drama. I knew I should sit quietly out of respect for everybody else in the meeting but the pain was unbearable. He was talking to somebody but glanced towards me. I was trying to get his help. As the pain rushed through I kicked out at my flags which were on the floor and before I knew it a well built, strong man was standing before me. He grabbed me round the top half of my body and began carrying me out of the meeting. I screamed with all my might as I was being wrenched from the 'Father' I desperately needed. Just because I was reacting did not mean I was rebelling. My screams went unheeded and I was carried out of the church with arms and legs outstretched while begging for release for all I was worth and grabbing the upper part of the wooden door whilst staring at the actor on the stage. I longed for him to help but he did not.

'Crucify her! Crucify her!' he and the congregation jeered in their silent witness.

Once out in the small front porch Raymond arrived and, pointing a finger in my face, told me off for my behaviour. I was then carried into the lounge and the door was blocked by the bouncer as he stood in the way of my returning to any hope of getting healed. Once the initial impact of my heart tearing was over I would have relaxed. I often told Raymond that all he needed to do was lay a hand on my head. I would go under the power of the Holy Spirit and be okay. I thought they were used to that kind of behaviour with a healing ministry. Soon Roberta entered the room with Brian. I liked Brian but he did not have very much to do with me. They were not coming to help but to shut me up. The bouncer continued to block me despite my trying to prize him away from the door. He was a wall of concrete.

'Let me back in, let me back in. God will heal me.'

I gave up, falling completely apart at the traumatic handling and lay on the floor until a measure of calmness returned but the meeting was going on and I was missing out on such an important issue in my life. Eventually, I sat on the sofa with Roberta on one side and Brian on the other,

'Why… wh.. wh .. why... wh, wh, why are you treating me this way?'

My body heaved again with the sobbing. My back arched backwards with the agony. All of a sudden I felt like Jesus Himself who had been so cruelly nailed to the cross and betrayed by the church I so loved. Why did Raymond not rescue me? Where was the compassion in any of my God forsaken life? Time went by and I was convinced the meeting must be almost over.

'Please let me go back in. I'll be alright now.'

At last, because the guest speaker was finished but the meeting not quite over, I was allowed back into church. They opened the door and I was guarded heavily from going through the front entrance,

'Please let me in.'

'No, you must sit at the back.'

Lashed by those words, I had no choice. What did they know about such agony?

'You have to walk round the building, not through it.'

'Okay.'

I walked with Brian in resignation; all trust in him gone. Raymond was speaking and seemed not at all moved as I began to sob my heart out again at the back. A lady came over and put a hand on my leg as if to sympathize but I was beyond comfort. Brian told me to go home without seeing Raymond but, like a small child having been cruelly separated from its parents, I could not leave without a hug. Brian sat on the wall outside trying to reason with me but to no avail.

'I'm not after him in a wrong way, I need a father,' I begged yet again.

Brian used all the force of his gentle personality to get me to go home in such a condition without a hug from Raymond but gradually succumbed.

'If I go in and ask Raymond, promise me you won't speak to him, just have a hug.'

'Okay.'

'I'll see what I can do.'

Not long afterwards Raymond emerged and quickly gave me a hug, then left. My world collapsed further and I was left desolate. God had told them just like He had told the fellowship in Mackton what I needed but they in no way wanted to give it. Why they would not give me what I asked for when it would heal me is beyond my comprehension. And it is not just boys and men that need a pure father's touch!

'It's all what YOU want,' they usually said.

No, it's what I NEED, even God says so.

A relatively new man to the fellowship spoke to Raymond in my hearing one Tuesday prayer meeting and explained that he had a picture of me. That I was like a shell but when he looked inside there was nothing there. In his giving this God was trying to vindicate me. I suppose if you are so stuffed with demons how can there possibly be room for yourself? Just a constant yearning to get rid of the things.

In time I recovered from that episode but Raymond was not going to budge concerning me. I had to behave in the way he demanded, which meant covering up the pain instead of dealing with it. The gentle compassion I received at the beginning was tampered with by Satan and came to an end by his manipulating others, forcing his thoughts into theirs.

If I was an inconvenience, people simply walked away or gave advice that I could not do anything with.

Chapter Ten

Australia

My trip to Australia was upon me. Way back in June Raymond promised to drive me to the airport. He had become reluctant but I insisted he keep his word for my sake that I would not have to suffer the unbearable rejection and disappointment. He said he would let me know and when he did it was around five in the afternoon on the day of departure. I had to leave at five thirty. He arrived with Oswald and Scarlet *(the member of the congregation who had taken me to the first ever meeting there).* Oswald and Raymond, remaining ignorant to any desire of mine, sat in the front. It had been my dream, as usual, to go to the airport with 'parents', in other words somebody I felt I belonged to and as he was my pastor then it was him. I said nothing and felt I was being driven to prison rather than the airport and could not talk because of the atmosphere created by my spiritual carers. Oswald talked for most of the two hours journey and Scarlet slept. I watched the glorious sunset and Raymond too loved it, he announced voluntarily. I said nothing then stared at something near the roof of the car.

'Are you okay, Rachel?' asked Raymond.

'Yes, I just wondered what that was.'

He explained what it was but I was unable to listen. That was all the verbal contact I had with any of them for the entire journey. *Is he scared of Oswald?*

On arrival at the airport I was dropped off and given a quick hug,

'Give a hug to Oswald,' Raymond ordered.

I obeyed reluctantly. They returned to the car and I was left to continue walking alone to the compound. Raymond's oval, expressionless face peered from behind the windscreen as he approached the level crossing; he waved to let me cross. Such a cold departure caused me to feel like a crushed rose whose thorns turned inwards and embedded into its delicate interior stem. *They hate me.* I wondered why it was considered normal for families to enjoy the closeness I yearned for and yet my yearning was considered an unforgiveable sin. I braced myself against the pain and made my way towards the special needs counter. We took off at ten thirty and soared the London skies. The flight was eventless. We *(the passengers and I)* disembarked at Hong Kong and, after about an hour, re-embarked on the freshly fuelled plane. My legs were swollen and jet lag accompanied them. When I got off the plane in Australia and picked up my luggage nobody had arrived to pick me up as had been arranged. I wandered around with the lump in my throat until eventually Vincent, a member of the ministry team, showed up. A girl I knew arrived on another plane so we journeyed together across the sunny morning's Australian roads towards Howmansworth. It was a forty degrees centigrade welcome. My billeting host, Darlene, greeted me at the immaculate ministry church site with a broad smile. I was struck by the heavenly atmosphere and gloriously large prints and paintings of tranquil flowers and scenes. A taste of luxury and sterility pervaded throughout as the pure cream walls surrounded the spacious main hall. The anticipation of getting set free was high but jet lag, the threat of a virus and cold sores, no doubt picked up on route, made it difficult to appreciate. Another two ladies joined us and Darlene took us all to her house to unpack and rest until the following day.

The worship and meetings were well orchestrated and the Holy Spirit was present at all times, even the staff looked angelic. Half way through the week one of the men volunteered to take us out for a day's trip. He chose Mornington Peninsula; a magnificent resort with turquoise sea and miles of heath land. The beach curved slightly as far as the eye could see. As I watched below towards the ocean from where we had climbed, one of the girls who had wandered down the crags looked like a busy ant. An experience I would never have ever dreamed possible came to an end and one I would definitely look back upon as one of those golden domes.

Back at the school during one of the meetings Evelyn taught about the part of Freemasonry where a man is symbolically placed into a coffin. I began to manifest and as I did so slid off the chair. As I fell to the floor my arms automatically crossed in front of my chest and I started to choke. That is the exact position they use during a Freemason's initiation ceremony.

I found clues to Freemasonry being in my family history when researching my family tree on my mother's side. One man, who had been a bard in the mother lodge in Scotland, had married my first cousin three times removed, that is three generations back in history. If he had married such a close cousin then my forefathers could well have been friends and associates of that same lodge. Because the man was famous his recording of certain events, being published in a book, could be easily found but not my forefathers. These would have to be researched in a longwinded fashion. On my father's side, though I found interesting and sometimes influential people, I found nobody famous but on visiting the graveyard where certain forefathers were buried I found skulls sitting on top of other people's gravestones and other bizarre features that spoke of a really dark history. If our forefathers had not renounced and forsaken those 'sins' then it is left to subsequent generations to do so and in doing so the entire family can eventually be set free. It was proving to be a very long battle to get free from the bondages of the terrible occultic strongholds because the enemy puts up a fight and there is no apparent freedom. When will I know I am completely free? I remind myself constantly it is when my body receives its physical healing as God had promised many years ago and I become like a normal human being. One friend pointed out while we were attending Matthew Minnerton's meetings that I did not even resemble one.

'I'll be back again next year,' I told Evelyn.

We waved our goodbyes and boarded the minibus for the airport. Most of the other English delegates took off to England or the countries they had come from. I took off for another part of Australia to spend some time with Richard and Emma. My time with them was hectic as I reasoned that perhaps it would be the one and only time. Richard and Emma were exhausted after the two weeks touring different places, including a bush walk and seeing wild kangaroos. When the time came for us to part company they drove me to the airport. I was sorry to be leaving.

I texted Raymond a few days previous to leaving, wondering if he would pick me up at the other end. He only replied at the last minute to say,

'Somebody will meet you at the airport.'

Mounting the skies in the jumbo jet I glanced out of the window. The shadow of the plane, encircled by a rainbow, moved across the tops of the clouds. I videoed it then relaxed for the long flight home. It was Scarlet who picked me up. Back at home I downloaded my videos and while watching them noticed a cloud the shape of Australia with the shadow of the plane flying back in. I captured the still image and surmised that God was telling me to return the following year.

On returning to church I continued to have hard times and crying out to God to help get me right so I could enjoy the people in the church. Sometimes it went well but Raymond was still bothered that he was the only one I could cope with imparting the Holy Spirit to me. I had to leave him to his own interpretation as to why and carry on the best I could. If I had been able to leave him alone and submit it would have been better but I could not.

New people continued to come to the fellowship and that included ones that were sympathetic to praying for Israel. Around Christmas I thought of hosting a Passover celebration in April and spoke to one of the girls about it. I asked Raymond to attend but he declined. Whatever reason he or others gave me for his answer I was convinced it was because of me. It seems that people put their dislike of me before their love for God. Nevertheless, Raymond gave his permission and I took full responsibility for the event. It took three months to organize and create booklets. It certainly gave me something worthwhile to do and, because of what I had suffered at the Synagogue, I wondered if God really was pleased with the venture. I prayed,

'If you are pleased with this Passover meal please show up powerfully at the next Sunday service to show Raymond that You are.'

After all, Passover is a Jewish feast and Gentiles seem to think it a foreign thing to celebrate Jewish feasts. However, he did promise to poke his head in on the day.

I laid the tables with alternate blue and white tablecloths and set the tables to precision. Another lady, Flora, helped for two days to prepare the meal. I choreographed dances about the Passover and those involved had practiced from time to time. Whilst preparing the food on the day of the meal Flora went off to get a bottle opener from Raymond's house and I was left in the kitchen. The sun shone hot so we left the door open to cool the air. Flora was gone a long time and as I anticipated her return I was unmoved when I heard a certain noise coming from the hall. A couple of minutes later, when she did not walk into the kitchen, I looked out. There was no sign of her so I got back to work. When she did return she stared at me for a while in silence. Raymond only lived round the corner, I thought, though I had never been to his house. Neither of us spoke. I thought her behaviour rather strange but we carried on with the preparation as before. At five o'clock the dancers turned up. Scarlet was one of them and asked,

'Where's your DVD player, Rachel?'

'It's out there on the table.'

'No, it isn't.'

With that I searched every nook and cranny and came to the conclusion the noise I had heard was somebody stealing my player. I could not phone the police as it would have interfered with the preparation. Scarlet went home to get her DVD player but it was not as good a quality as mine. Despite that, the evening went much better than anticipated and Brian, who had accompanied us to represent the leadership, thoroughly enjoyed himself and said what a great evening it was. Somebody's son took an amateur video of the evening and before the service the following Sunday I made certificates for everyone as a commemoration and those who wanted a DVD bought a copy for three pounds. I designed the holder insert of the DVD to match the certificate and gave Raymond and Gail a copy free of charge.

On Sunday morning I wondered if God would show His approval and was not disappointed. Raymond was well pleased with the power and later I explained why God had come. His face, though, remained pensive.

Not long afterwards the church started planning to go to a Bible camp far away, to be held in the summer. I put my name down for it. The previous year Raymond took the youth to a different camp up North but the adults were left. I particularly felt left out.

After all, I had a whole life to make up on and had never enjoyed my teenage years. I longed to join the youth and enjoy the security of those in loving, caring authority. To quell the pain I booked into Purple Heathers from where I texted Raymond to see if they arrived safely. He refused to reply which made my insecurity worse. I was unable to accept the rejection so persisted with my texts until he finally replied to the affirmative.

Raymond did not want me to go to the Bible camp. I wanted to travel with them and feel like a family.

'I'm not organizing it,' he stated.

'How far is it from the station?'

'Oh, you can't get there easily. You need a car.'

Nobody was organizing it. The single people had to make their own arrangements but I felt too vulnerable. If I wanted to go though, I had to comply. Christine phoned eventually to say,

'I've got a lift with a couple and there's space if you want it.'

Reluctantly, I took the space and we drove the long way to the Bible camp. When we arrived at the ticket office I discovered that as I had not booked a place with my church for my tent,

'You will be put into the overflow field.'

My stomach fell to the ground and my reactions were not at all Godlike. The woman tending me seemed sympathetic but another one fumed with anger because of my behaviour. I longed for a morsel of comfort and understanding but normal people only see through normal eyes and cannot identify with gross internal suffering. Inwardly, I longed for Raymond to arrive but I was sure the incident would be reported to him and I lose even more favour. Christine waited until finally we were allowed to go over to the overflow field. Being bold she put her tent inside the main field, just outside the dreaded field and we were told we could stay there but would have to move if there was no space for those who had booked. Half an hour or so later Raymond arrived with his family and impressive caravan but he drove right past us without a word and the lady in charge accompanied him on foot. He drove off slowly, talking to her with the window of his car rolled down and I knew I was being not very kindly talked about. Raymond was allocated an area quite a distance from where we were. My heart tore some more and I died again, having imagined playing games of football and a family time that I had never had with my own family but they wanted to be left alone and discard any duties toward me. The lady he had spoken to tried to accommodate my disturbed behaviour and listened to my story. She escorted me over to her tent and then on to the canteen. There she talked with me some more and told me what I must do,

'Stay away from Raymond and Gail.'

Looking over her shoulder I saw them sitting with others from our fellowship and talking with them but I was to pass them by as I left the place as if I did not know them. I could not and why should I? *They're talking to everybody else.* When we finished our conversation I left but was magnetized in the direction of my pastor. I do not recall if I said goodnight to them but the lady reprimanded me,

'You deliberately walked over in their direction.'

Lost for words at the injustice of being treated like a leper I dragged myself around as though weighed down by a heavy anchor. The more I did not smile the more the cold shoulder but even if I did try to smile I was still not accepted. I questioned my looks more than once and felt I did not stand a chance of being accepted. The more I was rejected the more I felt there was something very bad and evil about me so kept looking for ministry to get rid of it but never could.

Despite trying to keep away whenever Raymond showed up I just wanted to be there. Even though he was nasty towards me he continued to be a loving, affectionate person towards others. He was a man of God, filled with the Holy Spirit, joy and carried a healing atmosphere? The following day after they settled in he and Gail came over to say hello but Raymond was careful not to give me much attention. He addressed most of his conversation to Christine and others from the fellowship who had camped nearby.

During the meetings I danced in the worship as always and borrowed a flag from somebody. Dancing was not the same without one. Raymond had advised me not to take my flags. When he had accepted that I was going to attend the Bible camp he told me at the previous Tuesday evening's prayer meeting,

'You are going to see something.'

I wondered what it would be and during one worship session I did see something. A picture of a waterfall was put up on the overhead screen. Part of the water was shaped like a person holding a tree and, pointing it out to the woman next to me, I knew it was Jesus and what I was meant to see. Later on during ministry as I was lying on the floor I heard God say,

'Come into the waters with Me.'

I tried to share the revelation with some of the leaders of the camp but they passed it off without even a smile as,

'That was probably just for you.'

If it was anybody else they would have got pride of place and an invitation to share the picture with everybody. Afterwards, I asked for a copy to be sent to my email so I could print it out.

On the final evening it was announced that a fire tunnel, instead of a prayer line, would take place. I did not like those because we had to duck underneath many pairs of arched arms and they belonged mostly to strangers who prayed very quickly with as little as one word or none at all. I stood, refusing to enter then glimpsed Raymond standing alone at the edge of the tent. Why was he not in the fire tunnel? I walked over to him but he became uneasy and demanded that I go into it so off I went, reluctantly. I experienced nothing the first time I went through but on one repeat round I was surprised. It felt like somebody invisible had taken hold of my left leg and swung it about. I had often watched that happen to others but never experienced it before. I did not like it one bit and became confused as to whether it was God doing it or not.

The following day a couple from my church offered to give me a lift home. The couple who brought Christine and I had already left and Christine had found a space in somebody else's car. When packing away I kept glancing in Raymond's direction in case he went home without saying goodbye. He did drive past but only stared out of the window and was gone. I stared back in disbelief as I watched him drive towards the gate but thankfully he stopped. I ran towards it and eventually found him talking to people inside one of the buildings. On seeing me he said,

'Sit down,' in a welcoming tone.

What? I sat for a while and he continued to talk to the others. Gail was also there but said nothing. Becoming uncomfortable that I was listening to their conversation I announced,

'I only came to say goodbye.'

That was all I needed. Why do people always assume the worst? I left their presence to find the couple who offered me a lift. We had a good time on the way home. The Holy Spirit was with us and for the first time I laughed. A man named Harris was laughing too as the Holy Spirit seemed to be tickling him. After a visit to a castle we found a quaint pub called, 'The Lamb' and stopped for a meal there. I ordered soup and when it arrived, being prompted by Harris's experience, I wondered aloud,

'Does God have fun with us?'

Then addressing Him I invited,

'Come into my soup.'

I was sitting at the table on a long bench that stretched the length of the room against a wall and suddenly burst out laughing, fell sideways and with difficulty sat back upright. When dinner was served I stared at my potatoes and asked,

'Does anybody want to taste my tomatoes?' and burst out laughing again.

The laughter was similar to what I experienced years before in the Rich and Richer store. Polly, who was fairly new to the fellowship, sat beside me to prevent me from falling again. I would have helplessly rolled around the floor otherwise.

'Does anybody want a drink?' asked Barney *(Polly's boyfriend)* after dinner.

'I'll have an Appletize, please?' I answered, then a little puzzled added, 'I don't think God would do something like make me go limp again with a drink in my hand,' but as soon as Barney handed me the glass I went limp a third time, yet was in full control. Following that we still had a fair drive before reaching home and as we approached an airport Polly beckoned us to look out of the window to her left. Three heads peered upwards,

'It's a lion!' we exclaimed all at once.

There, in the shape of a lion's face, was a huge cloud.

'Well, we could not have mistaken that as we all saw it,' pointed out Harris.

A few nights after returning from the Bible camp I had a dream of being in a certain place. Raymond and Gail approached me with what looked like a long list. Gail handed it to me. I read its contents; reams of negative things I had done. The only words I recalled on waking were,

'Leave us alone.'

Demons normally say that to Jesus. In the dream I went into a deep depression resulting from the merciless remark. After the depression, still in the dream, I went to a conference where a well known preacher was standing on the platform. When he invited people forward for prayer I went also and started to shake and cry. The preacher walked over to me immediately, kissed me once on each cheek, gave me a hug and told me,

'You don't have to stay somewhere where you are treated so badly.'

I came off the platform to where Scarlet was sitting and told her what the preacher had said. She said it was not right for him to have said that. We left, emerging into the dark night. I looked towards the sky. Just opposite was a cloud the shape of a lamb and, staring at Him, I wondered if He was there for me. He lifted his two front legs, waved them sideways at me and then was gone. On waking, I pondered the dream and at the following Tuesday evening prayer meeting told Raymond about it. He staggered a little when I told him what the preacher had said. I felt sorry for him as I had done towards my father when we had run away from home but there was no change in his attitude.

I had spent thousands of pounds going to ministries offering freedom but my attempts to improve were not taken into consideration and certainly never praised. Gail had said,

'If we praise you, we would have to praise everybody.'

Regardless, I still carried on at church and it was almost time to be preparing for Australia again.

'Do you know anybody who can take me to the airport?' I asked Raymond.

'I can't,' he said, then explained why.

I was not convinced his reason was genuine but that he really did not want to help. My hopes were high that he would drop all judgment against me. A week or two later he reserved the front row of the left hand side of the church for the leaders.

'Have you done that because of me?' I asked him.

'I just want my leaders to sit there.'

'So it doesn't matter about me or how I feel?'

The infliction of pain was so acute that I went for a walk round the block but first I put some of my things on a seat on the front row of the other side where the youth sat. I danced as usual with my flags and tried not to hurt but felt the conflict keenly. Was I not doing what God wanted me to do? Dancing with all my might, worshipping Him? Opening my spirit up to receiving whatever He had for me in the way of healing and deliverance? Was the progress I had made not good? I still had much more to improve in which would come in time, just as it had taken time to reach that point. The following Sunday I woke early and prayed in preparation for the meeting.

'Lord, what if they stop me from sitting on that side now?'

I planned to put my things on the next available seat behind the youth and not react in any way. Raymond picked me up, as he had been doing for some time, outside Minnie's *(an old lady)* house a few streets away from me. I wandered into the church and, sure enough, there was a reserved note on the seat. Despite the prayer time I was unprepared for the effect of the move they had made. I made my way to the back of the church to talk to Raymond.

'Why have they put a reserved notice on the other side now? It is against me, isn't it?'

'I want that side for the youth. Soon I will have leaders right up to the fourth row.'

Again I took a walk. When I returned Raymond was on the doorstep looking smug with Georgina and Meg, a member of the congregation who had been with the fellowship from the start, by his side. *Why is it so hard just to be loved, wanted and accepted?* That evening as I waited outside Minnie's for Raymond to pick us up, he did not show. I rang Minnie's doorbell and she invited me in. We waited for a long time, unable to get through to Raymond's phone but eventually Minnie's phone rang. It was Brian to say he would be picking us up. I was anxious about what was going on with Raymond. When Brian picked us up he explained that Raymond had cut his finger really badly and was being treated at the hospital. I was in turmoil but dared not show it as it was not wanted. Deeply concerned I hoped Raymond would be able to come to the meeting. He did come later on and after the meeting I made my way to see how he was and many others stood around him also. He ignored me but explained to the others how he had been playing with his dog and that the dog missed the ball and grabbed his finger instead. His teeth punctured so deeply that blood filled Raymond's palm. I had been asking for an appointment for many weeks with him but he had refused. I wanted to discuss my second trip to Australia and to ask if I should go. After explaining his predicament to the others he looked at me and said in an angry tone,

'You wanted an appointment to see me. Well, you have one tomorrow morning at ten, in the office.'

He must have thought it was my fault that the dog bit him. *'It is a dreadful thing to fall into the hands of the living God',* Hebrews 10:31. I remembered Samuel Mushi's broken finger when he hurt me too. God does say not to touch His anointed and to do his prophets no harm but also He says He is a defender of orphans and widows. It certainly was never my intention for Raymond to suffer because of the way he treated me. I longed for him to change his attitude and maybe God did too. The following morning in his office I felt stripped to the bone myself by his scathing words and when I could take no more I burst out crying. They admitted the issue with the chairs was about me and Gail added,

'You are a distraction with your flags.'

I explained how her singing was a blessing and it seemed new to her that I thought well of her. They misunderstood me badly but was she about to change? I hoped desperately she would. Raymond motioned for her to sit beside me. She did but I could not be comforted.

A few mornings later Scarlet, accompanied by another lady, drove me to the airport en route to Australia. There was an emptiness in my heart that Raymond had not. From his and the other leaders' point of view I was simply a troublemaker, not a woman who had been so ravaged by life that she could not function properly anymore.

Nothing much happened when in Australia the second time but there was a time of ministry for those who were facing persecution in their churches. The Holy Spirit fell on me at the mention of it and without anyone praying I fell to the ground. God had not abandoned me as my church had.

After the school, as with the previous year, I went to stay with my brother and sister-in-law. My sister-in-law had lost much of the use of her legs since then due to an investigative operation and had also become half blind in one eye because of glaucoma so any touring, except locally by car, was out of the question.

A few days before it was time to leave I texted Raymond for a lift. It was not forthcoming and in the resulting pain I texted Scarlet. At first she was reluctant to fetch me because she was busy preparing for some event but after a few messages between us she changed her mind and offered to pick me up saying,

'You see, God does love you.'

I was not convinced because why would He not arrange for somebody to pick me up before I left for Australia? I felt incredibly abandoned but extremely relieved with Scarlet's offer. Raymond would have no difficulty picking up his own children, as I had observed but for me it was a different matter. It all boiled down to the rules of the church and I find words hard to describe that kind of cruelty being handed down to vulnerable, broken people.

'I'd have to do it for everyone,' Raymond had said.

'Well, everyone isn't asking. I am asking.'

In fact, I was begging.

After a more restful time from the previous year with Richard and Emma we were off to the airport for my departure. Richard helped pack everything into the case but surely it would be too heavy. The weighing in staff confirmed my suspicion.

'We'll have to take some things out,' I said.

When Richard tried to open the case, however, the combination padlock jammed and no amount of trying to get the number sequence right budged it. Time was running out and I ran around the airport looking for a lock cutter but to no avail.

'Why don't you pray, Rachel,' suggested Emma.

'I have done already.'

I took hold of the lock in my hand after my brother had already tried so many times to open it and told God with as much boldness as I could muster,

'I *know* You can do it.'

Not a second later I looked down and the lock had sprung open a miraculous one hundred and eighty degrees. I had not heard a click nor felt anything. Thankfully, there was still time to have a coffee together and say our goodbyes.

Rumbling fear and tightening of my stomach were ever present because I was unsure of the reception facing me on my return to church. I texted Polly to see if Raymond did not want me back. She assured me that both she and Barney would be there to support me.

At Melbourne airport, where I had to change planes, I bought presents that I had promised people and a tie and long handled dog toy for Raymond so his finger would not be bitten again. I longed for reconciliation and had already bought Gail a worship CD from the conference.

Just one day after my return a couple from Canada, Ambrose and Jade Noston, came over to do a worship conference at the church. The first evening had been cancelled so it gave me a chance to rest. The following evening I felt ill and jet lagged so sat for some of the meeting with my head in my arms but I was worshipping God as best I could. Later, despite the way I felt, I danced with all my might but there was no room to wave a flag. Raymond had changed the church around while I was away. The platform was at the opposite end. It felt odd. Ambrose beckoned me to one side and after conversing with him the first thing he said was,

'You don't have to stay in a place where you are so cruelly treated.'

I wondered if it was a set up as I had told Raymond about the dream. I had mentioned the dream to one of the staff in Australia and wondered if the Devil had been trying to get me out before I received a breakthrough in the situation but during one of her messages Evelyn had said that a double kiss was one of betrayal. I explained to Ambrose how I loved Raymond and Gail but that Gail had not spoken to me for two years. A few months before the meetings with Ambrose and Jade, Gail had an experience where God brought her attention to a dying snail. He told her to take it indoors and caress it for a few days. After a struggle with the idea, she obeyed. To her amazement the snail revived. I thought she would then have understood how to treat those of us who were snail like but it had not materialized. Could this have been a continuation of communication from God about my shell like existence, through Barney, months earlier?

There was no way I wanted to leave them but clung to the hope that we could make it through and wondered if everything was going to be alright after all as Raymond gave me a hug on my way in. Later in the meeting an opportunity for prayer was given, nobody prayed for me but as I was feeling ill and seen Raymond walk across the front and then standing alone I stepped out of my place and, feeling that things were going to be fine, asked him to pray for me.

'Have you already been prayed for?'

'No.'

He laid a hand on my head and I 'went down' under the power of God. I lay feeling secure, content and relieved that I was accepted again. I opened my eyes thinking Raymond was sitting in the front but Gail had taken his place. He had moved to the row behind so the attitude against me had not been resolved. I felt crushed again. *Why can't they just leave me alone to get well in my own space?* My behaviour was quite normal for somebody who had been treated as I had. I had read books where other people had found amazing loving people to care for them and they made it in life. I ignored what they were doing to me and stood up when Raymond suddenly announced,

'We're going to have a fire tunnel.'

I dreaded the thought as it meant all the other ministers, who had wanted me to leave the church in the early days, would be praying. Raymond was the only one I was still trusting in my childlike way. I went through the fire tunnel. Nothing happened. Again and again I went through it but still nothing happened. Then suddenly, while standing alone doing nothing, a cold breeze blew over my hands. It was usually a sign from God that something was about to take place. As I stared into space Georgina rushed towards me and in a threatening tone said,

'Rachel, next time I see you going and asking Raymond for prayer I'll throw you out.'

'Who told you, you could say that?'

'I did.'

She was a favourite of Raymond's, probably because of being Brian's daughter. I could take no more. How could I stay in a place where Jesus was being proclaimed as a God of love and yet there she was with the Devil's fork in her heart? It went straight through mine. I went to Ambrose who was packing his things away and explained what happened.

'Who said that?'

'Georgina.'

'Go and tell Raymond when she isn't there.'

I approached Raymond but as I did so Gail came between us to give him a hug and Georgina also came to eavesdrop.

'Do you want me?' asked Raymond indignantly.

Because of fear I had also mentioned it to Roberta who was standing by, as I longed to be rescued. I told Raymond what Georgina had said, to which he replied,

'If you do not obey, just like a criminal you will have to be disciplined.'

'Is it a crime to ask for prayer?'

Leaving him, I grabbed my flags one by one out of the cardboard stands that I had made and left the building with them. Somebody asked,

'Where are you going with those flags?'

'They're mine.'

I was totally shocked, confounded and absolutely desperate. Flora, who had helped me with the Passover meal, offered to give me a lift home and stayed until I was a little calmer. I texted Raymond the following day for reconciliation, he texted back,

'We'll be there about two thirty.'

I wondered who would be with him, put a praise CD on to charge up a protective atmosphere and let them in. As Raymond and one of the men walked along the hall I felt an invisible veil drape over me for protection but did not tell them about it. I sat calmly on my settee and listened to Raymond telling me he was not prepared to have me any longer.

'I'm a very hard man,' he said.

After much appealing from me and explaining that he had done so much to improve me he still was unmoved. When finished he stood to give me a hug.

'What's that for?'

'I want to give you a hug.'

I thought Ambrose's chat was the kiss on the cheek betrayal but the hug must have been the double one. And so I remained at home for quite a few weeks trying to come to terms with yet another plight.

Christmas Eve arrived and I was determined to let the people of the fellowship know I had not forgotten them, that I still loved them. I wrote out many cards and walked to the church to post them. A little fear was present so I pushed them through the letter box and left before anybody could catch me doing a good turn. With two cards left to deliver to a couple of elderly ladies I wandered round to one of their houses, about a quarter of an hour's walk. As I approached the first lady's house Raymond drove up. Rita opened her front door as I reached it. She accepted my card. Raymond got out of the car and stood by the gate. He greeted me with a hug.

'When can I come back?'

'Go to another church.'

'I will never go to another church again. Yours is the best I have ever been to.'

'Happy Christmas.'

'I'm praying to come back to church,' said I, pleading with my eyes.

He stared into the distance, then replied,

'We'll see.'

We parted company.

My diary entry for 30th December that year reads:

'Last night I asked God to wake me up if He wanted me to go to church. I had had an urge to go all day yesterday. Waking at eight thirty in the morning was a sure sign to go. It was sunny and relatively warm, though I needed to wear gloves. The rims of dark brownish clouds surrounding the blue sky were topped with white. I was a bit fearful so texted Richard and Emma for support.

I had planned to arrive at church late so as not to be seen and start my journey home as soon as worship ended. I had bought Jane (a girl who also needed deliverance) *a birthday present and taken it with me to give to her in case I saw her. I also took my book draft to read in case I decided to continue with it outside. I only wanted to be near the fellowship I loved and missed. Alas, when I arrived and was getting close to the church people I knew were going in. They must have reported seeing me because shortly afterwards Meg came out, looked right and left, then disappeared back inside. She probably told Georgina because she also came out and so my privacy was broken. I had not planned to talk to Raymond, just to be near the fellowship and worship but because they had seen me I decided to stay.*

By the time Georgina came out I was on the pavement singing quietly to myself in worship. I paced up and down outside worshipping for the duration of the service in full view of my guards. I prayed for God's love and Holy Spirit to come down on the service. At one point I took my glasses off and worshipped feeling the presence of God and a smile form on my face. The sun was shining again after a spell of cloud blocked it from view.

When the meeting was finished I waited to see if Jane would arrive but I also thought I could get a lift home. I did see Jane and gave her the present. Raymond came out of the hall in an entourage of people. I guess because he was running from me. I don't know why he should because I wasn't even going to talk to him unless he spoke to me. As I gave Jane her present I walked up the road with her and another woman and said,

'Well at least I've given it to you now.'

I was about to walk home and, even though I was hidden by a big car, I noticed Georgina looking to see if I had gone. She and Meg had been outside for the entire meeting – chatting and joking. Their eyes were on me but mine were on the Lord. A group had gathered behind me and I turned to them. By then Georgina and Meg had joined them. The group consisted of Georgina, Meg, Pricilla (Georgina's mother) *and a young lad. I approached them,*

'Excuse me, what have I done to you to cause you to treat me this way?'

'Nothing,' replied Georgina.

'Do you think Jesus would be very happy that you are treating me like this?'

'Raymond has given his instructions. He doesn't want you here. You are not welcome here.'

'This is my home.'

'It isn't your home,' said Meg.

'Yes it is, in here (I pointed to my heart) *it's my home. Raymond has done so much. I'm nowhere near as bad as I was when I came.'*

They answered nothing. Thomas Breekin, a quiet man who was usually working at the sound desk and one of the leaders, drew alongside me and marched me a few steps away from the building.

'Listen to me or I will get cross,' he said. 'If you keep coming here walking up and down outside I'll get a restriction order put on you and stop you from coming anywhere near the area.'

'I'm not doing any harm.'

'Your phoning Raymond at midnight, texting.'

'That was all two years ago.'

They are keeping a bad record even though they have tried to help me. And I have done my best too. Besides, Raymond gave full permission to phone him any time. Before I walked away I tried to show him my autobiography. He said,

'I'm not interested.'

Well, one day he might be or wish he had.

I looked towards Georgina after Thomas told me to go home. I had told them all I was there for reconciliation but they refused it in return. Holding my hand out to Georgina, I said,

'I want to be reconciled with you.'

Her lips trembled (another thing I said was that I would never wipe the dust off my feet from them and that I loved them). *I gave her a hug and she readily hugged me back. I turned to Meg.*

'I'd like to be reconciled to you too.'

She turned away. Her lips were quivering also and she looked as though she was about to cry. I offered my hand and we hugged briefly. I walked home in the sunshine. It's a shame they never really got to know me or care less to really help. You just shout at the wounded and expect them to get well and change. They are all in God's hands now. I texted Raymond, imploring him to take me back but he texted back,

'That's the end of another chapter.'

Right. Write.

Afterword

My sister Margaret informed me she had written her autobiography and that was an enormous encouragement to get mine finished. Raymond's last text pushed me further, Thomas Breekin had more than likely told him I offered him my autobiography, prompting that text. Since that last text I sat to write one thousand words per day. The book I started in 1993 has now been completed. My time with Raymond and Gail had to be the final chapter of this volume.

Is my book and a healing revival taking place in Florida, USA, and said to be coming to the United Kingdom going to be a springboard to a better life? Only time will tell. I remain with my Arms Outstretched and with Jesus' Arms Outstretched towards me.

Book three will describe any achievements I have made since and will include any omissions from this book, yet to be written. After four hundred pages of writing I faced the challenge of dividing my book, Arms Outstretched, into two, the first one being called, 'Is Anybody Out There?' A triumphant, monumental task of writing, editing and self publishing I thought would never materialize is finally here.

May God's purpose for my books being published come to fruition.

DID3100186

L - #0459 - 010621 - C0 - 234/156/13 - PB - DID3100186